T·H·E Y·O·U·N·G L·U·K·Á·C·S

T·H·E Y·O·U·N·G

Lukács

L·E·E C·O·N·G·D·O·N

THE UNIVERSITY OF NORTH CAROLINA PRESS

Chapel Hill and London

Both the initial
research and the publication
of this work were made possible in part
through grants from the National Endowment for
the Humanities, a federal agency whose mission is to
award grants to support education, scholarship, media
programming, libraries, and museums, in order to
bring the results of cultural activities to
a broad, general public.

Library of Congress Cataloging in Publication Data

Congdon, Lee, 1939–
The young Lukács.

Bibliography: p.
Includes index.
1. Lukács, György, 1885–1971. 2. Philosophers—
Hungary—Biography I. Title.
B4815.L84C66   1983   199'.439   82-11162
ISBN 0-8078-1538-1

To the Memory of
My Mother and Father

C·O·N·T·E·N·T·S

Preface ix

Acknowledgments xi

Abbreviations xiii

Introduction: Alienation 3

PART I. IRMA SEIDLER: TRAGEDY 13
Chapter 1. The Drama 15
Chapter 2. The Essay 40

PART II. LJENA GRABENKO: UTOPIA 71
Chapter 3. Heidelberg 73
Chapter 4. The Great War 96
Chapter 5. The Russian Revolution 118

PART III. GERTRÚD BORTSTIEBER: DIALECTICS 145
Chapter 6. The Hungarian Soviet Republic 147
Chapter 7. Vienna 168

Conclusion: From Tonio Kröger to Naphta 187

Notes 189

Bibliography 207

Index 223

This is a historical and critical study of a major twentieth-century thinker. Georg Lukács's early writings work a special kind of spiritual magic because they project a mirror image of his struggle with a problem that continues to bedevil modern man—the problem of alienation. Much, indeed, has already been written about the young Lukács, but the chance discovery in 1972 of his pre-1917 manuscripts and correspondence—in a valise he had placed in the Deutsche Bank of Heidelberg on 7 November 1917—has made possible for the first time an authoritative intellectual biography.

My principal purpose has been to retravel with Lukács his road to Marx. To that end, I have directed attention to the interrelationship between the ideas he entertained, the world in which he lived, and the conditions of his personal existence. Lukács's understanding of Simmel, Dostoevski, and Hegel, for example, was profoundly affected by the world of fin de siècle Europe, the Great War, and the Russian Revolution. And his own ideas were in the most literal sense expressions of his relationships with three women—Irma Seidler, Ljena Grabenko, and Gertrúd Bortstieber.

My other purpose has been critical. This is as Lukács would have had it, for he insisted that one should take sides and he derived satisfaction from the controversies that swirled around his head almost without ceasing. Although I harbor some sympathy for the young Lukács and his enthusiasms, I have attempted to show how it happened that a brilliant and sensitive man "started out with the idea of unrestricted freedom and . . . arrived at unrestricted despotism." I borrow these words from Dostoevski's *The Possessed*, because it was the great Russian writer who understood best that the defense of revolutionary murder was rooted in the passion for justice.

A · C · K · N · O · W · L · E · D · G · M · E · N · T · S

In the course of writing this book, I have benefited from the wisdom and kindness of a great many people, several of whom I should like to thank publicly. At every stage, W. Bruce Lincoln of Northern Illinois University has served faithfully as adviser, critic, example, and friend. During my graduate years in DeKalb, Albert Resis called my attention to Lukács's life and work and Michael Gelven deepened my understanding of the German philosophical tradition. Since then I have been fortunate to receive encouragement from Samuel H. Baron, Daniel Bell, István Deák, Paul Gottfried, William M. Johnston, John Lukacs, and Hans A. Schmitt. Among my Hungarian colleagues, I am particularly indebted to my friend J. C. Nyíri, professor of philosophy at the University of Budapest. György Litván and Miklós Lackó, members of the Institute of History, selflessly shared their vast knowledge of twentieth-century Hungarian intellectual history. Erzsébet Vezér and Éva Gábor alerted me to numerous important sources, and Ferenc Fehér, one of Lukács's most able students, spoke openly and in detail about his mentor's remarkable career. Ferenc Jánossy, Lukács's stepson, kindly granted his permission to cite material I obtained in the Lukács Archives, where Katalin Lakos and her expert staff aided me in innumerable ways and made my days in what was once Lukács's apartment pleasant and rewarding. In the same way, the librarians at the Széchenyi National Library, the Hungarian Academy of Sciences, and the Ervin Szabó Municipal Library were invariably competent and courteous. In Vienna, I profited from a long discussion with Tibor Hanák, and in London the late Arnold Hauser received me at a moment when he was recovering from a heart attack.

In addition to these colleagues and friends, various institutions have aided my work. Along the way, I have enjoyed generous support from Northern Illinois University, the Fulbright-Hays Faculty Research Abroad Program, the International Research and Exchanges Board (twice), the American Council of Learned Societies, the National Endowment for the Humanities, and James Madison University. Even with backing such as this, however, I found it necessary on more than one occasion to turn to my late father-in-law, Dr. Howard J. Buchner, who cheerfully helped me through difficult times and expressed the kind of confidence that inspires even greater effort. Without him, I might not have completed my work.

For permission to republish material that appeared originally in somewhat different form in *Continuity* (no. 1, Fall 1980) and in *Austrian Philosophy: Studies and Texts* (1981), I am grateful to the Intercollegiate Studies Institute and the Philosophia Verlag respectively.

Finally, I am eager to thank my wife and children—Carol, Mitchell, and Colleen—for their love, patience, and understanding. I have indicated my debt of longest standing in the dedication.

Lee Congdon
Princeton / February 1982

A·B·B·R·E·V·I·A·T·I·O·N·S

GK

Geschichte und Klassenbewusstsein:
Studien über marxistische Dialektik

IM

Ifjúkori művek, 1902–1918

MD

A modern dráma fejlődésének története

UM

Utam Marxhoz, Volume I

T·H·E Y·O·U·N·G L·U·K·Á·C·S

Was für eine Philosophie man wählt,
hängt davon ab, was für ein Mensch man ist.
FICHTE

Alienation

Alienation in the Home

György Bernát Lőwinger (Lukács) was born in Budapest to "a pure Jewish family"[1] on 13 April 1885. His father, József Lőwinger, began his life in the southern city of Szeged, the son of a quiltmaker who could scarcely write his name.[2] In order to contribute to the family income, young József withdrew from school at the age of thirteen and went to work in a bank. Moonlighting as a free-lance bookkeeper, he yet found time to study languages, history, and economics. At eighteen, he obtained the position of chief correspondent at the Anglo-Hungarian Bank in Budapest, and, at twenty-four, he was named director of a branch of the Anglo-Austrian Bank. In 1906, he would become director of the Hungarian General Credit Bank. He was, in sum, a self-made man who never forgot what it was to be poor and who generously helped those, like his son, who pursued worthwhile, but less lucrative, professions.

József Lőwinger's grandfather on his mother's side was a well-known Talmudist, from whom Lukács believed he had inherited his love of learning and his philosophic inclinations. His own father was not, however, religiously inclined and did not identify himself with the Jews. On the contrary, he was an advocate of assimilation, magyarizing his name to "Lukács" in 1890. In keeping with the policies of Hungary's ruling Liberal party, Lőwinger-Lukács's willingness to identify with the Magyars was accepted as evidence of his loyalty; henceforth, as far as official Hungary was concerned, the elder Lukács *was* Hungarian. In 1901, he was ennobled (effective retroactively to 1899) as József Szegedi Lukács.

As a boy, Lukács rarely saw his father, who was obliged to work long hours at the bank, and he never established a close relationship with him. For his part, however, the elder Lukács was very fond of his son, acting as his Maecenas and never failing to encourage him in his work. If anything, he provided too much encouragement, because Lukács soon began to be annoyed by his father's incessant talk of the importance of success. Although willing to see his son pursue his literary and

philosophic interests, József Lukács emphasized repeatedly how necessary it was to publish and to secure an academic position: "Look here,
my dear son," he wrote in 1910, "outer successes and results are also
important in life, because it is often impossible to draw the line between
outer and inner successes."[3] In reaction to his father's view that success
validated one's enterprises, Lukács adopted a "last of the Mohicans"
point of view. In James Fenimore Cooper's famous book, he found
support for his conviction that the defeated could be justified as "over
against the merely formal conqueror."[4]

If, however, Lukács's relationship with his father was cool, that with
his mother was icy. Adél Wertheimer was raised by her uncle in Vienna;
not uncultured, she spoke several languages—German being her mother
tongue—and was accomplished at the piano. Yet her daughter conceded
that her learning was very shallow. She was known to speak of books
she had never read and seems to have dedicated most of her time and
energy to the social life of the capital. Perhaps it was because of this
lack of seriousness and because of her obvious preference for her first
born, János,[5] that Lukács developed, from his earliest years, an intense
dislike for his mother. In the last year of his life (1971), he still remembered her and his elder brother unkindly: "In childhood, my mother
governed the atmosphere and ideology of our house. My brother belonged, almost as the focal point, to this atmosphere; he was regarded
as a very influential child, next to whom I was completely in the background." Summing up his relations with the members of his family, he
wrote: "At home: absolute alienation (*Entfremdung*). Above all mother;
almost no communication. Brother—none at all. Only father and—
peripherally—sister."[6]

Nor did the young Lukács make any attempt to disguise his feelings,
and his refusal to extend to his mother any formal courtesy further
alienated him from his father. In a letter of 1910, for example, the elder
Lukács rebuked his son for failing to send his mother a birthday greeting.[7] This total estrangement from his mother made Lukács particularly
sensitive to those experiences of alienation that are more universally
shared and, at the same time, contributed to his longing for a female
companion, the search for whom constitutes the major theme of this
study.

Lukács was further alienated from his family by what he later described as "the conception of protocol" that structured life in his home.[8]
From the beginning, the forms of social life seemed to him empty and
without meaning, and he appears to have taken delight in refusing to
observe them. His sister remembered, for example, that he would not
greet guests who came to visit the Lukács home. That this initial rejec-

Adél Wertheimer about 1900
Courtesy Magyar Tudományos Akadémia Filozófiai Intézet
Lukács Archívum és Könyvtár
(Lukács Archives and Library, Institute of Philosophy,
Hungarian Academy of Sciences), Budapest

tion of social forms provided the background to his subsequent critique of bourgeois society, Lukács himself had no doubt: "From childhood rejection of protocol to concrete critique of society, a slow, scarcely-conscious interval."[9]

At the highly regarded Evangelical Gymnasium where his parents enrolled him, Lukács continued to experience life as protocol. Moreover, it was at the gymnasium that he became convinced that the Hungarian ruling classes (the magnates and the gentry) had enlisted Hungarian literature, music, and art in the service of a semiofficial ideology compounded of Magyar nationalism and conservative Christianity. Too many teachers praised piety and patriotism more than creativity and independent thought. "I won't even speak here," Lukács wrote years later, "of how poor this school was from the point of view of essential instruction."[10] The world of school was as little calculated as his family's social world to inspire affection in a restless spirit, and Lukács later claimed that "very early, I was ruled by feelings of strong opposition to official Hungary in its entirety." His opposition, he maintained, extended from politics to literature.[11]

Alienation in Hungary

In view of his subsequent political commitment, it is well to point out that Lukács's initial opposition to Hungarian politics was not nearly so great as he later maintained. As he was coming of age in the early years of the twentieth century, Hungary was governed by the Liberal party that dominated the era of dualism (1867–1918). Inspired by the great liberals who engineered the *Ausgleich* with Austria in 1867—Ferenc Deák and József Eötvös—the Liberal party represented a merger of Deák's followers with those of Kálmán Tisza, who originally preferred a personal union only. Tisza was to direct Hungary's political fortunes from 1875 to 1890, the years that witnessed József Lukács's meteoric rise to prominence. Although not very liberal with regard to the franchise and the subject nationalities, Tisza's party did deserve its name with respect to economic development and its treatment of the Jews. In few if any European states did the Jews enjoy as much tolerance as they did in pre-World War I Hungary.

Because of their support of the national cause during the revolution of 1848–49, Hungary's Jews won the gratitude of the Magyars. In the summer of 1848, a bill of Jewish emancipation was introduced that was enacted into law the following year, on the eve of the collapse of the revolutionary government.[12] Forged in the crucible of a failed revolution, this act was little more than a gesture of goodwill, but it did constitute a moral commitment on the part of the Magyars, and in the aftermath of the *Ausgleich*, on 22 December 1867, a new law of emancipation was enacted. The Magyars assumed that the Jews would assimilate and contribute to the strengthening of the Hungarian nation, and they were not disappointed. By the end of the nineteenth century, three-quarters of Hungary's Jews had "magyarized."[13] And for those who elected to identify themselves as Magyars, opportunities were great, József Lukács being a case in point. Thus the Jews had every reason to be satisfied with the Liberal party; indeed, Lukács's father was a friend and devoted follower of Kálmán Tisza's son István.

Although the young Lukács never shared his father's enthusiasm for liberalism, he preferred a continuation of Liberal party rule to any visible alternative. Such an alternative presented itself in 1905, when István Tisza (then minister president of Hungary) ordered a national election, confident of victory. To almost everyone's surprise, a coalition of five parties, led by Gyula Andrássy (son of the former foreign minister of the monarchy), Ferenc Kossuth (son of the hero of 1848), and Albert Apponyi, won the election. For the *Ausgleich* and for Franz Josef, the coalition's victory was unwelcome, because talk of independence, encouraged by Norway's separation from Sweden in the same year, was once again in the air. When leaders of the coalition presented the king with a list of demands aimed at further reducing Austrian authority over the Hungarians, Franz Josef appointed as minister president Baron Géza Féjerváry, a *Kaisertreu* Magyar general, and when parliament refused to recognize this government, it was prorogued. Tension between Hungary and the crown was greater than it had been since 1849.

In a letter of 25 June 1905, Marcell Benedek, one of Lukács's friends, asked for his assessment of Tisza and Féjerváry.[14] Filled with national fervor, Benedek sympathized with the coalition and assumed that Lukács did as well; but although Lukács's reply has not survived, Benedek's angry letter of 30 July 1905 leaves little doubt that Lukács did not share his friend's enthusiasm.[15] And in a letter of 4 August, Benedek rejected Lukács's charge that the coalition was anti-Semitic. "But you who know me," he wrote, "you don't think that I am now joining the anti-Semites? . . . Eighteen-Forty-Eight made of the Jews human beings. In Hungary today, their situation is better than it is anywhere else, and yet, with the exception of the Lengyels,[16] there is not *one* Jew of our acquaintance who would side with the [Hungarian] nation in this struggle." Benedek also argued that Tisza's Liberal party was "liberal" only vis à vis the wealthy Jews. When it came to appointing a Jew to a university professorship, it was an altogether different matter.[17]

The coalition seemed to be on the brink of leading Hungary into yet another revolutionary war against the Habsburgs in an effort to overthrow the Compromise of 1867, to which the Liberal party was committed. For the Jews, this was not a welcome prospect, because they had done very well in Dualist Hungary. Moreover, Kálmán Tisza had opposed the political anti-Semitism of a member of his own party—Győző Istóczy—and declared his intention to protect the rights of all Hungarian citizens in the wake of the anti-Semitic agitation triggered by the "ritual murder" trial in the town of Tiszaeszlár in 1882. The anti-Liberal coalition was, on the other hand, an unknown quantity. Not every member of Ferenc Kossuth's Independence party was above pandering to the anti-Semites, and attacks on the Tiszas were sometimes anti-Semitic in tone.[18] Hungary's Jews recognized that as liberalism lost its monopoly as the ruling ideology, a new and potentially dangerous ideological situation was in the making, and they did not want to take any unnecessary chances.

The growth of anti-Semitism in Hungary can be traced in large part to the massive immigration of Jews from the east—Rumania, Russia, and Galicia—that even Ferenc Deák had attempted to forestall. To these Jews, liberal Hungary must have seemed the Promised Land, but as they became ever more conspicuous in Hungarian economic, professional, and intellectual life, many of their new countrymen became receptive to anti-Semitic propaganda.[19] Lukács was aware of the increasingly threatening atmosphere. He knew, for example, of the anti-Semitic "Cross Movement" at the University of Budapest, and, like all Hungarian Jews, he had read of the Dreyfus affair and had witnessed the advance of anti-Semitism in Vienna, signaled by the decline of Viennese liberalism and the rise to power of Karl Lueger and his Christian Socialist party. In the imperial capital "the forces of racial prejudice and national hatred, which the bearers of liberal culture, Jew and Gentile, had thought dispelled by the light of reason and the rule of law, re-emerged in terrifying force as the 'century of progress' breathed its last."[20] Lukács was sensitive to the crisis of liberalism and what looked to be a process of Jewish dissimilation. If Magyars were to refuse to recognize Jews as brothers, for all practical purposes they would cease to *be* brothers. Thus, though he never accepted his father's liberal view of the world, he, like Freud in Vienna, recognized that he belonged to the group most threatened by the new political forces—Jewry.[21]

More than Hungarian politics, it was Hungarian culture with which Lukács found himself at odds. To begin with, he felt constrained by the cultural provincialism that was reflected so faithfully in his classes at the Evangelical Gymnasium. Because of his experience there, his attempts to free himself "from intellectual bondage to official Hungary emphasized praise for international modernism, in opposition to Hungarianness (magyarság), defined in narrowly conservative terms."[22] The premium that Hungarian critics placed upon the "Hungarianness" of literary works dated to the second half of the nineteenth century and was the outcome of the profound sense of loneliness experienced by the Hungarian intelligentsia as a result of the isolation of their language.[23] That language is Finno-Ugrian and is unrelated to the Indo-European languages spoken by the majority of Europeans. Furthermore, Hungarians never forgot that Herder had prophesied that Magyar would eventually disappear entirely.

Determined to preserve a Hungarian culture and hence a national identity, and fearful of the increasing national consciousness of the Slavic peoples under their rule, many of the cultural leaders of Dualist Hungary subordinated aesthetic to nationalistic judgments. Pál Gyulai, influential editor of the Academy-sponsored Budapesti Szemle (Budapest Review) and leader of the "literary Deák-party," considered service to the nation to be a major criterion of excellence, and Zsolt Beöthy, with whom Lukács was to study, "regarded literature as an expression of national character, so that literary history became 'a compendium of national documents, an auxiliary science to political history, an illustrated album of national life.' "[24] And if nationalism was the chief virtue in writers, "cosmopolitanism" was the chief vice.

Although Lukács shared his countrymen's experience of loneliness and alienation, he was convinced that no literature worthy of the name could afford to ignore the best representatives of foreign traditions. "Hungarianness" need not be conceived in narrow terms. Thus in his fifteenth year, he began to acquaint himself with the literature of Scandinavia (especially Ibsen), Germany (from Hebbel and Keller to Hauptmann), France (Flaubert, Baudelaire, Verlaine), and England (Swinburne, Shelley, Keats).[25] From the first, Lukács was drawn to these outsiders, men whose thoughts were out of season.

There was yet another reason for Lukács's estrangement from official Hungarian culture—its unphilosophic, a-theoretical character. "In Hungary," he wrote in his first book, "there never has been and there is not now a philosophic culture—at best, only isolated and lonely thinkers."[26] In this judgment, too, Lukács was correct. It was as if their nation's precarious geographic location and tragic past had persuaded Hungarians of the irrelevance of abstractions and the consequent importance of concrete, historical experience. The glaring contrast between the failure of 1848 idealism (the revolution) and the success of 1867 realism (the *Ausgleich*) could only have reinforced that persuasion. Two of the greatest and most characteristic works produced by Hungarian culture in the second half of the nineteenth century—József Eötvös's *The Influence on the State of the Ruling Ideas of the Nineteenth Century* and Imre Madách's *The Tragedy of Man*—witness to the unphilosophic character of Hungarian culture.[27] Convinced that such a culture could never achieve greatness, Lukács looked to foreign traditions, particularly to the philosophic culture par excellence—German culture.

Alienation in the Modern World

Alienated from his family in general and his mother in particular, sensitive to the growth of anti-Semitism in the Austro-Hungarian monarchy, and hostile to official Hungarian culture, Lukács was an outsider. He felt therefore an elective affinity for those fin de siècle thinkers who first identified the major themes of twentieth-century existence: the crises of liberalism and individualism; the revolt against positivism; nihilism; alienation; the quest for community; the decline of the West. To be sure, for the vast majority of Europeans, the illusion of progress would be sustained until the shattering experience of the Great War, but men such as Tocqueville, Burckhardt, Baudelaire, Flaubert, Nietzsche, Tolstoi, and Dostoevski did not need the war to alert them to the impending crisis. Living in the same world inhabited by those who believed in progress, they looked deeper, reacting "to precisely the same elements of modernity which figured so prominently in the major expressions of the vision of Western progress: industrialism, technology, mass democracy, egalitarianism, science, secularism, and individual liberation from traditional values."[28] Central to the darker side of the nineteenth century, in Lukács's view, was the problem of alienation.

Perhaps no single book exposed the problematic character of liberal individualism so devastatingly as Ferdinand Tönnies's *Gemeinschaft und Gesellschaft* (1887), a study with which Lukács was well acquainted[29] and from which he learned that individualism had brought about the destruction of human "community" and the creation in its place of legally defined, impersonal "society."[30] In a community, close family relationships, above all that of mother and child, formed the basis for wider, equally organic, if less intimate, associations. One's place in a village or a town, the typical locale for a community, was assured, just as it was within the context of the family. In a society, on the other hand, "everybody is by himself and isolated"; the city was "typical of *Gesellschaft* in general."[31] Estranged from his family and living in Austria-Hungary's fastest-growing city, Lukács was impressed by Tönnies's understanding of the alienation engendered by modern life. For the same reasons, he was attracted by the work of Georg Simmel and Max Weber, who had directed their attention to the human estrangement produced by the anonymity of urban living, the impersonal relationships dictated by a money economy and industrial capitalism, and the continuing "rationalization" of existence—the "iron cage" from which there was no escape.

The modern experience of alienation that so fascinated these German sociologists is deeply rooted in Western culture. Like so many of his generation, Lukács was the heir "of a very old and expanding tradition —pagan and Christian, mythical and metaphysical, religious and secular—that it is the lot of man to be fragmented and cut off, but haunted in his exile and solitariness by the presentiment of a lost condition of wholeness and community."[32] This tradition had been very much alive during the Romantic era, particularly for the German writers and philosophers to whom Lukács was inevitably drawn, and just as their presentiment of a restored community was often symbolized by union with the feminine other, so Lukács's dream of community was intertwined with his desire to become one with a woman, someone who would fill the void left by his mother. In his earliest years, he despaired; regarding alienation as the *condition humaine*, he espoused a tragic conception of life. Only when, out of the crucible of a great personal tragedy, he came to believe that alienation might be overcome, did he begin his own existential and ideological "quest for community"[33] that would end only with his marriage to Gertrúd Bortstieber and his studies in Marxist dialectics.

Irma Seidler: Tragedy

Irma Seidler about 1908
Courtesy Magyar Tudományos Akadémia Filozófiai Intézet
Lukács Archívum és Könyvtár
(Lukács Archives and Library, Institute of Philosophy,
Hungarian Academy of Sciences), Budapest

Passport photograph of György Lukács, 1917
Courtesy Magyar Tudományos Akadémia Filozófiai Intézet
Lukács Archívum és Könyvtár
(Lukács Archives and Library, Institute of Philosophy,
Hungarian Academy of Sciences), Budapest

C·H·A·P·T·E·R

1

The Drama

The Thália Theater

Lukács's experience of alienation accounted for his fascination with the drama. In an effort to understand his sense of loneliness and his inability to establish a close relationship with the members of his family, he focused his attention on that form of art that portrayed the human condition as the dialectical playing out of the struggle between men. For the drama, man was indeed a "social animal," whose destiny was revealed in his relationships with his fellows, and hence, as Lukács pointed out in a 1906 essay, dialogue was its essence. "The relationship of human beings to one another; the scarcely audible cadences of their drawing nearer to one another and moving away from one another emanate from it."[1] At the theater, Lukács witnessed the ritual rehearsal of those problematic relationships that defined human existence, and as a member of the audience, he was able to experience an identification with others that was impossible for him in the world outside.

At home, Lukács read every drama he could find. He admired greatly Ibsen's *Ghosts*, which in his view represented "the new tragedy of fate concerning the futility of everything, the inevitable lateness of all knowledge, the eternal foreignness of people confronting one another."[2] Inspired by the Norwegian playwright, he began to write dramas, all of which he judged to be failures.[3] The painful experience of self-criticism led him to literary criticism and he soon came under the influence of Alfred Kerr, who had been an early champion of Ibsen's work. Eager to try his own hand, Lukács secured, through family connections, an assignment as drama critic for *Magyar Szalon* (*Hungarian Salon*), a small-circulation paper.[4]

The reviews and criticism that Lukács published in the *Magyar Szalon* were impressionistic. Informed by no theory of literature or critical method, they represented Lukács's personal judgments and impressions, which were remarkably mature and well-informed for a young man of seventeen. In general, Lukács was highly critical of the plays performed in Budapest's theaters. He once referred to the National Theater as the "Sardou" Theater, because of its penchant for the plays of Victorien Sardou, a popular but shallow playwright of the fin de siècle. In a purposely brief review published in April 1903, he began: "The most boring month of this very boring year. Simply nothing." And in a review of a prize-winning play by a Hungarian playwright, he fired this verbal salvo: "The author's mistake is great: he believed this piece to be good. That of the Academy is greater: it put in writing that it was good. That of the National Theater is the greatest, the inexcusable: it performed it."[5]

Nor did Lukács spare Budapest's theatergoers. "To enthuse over classical purity and to frequent French farces: this is the character of our public. In principle: the classics, those that are ethical. In practice: the Comic Theater, because sometimes it is also necessary to amuse oneself. Read: if I go to the theater ten times, it is necessary ten times 'sometimes to amuse oneself.' "[6]

Though thoroughly disgusted with theater life in Budapest, Lukács was well aware that opposition to the modern drama was a European phenomenon. State and commercial theaters were the same everywhere in the world, he told Marcell Benedek, but at least the French and Germans had avant-garde theaters.[7] Lukács had in mind André Antoine's Théâtre Libre in Paris and Otto Brahm's Freie Bühne in Berlin. Begun in 1887, Antoine's theater became the prototype for almost all avant-garde theaters, and because it was financed by subscription, it was legally a private organization and could not be placed under the restrictions imposed upon state theaters. Although he wished to perform any modern work of merit, Antoine came to be closely identified with naturalism and realism. Brahm's great discovery was Gerhart Hauptmann, who established himself as a major dramatist on the basis of early naturalistic plays such as *Before Sunrise* (1889) and *The Weavers* (1892).

Inspired by the success of Antoine and Brahm, Lukács suggested to Benedek that they create a countercultural theater in Budapest. His friend was enthusiastic about the idea, and together they recruited László Bánóczi, the lawyer son of József Bánóczi, professor of philosophy and literary history at the University of Budapest. The major problem confronting the three young men was that none of them had any practical experience in the theater, and they were fortunate that Sándor Hevesi, a talented assistant director at the National Theater, got wind of their plans and, eager for more serious challenges, agreed to work with them. As Lukács acknowledged fifty years later, his and his friends' dream would have remained just that had Hevesi not come to their aid.[8]

Lukács's next step was to invite interested professors and students to a meeting organized to discuss the possibility of turning the dream of a new theater into reality. The plan captured the imagination of many of Lukács's most able fellow students, among them Bálint Hóman (later a distinguished historian), Herbert Bauer (Béla Balázs), and Zoltán Kodály, and on 20 April 1904, these young men founded the "Thália Society." László Bánóczi became the society's president, and he, Benedek, and Lukács formed the "artistic committee."[9]

The aim of the Thália Society, according to its by-laws, was "the presentation of those dramatic or other performable works of art, old and new, which are not included in the repertoire of Budapest's theaters, but which nevertheless possess great artistic or cultural value and interest."[10] As this statement indicates, the leaders of Thália defined "modern" not in temporal but in artistic terms. As Thália's designated artistic director, Hevesi promised that the theater would bring to the stage those dramas that were modern in the loftiest sense of the word: those that evidenced artistic truth. Thus Hevesi put society members on notice that Thália did not intend to emblazon "naturalism" or any other ism on its banner in the manner of the Freie Bühne. "Beyond any doubt, every kind of [dramatic] piece possesses its own style, tone, color. Truth in dramaturgy, truth in acting: thus one can summarize succinctly the Thália Society's program."[11]

In keeping with his determination to avoid identification with any one school or movement, Hevesi proposed to place four one-act plays, each written in a different style, on Thália's first bill. On opening night, 25 November 1904, the audience witnessed Goethe's *Brother and Sister* (idealistic romance); Georges Courteline's *Le commissaire est bon enfant* (farce); Edvard Brandes's *A Visit* (realism); and Paul Mongré's *Artz seines Ehre* (comedy). As Hevesi wrote to Lukács: "Three new writers and four distinct styles; that suffices for an amateur society's first step."[12] As a result of its public and critical success, Thália advanced a second step on 12 March 1905, when it performed Strindberg's *The Father*, a play inspired by what the author regarded as Ibsen's excessive sympathy for women. Hevesi, Lukács, and the other leaders of Thália thought it important to present a modern bourgeois tragedy at a time when tragedy was out of fashion.[13]

On 12 April 1905, Thália presented what was to become its most successful play—Friedrich Hebbel's *Mary Magdalene* (1844). This was a favorite of Lukács's and was performed at his urging. It concerns Klara, the daughter of Meister Anton, a cabinetmaker. In order to "prove her love," she is compelled to yield to her fiancé, whom she does not love, and when it is learned that she is pregnant, she is rejected both by her fiancé and by the man she does love. Suspecting the truth, Meister Anton makes his daughter swear that she is still a virgin and tells her that he could not survive the kind of scandal that illicit sex would occasion. With no one to whom she can turn, Klara kills herself. In the introduction to a Hungarian translation of the play published in 1917, Hevesi pointed to the play's central insight: "From this bourgeois morality the elevating sentiment of forgiveness, the true freedom of love, is missing. . . . This morality had hardened into convention. . . . And this bourgeois morality—which was later to be the subject of so many of Ibsen's dramas and of Shaw's comedies—in this play of Hebbel's . . . gathers its martyrs with the power of ancient fate."[14]

Despite, however, Thália's initial successes, the theater was unable to find a permanent home. The established theaters were reluctant to offer their stages and when, on occasion, suitable accommodations were found, the police often revoked the original permit, usually on the grounds that the theater performances constituted a fire hazard. The situation worsened markedly after February 1906, when Bánóczi, inspired by the German Freie Volksbühne, concluded an agreement with the Hungarian Social Democratic party to organize a series of workers' performances, which were held in trade union buildings, workers' homes, and restaurants.[15] Lukács was particularly proud of this initiative, but as alarm spread in official circles, even more determined attempts were made to force the rebel theater to close.

To be sure, the increasingly heavy-handed interference of the municipal government did elicit protest. The Christmas 1907 number of the *Budapest Journal*, for example, published a mock drama ("Thália's Tragedy") that highlighted the theater's difficulties in obtaining official performance permits. But the piece only strengthened the opposition's resolve. Faced with the government's mounting political fears and the personal jealousies of men such as the Comic Theater's László Beöthy, Thália's fate hung precariously in the balance.[16]

In desperation, the theater took to the road, giving performances in such provincial cities as Eger, Szeged, Veszprém, and Pécs. But no serious Hungarian theater could survive without a Budapest home, and

Thália now had other difficulties; its most talented actors began to receive attractive offers from the established theaters, and, as Benedek confided to his diary, one could scarcely fault them for accepting more lucrative and secure positions.[17] Hevesi's defection was the final blow. In a letter of 7 August 1908, Bánóczi informed Lukács that Thália's guiding genius had become head director at the National Theater.[18] Weary, beaten, and without money, Thália gave its final performance on 28 December 1908; it had given 142 performances (thirty-five works by twenty-seven authors) during the four years of its existence.[19] But statistics do not tell the whole story, for Thália had introduced the Hungarian public to works of the founders of the modern drama: Hebbel, Ibsen, Strindberg, and Hauptmann. Thus it had written an important chapter in the history of Hungary's emerging counterculture.

Hauptmann, Ibsen, and Tonio Kröger

In a letter dated 5 August 1906, Bánóczi directed Lukács's attention to a competition being sponsored by the literary Kisfaludy Society: "Dear Gyuri [familiar form of György], I read in this evening's *Magyarország* (*Hungary*) that the Kisfaludy Society is proposing among other things the following subject for an essay competition—an exposition of the principal directions of playwriting during the last quarter of the nineteenth century. The final date for submission is 31 October 1907."[20] Lukács viewed the competition as an opportunity to further his studies of the drama and at the same time prepare a dissertation for his doctorate in literature. True, he was within two months of taking a doctorate in political science—a prerequisite for a responsible position in the Hungarian bureaucracy—under Bódog Somló at the University of Kolozsvár,[21] and he had already accepted a position with the Hungarian Ministry of Commerce.[22] He must, however, have known that it would be a short-lived career; recognizing that he was unsuited for such work, he soon resigned to pursue his interests—literature, philosophy, and cultural history.

His views concerning the drama had matured since he published his impressionistic pieces in the *Magyar Szalon*. This was due in part to the opportunities he had to attend performances in Budapest, Berlin, and Vienna. In major essays on Hauptmann (1903) and Ibsen (1906), he first turned to the theme that was to be central to all of his work before the great existential crisis of 1911–12: tragedy and the tragic sense of life. In "The New Hauptmann,"[23] Lukács argued that the German writer had not rested content with the critical and popular success achieved by his early naturalistic plays. *Michael Kramer* (1900), *Der rote Hahn* (1901), and *Der arme Heinrich* (1902) heralded the arrival of a new and greater Hauptmann. Unlike his younger self and other naturalists, this new Hauptmann, according to Lukács, was dissatisfied with a superficial, nonmetaphysical view of reality. He knew that, behind the last gates, the final secrets, the great powers, lay hidden, and if men attempted to force these gates open in vain, those powers were not for that reason less real. If men could not perceive them, they experienced the effects of their will. Based upon his new metaphysical, antinaturalist vision, the new Hauptmann took a far different view than he once had taken of politics and the social question. "He once shook the tree of the already decayed society and showed its fruits, but he no longer does this. Whatever must happen, he now says, let it happen. It is interesting to view what happens, but not worthwhile to take part in it. The oppressed are worth no more than the oppressors." The final words are those of a character in *Der rote Hahn*.

Though he did not use the words "essence" or "form" in this essay, Lukács had already arrived at a metaphysics of tragedy. The new Hauptmann was praised for abandoning his early naturalism and for seeking the essence, the ultimate metaphysical reality behind appearances, and that reality, though never known to us directly, could be inferred from a close observation of human existence; among the awesome metaphysical powers that determine our lives, the most obvious were death and love—both of which engender those existential tragedies that are inescapable.

On this view, the "social question" posed and implicitly answered by the naturalists was a misguided and trivial substitute for the true social question. It was misguided because it failed to recognize the irresolvable, tragic nature of injustice; it was unable to understand that the tragic condition of the world was a metaphysical and not simply a historical reality. It was trivial because it failed to locate the social question within the relationships between human beings—in the failure of human beings ever truly to make contact with one another.

Three years later, after the death of Ibsen, Lukács published "Reflections on Henrik Ibsen,"[24] a pivotal essay in which he characterized the age in which the playwright lived as an age of alienation. Ibsen's work, he argued, emanated from the suffering experienced by great and lonely men. Like Baudelaire, Flaubert, Grillparzer, Schopenhauer, and Kierkegaard, Ibsen was born too late; in a time of rationalism, he possessed the sensibility of a Romantic. But Lukács recognized that the Romanticism of Ibsen and others of his generation differed from that of the early nineteenth-century Romantics. Whereas the latter were inspired by a great faith in man and the world, the former had lost their faith and had become bitterly disillusioned. They despised their own time, but they felt themselves to be impotent in the face of it. Hence, they turned from life, fearing disappointment; Romantic sensibility was rechanneled. Instead of belief, there was radical doubt about everything. "Romanticism *à rebours*. The earlier Romantics were adventurers, Ibsen and those like him were solitary figures; but the basic sentiment is the same in all of them."[25]

At this point in the essay there is a break. In what followed, Lukács praised Ibsen as a great tragic dramatist who had in fact transcended this "Romanticism *à rebours*." One is left with a sense that some stage along Ibsen's life's way has been omitted, as indeed it had been. In the chapter on Ibsen in his *History of the Evolution of the Modern Drama*, Lukács made good this omission; hence, in order to make sense of the important second half of the Ibsen essay, we must turn briefly to Lukács's description of Ibsen's development in the drama book. There Lukács asserted again that Ibsen had begun his career as a disillusioned Romantic, only to become a revolutionary and an anarchist who wished to overturn the world. Finally, he became "a great tragic poet—all-seeing, all-understanding, clear-eyed, and with a wounded heart." And what is perhaps most significant: "His evolution is typical of contemporary man, save that not everyone continues to the end of the road. Most remain at an intermediate station. Only the most extraordinary reach the last step—resigned and heroic understanding of the tragic necessity of the laws of life."[26]

In the second half of his "Reflections," Lukács discussed the tragic vision of the mature Ibsen, characterizing the dramatist's later work as the apogee of the "analytic" drama. In this drama, which is at least as old as *Oedipus Rex*, all the important events of the plot have taken place before the curtain is raised and cannot therefore be altered. It is precisely this that gives the analytic drama its atmosphere of necessity. In the "synthetic" drama, on the other hand, every significant event occurs on stage. Arguing that the form chosen by a dramatist is a function of his Weltanschauung, Lukács maintained that the choice a dramatist made between the analytic and synthetic exposition was inextricably intertwined with his view of free will. Hence, for the Greeks, who did not believe in freedom of the will, the analytic exposition was the appropriate dramatic form, while for Shakespeare, the synthetic exposition was dictated. Though properly respectful of the great Elizabethan, Lukács left no doubt that he regarded the classic Greek tragedies as superior models for the modern drama.[27]

In his concluding paragraphs, Lukács turned to one of the principal leitmotifs of his early years: the alienated relationship between man and woman, art and life. In Ibsen's world, he pointed out, couples are tragic, their tragedy consisting of their foreignness one from the other. Indeed, the inability of men and women to bridge the existential gap that separated them was for Lukács the paradigm of the universal tragedy of human alienation, and he explored this theme with anyone he thought capable of understanding, witness a letter (dated 7 March 1909) from his friend Hilda Bauer in reference to previous discussions. She wrote: "Well I know, Gyuri, that human beings are unapproachable, that their souls are as far from each other as the stars; only their remote radiance reaches one to the other. I know that human beings are islands surrounded by dark, great seas, and thus they look across to one another, yearning but never reaching one another."[28]

In the Ibsen essay, Lukács put it this way: "Eternal, irreconcilable adversaries; they who were intended for each other, the man and the woman, art and life" (*IM*, 103). Man was the creative figure, the artist who had a work to perform; here "work" was understood in the German sense of "*Werk*," a word that connotes the incorporation of one's Being. Woman, on the other hand, represented the kind of spontaneous, unreflective life that man as artist could never share. Following Kant's and Schopenhauer's idea that art must be disinterested, Lukács believed that the artist (man) had to stand apart from life if he wished to create, for the moment he permitted himself to engage life, he lost that perspective necessary to creation. Ibsen's heroes, according to Lukács, experienced this profoundly tragic dualism, dramatizing Flaubert's dictum: "Un homme qui c'est institué artiste n'a plus le droit de vivre comme les autres." Lukács regarded himself in this light and he was not alone. In a letter of 3 April 1909, Hilda Bauer related to him a dream she had had, in which she came to Lukács's room on a pleasant spring evening and found him working at his desk. She asked him to accompany her on a walk, and when he refused, she seized his pen, trying in vain to wrest it from his hand. As he continued to work with icy resolve, she threw herself to the ground, sobbing uncontrollably until she died.[29]

As he prepared to begin work on a history of the modern drama, then, the twenty-one-year-old Lukács cast himself in the image of Thomas Mann's Tonio Kröger. In the 1962 foreword to a collection of his essays on Mann, he recalled that "the Tonio Kröger problem . . . was a major influence in determining the main lines of my own early work."[30] Tonio Kröger's "problem" was precisely this gulf between art and life, the gulf that yawns between a sensitive young man and those people, the vast majority, who live without reflection and soul-searching. This alienation was not something of which Tonio was proud or pleased; he viewed his existence as tragic, his detached objectivity as a curse, a sacrifice of life on the altar of art. He longed for "the bliss of the commonplace," to be innocent and full of life in the manner of Hans Hansen (whom he wanted desperately for a friend) and Ingeborg Holm (whom he loved), to be able to belong to the great, untroubled, happy community of ordinary men. "It begins," Tonio told Lisabeta Ivanovna, "by your feeling yourself set apart, in a curious sort of opposition to the nice, regular people; there is a gulf of ironic sensibility, of knowledge, scepticism, disagreement between you and the others; it grows deeper and deeper, you realize that you are alone; and from then on any *rapprochement* is simply hopeless! What a fate!"[31] Tonio loved life, which for Lukács meant "simplicity, simple happiness, contentedness, unproblematic submission to the course of things and engagement with human communities."[32] The Hungarian was soon to meet his own Ingeborg Holm—Irma Seidler.

The Theory of Literary History

Lukács received Bánóczi's letter concerning the Kisfaludy competition in Berlin, where he had gone to study with Georg Simmel, and it was in the imperial capital that he wrote "The Main Directions of Dramaturgy during the Final Quarter of the Last Century," a copy of which was discovered among the papers of the late Theodor W. Adorno. In his introduction, Lukács expressed his dissatisfaction with old-fashioned literary history and announced his intention to apply to the discipline the insights of sociology:

> No solitary writer has yet created a new dramatic form. Only in brief and intensely alive golden ages have truly vigorous and original dramas come into being. . . . There must be some more profound cause; there must be something in the age in question that compels the richly talented to view life in the form of dramas. In the past, literary history wished to explain everything exclusively in terms of literary causes and hence it did not even pose the question, much less provide an answer; sociology, on the other hand, grasps literary and artistic phenomena with rough hands, wishing to trace them back to simple economic facts—without success of course. The task of this work can only be to demonstrate the necessary character of this relationship and insofar as it succeeds in discovering it, to point it out in modern life and dramatic literature. If this succeeds, I believe that we will have

given an answer to the question posed: Is it possible to speak
of modern dramatic literature?[33]

Whatever the uses of sociology, then, Lukács was careful to dissociate
his method from any hint of reductionism. Sociology was to join hands
with aesthetics, not to replace it.

Lukács submitted his completed work to the judges on 30 October
1907, and it won the enthusiastic support of one of the society's leading
members—Bernát Alexander, professor of philosophy at the University
of Budapest. Alexander, himself of Jewish extraction, was a respected
teacher who worked in the Kantian tradition. He had become acquainted
with the Lukács family through the friendship of one of his daughters
with Mária (Mici) Lukács. In a letter of 21 January 1908, Alexander
told Lukács that he was "happy that by proposing the subject for the
competition I have some part in the creation of this excellent, monumental, fresh, and interesting work. It is almost certain that you . . .
will receive the prize."[34] A few days later, Lukács was indeed awarded
the Krisztina Lukács (no relation) Prize.

Having won this award, Lukács's hopes for a university career
soared, and he resolved to enlarge and rework his study and to submit
it for publication. The book, *History of the Evolution of the Modern
Drama*, published in two volumes, appeared in 1911, although Lukács
had completed it late in 1909. In fact, the first chapter of the book served
as a dissertation for his second doctorate (awarded October 1909)—this
time in aesthetics, with minors in German and English literature. In his
foreword (dated Berlin, 10 December 1909), Lukács wrote that the
work was based upon the same principles that had informed the prize-
winning study, but he added that "the historical and sociological borders
were extended and the analysis of form was deepened considerably."
Indeed, the book bore the unmistakable imprint of Georg Simmel's
philosophic sociology. Lukács had studied with Simmel in 1906–7 and
again in 1909–10, and under the sociologist's tutorage, he deepened his
understanding of alienation and his sense of the tragedy inherent in the
human condition.

In particular, Simmel's *Philosophie des Geldes* (1900) exercised a
great influence on Lukács. In this brilliant work of cultural criticism,
Simmel maintained that in money economies men came increasingly to
view the world as the sum total of commodities, and he attempted to
show the consequent impersonality and objectivity that defined human
relationships. In place of the intensely personal transactions that obtained in economies in which exchanges were made in kind, those based
on money exhibited the character "of a purely momentary relationship

that leaves no traces." Prostitution was but the most dramatic of such transactions.[35] Because in a money economy everyone accepted legal tender as a means of exchange, one was no longer obliged to offer some product desired by another in order to obtain the object of one's desires; this made possible much greater individual freedom, but as Simmel suggested, it was a freedom that isolated man from his fellows.

A money economy and individual economic freedom conspired to create capitalism. In order to increase his capital, the capitalist relied on mass production, which in turn required a division of labor. But this form of labor, as Marx had recognized, alienated the producer from his product because his essential self (his "soul")—what Simmel called subjective culture—could not fully be realized in the partial object he produced. In Simmel's view, this alienation of subjective from objective culture, the creative personality of the producer from the product of his work, was merely a particular expression of the general tragic fate that determined all forms of cultural activity.[36] Even in the realm of high culture, division of labor, euphemistically described as specialization, robbed men of any sense of personal fulfillment. As Simmel put it, "division of labor—which I understand here in its broadest sense, comprising division of production, dispersal of labor, as well as specialization—detaches the creative personality from the finished *Werk* and permits the latter to acquire an objective autonomy."[37]

Simmel was here describing what he later designated the "tragedy of culture"—the increasing alienation of objective culture (cultural products) from the subjective culture (soul) that inspired it; objective culture tended to take on a life of its own. But this, like every expression of alienation, was inevitable and irreversible—tragic in essence. Such a conception depended upon metaphysical assumptions, as Max Weber recognized when he wrote that "Simmel's ultimate *interests* are directed to metaphysical problems, to the '*meaning*' of life."[38] Nor was Simmel's metaphysics of tragedy an anomaly in imperial Germany; the work of Weber himself, Ernst Troeltsch, Max Scheler, and Ferdinand Tönnies was also dominated by a "tragic consciousness" that "proceeds from the all-governing conviction that in the end an unforeseen 'fate' and mysteriously operating 'powers' determine social and historical events."[39] This was precisely Lukács's conviction as he prepared his prize-winning study for publication.

In order to clarify the theoretical standpoint that informed the brilliant published version of his study of the modern drama, Lukács called attention to an essay he published in a festschrift for Bernát Alexander in 1910 entitled "Notes toward the Theory of Literary History."[40] There he relied not only on the work of Simmel but also on that of Wilhelm

Dilthey. Having heard the German philosopher lecture in Berlin and having read the epoch-making *Das Erlebnis und die Dichtung*, Lukács was impressed by Dilthey's understanding not only of individual works, but also of the spirit of the age in which they were written. To consider literature within a broader cultural matrix became one of his central ambitions.

After emphasizing the tentative nature of his "notes," Lukács defined literary history as an organic synthesis of aesthetics and sociology, of the absolute and the historical. When writing an aesthetics, one attempted to demonstrate those principles in accordance with which judgments of literary works could be framed without regard for the historical milieu in which they were conceived and written; such judgments made claim to timeless, universal validity. Obviously, this differed as an enterprise from literary *history*. Of histories of literature, Lukács identified two types: those that traced the immanent development of literature, the influences that earlier literary works exerted on those that followed, and those that examined the sociocultural milieu from which a literary work arose. Lukács preferred the latter approach, but in either case, there was a danger that transhistorical aesthetic judgments would be sacrificed. In uniting aesthetics and sociology, Lukács hoped to give due recognition to the historical genesis of a literary work without discussing it merely as a reflection of its time and without being forced to abstain from value judgments.

Central to his strategy was his focus on literary *forms* rather than *contents*. The latter were, in Lukács's judgment, quintessentially historical and they therefore quickly became foreign to readers living in a different time and place; he doubted, for example, that many of his contemporaries were able to understand much of the content of Dante's work. Forms, however, were not subject to the ravages of time because they derived from a priori postulates, or Weltanschauungen present in human consciousness; as metaphysical realities of the soul, they were timeless. Precisely because they depended for their effect upon immutable realities of the soul, according to Lukács, *Oedipus Rex* and *Antigone* were more alive than Euripides's plays, which were undeniably richer in content. The more closely, then, that a work approximated to "pure form," the greater and more universal it became. Pure form lay beyond place and time and was therefore free of historical particularity.

Insofar as literary forms were manifestations of metaphysical Weltanschauungen lying a priori in human consciousness, they were subject matter for aesthetics. But literary history, according to Lukács, was the synthesis of aesthetics and sociology. Hence, if forms were the subject of literary history, they had in some sense to be historical and thus open to sociological analysis, and this is precisely what Lukács claimed: "Form is that which is truly social in literature" because literature represented a communication of one man's experience to other men, all of whom lived in society and all of whom were subject to social influences. As these influences created in us certain feelings and dispositions and excluded others, those literary forms (the means of communication) that reflected those Weltanschauungen (a priori forms) that were most nearly compatible with the sentiments of a given age were likely to dominate that age.

Literary form was both an aesthetic *and* a sociological category; it was aesthetic (absolute and timeless) insofar as it embodied metaphysical Weltanschauungen rooted in the a priori structure of human consciousness, and it was sociological (historical and temporal) insofar as it could find historical expression only in an age in which the sensibilities generated in men by their social experience were compatible with the Weltanschauung it embodied. In order to avoid a confusion of terms, Lukács called the basic concept (form) of literary history "style." Insofar as style embodied a timeless form, a Weltanschauung, it was open to aesthetic value judgments; as a response appropriate to the age, it could be analyzed sociologically. In *History of the Evolution of the Modern Drama*, Lukács attempted to work this theory out in practice.

The Practice of Literary History

Lukács's *Modern Drama* was not only a literary history, it was also a work of cultural criticism. Taking his cue from Simmel and his own experiences, he regarded fin de siècle culture as symptomatic of the most profound human alienation. Without direction or conviction, ugly and rootless, modern culture had retreated into the superficial impressions of isolated, lonely individuals. From what was unmistakably an aristocratic perspective, Lukács inveighed against modern "mass culture" and "took a jaundiced view of industrial capitalism long before he became a Marxist."[41] In the final analysis, however, cultural criticism constituted for Lukács a metaphysical critique of timeless world views.

In the foreword, Lukács wrote that the study sought to discover whether or not there was a modern drama, and if so what its style (form) was and how it had come into being. What sort of dramatic expression corresponded to the intellectual and sensible world of modern life? As with every question of style, Lukács continued, this question was sociological in essence, but unlike past sociologies of literature that focused on the contents of artistic works and sought a direct connection between those contents and economic relationships, his study would examine the truly social in literature—the form.[42] But as we have seen, form was also an aesthetic (and hence a metaphysical) category. "On the one hand," Lukács later recalled, "in conformity with Simmel's example, I separated 'sociology' as much as possible from the abstractly perceived economic base; on the other hand, I saw in 'sociological' analysis only a stage prior to the essential scientific investigation of aesthetics."[43] On a more personal note, he pointed out that the book developed out of his experiences as a prime mover in the Thália Society:

> During the years 1904–1907, as one of the leaders of the Thália Society, I lived through the questions touched upon in this book while choosing plays, organizing, etc. Only when it became necessary to set those questions down on paper, when I wished to trace every single question back to more profound causes and regularities did the book become theoretical and its mode of composition conceptual. Hence, I am conscious of the fact that this book grew completely out of life, with which it is closely related. In publishing it, I hope the reading public too will perceive this relationship.[44]

Compared with the twenty-eight-page introduction to the prize-winning version of his study, Lukács now devoted more than two hundred pages to a section entitled "Questions of Principle." In chapter 1, "The Drama,"[45] he maintained that the subject matter of the drama was that which was enacted between human beings; in the greatest dramas these relationships were tragic. "The drama always reaches its apogee in tragedy; indeed, consummate drama cannot be other than tragedy" (*MD*, 1:19). But in order for the tragic drama to flower, the age had to be one in which the Weltanschauung (the metaphysical form) of writer and public was tragic—only when the "common *Erlebnis* of both is such that it can be expressed best in the drama and perfectly in the drama alone: the tragic *Erlebnis*" (*MD*, 1:55–56).

What social and historical conditions, Lukács asked rhetorically, produced this tragic *Erlebnis* (experience)? Because every culture was dominated by a particular social class, or more accurately, by that class's economic and political relations, the answer could only be sought in class history. A tragic age was "the heroic age of a class's decline, when people representing the highest capacities of a class, heroic types, perceive their typical *Erlebnis*, the *Erlebnis* symbolizing their entire lives, to be tragic collapse" (*MD*, 1:59). This was true even for the golden age of Greek drama, which Lukács described as "the manifestation attending the decline of the ancient Athenian residents, the *eugeneis*

class" (*MD*, 1:64). A class on the rise, on the other hand, did not perceive its life to be problematic; if it were struggling with another class
for social domination, it conceived of the sources of its difficulties as
causes that were temporary and hence subject to change. Under these
conditions, no serious drama was possible.

In chapter 2, Lukács turned to "The Modern Drama,"[46] which was
that of the bourgeoisie, just as contemporary culture was bourgeois
culture. In order to understand the essence of modern bourgeois drama,
it was necessary to ask in what relation dramatic man stood to other
men, because the drama was the genre par excellence of the relationships between human beings; there could not be an isolated man in the
world of the drama. More precisely, one was obliged to ask: "What
are the maximum possibilities of drawing near to one another and what
are the maxima of alienation?" The answer, according to Lukács, was
that in the contemporary world, loneliness surrounded each one of us.
The logic of the modern drama, then, led it to strive to become the
adequate expression of this tragic alienation; if it succeeded, it would be
tragic drama.

In section II, "Historical Antecedents," Lukács added a new chapter,
"The German Classical Drama," before turning to "The French Problem Drama." In the former chapter,[47] he traced the efforts of the greatest
German dramatists to create a modern tragedy of fate. Goethe and
Schiller sought "to attain the powerful, fatalistic inevitability of Greek
tragedy with the expressive possibilities of the modern drama" (*MD*,
1:260–61). That in the end they failed was due to the fact that for them
the problem of fate was still only an aesthetic problem, divorced from
life. Although they attempted to write tragedies, their Weltanschauung
was not tragic, because they lived in an age that witnessed the *rise* of
the bourgeoisie. In *Mary Stuart*, for example, Schiller weakened the
tragic purity of his story by emphasizing Mary's culpability, the sins of
her youth. Without a tragic Weltanschauung, one that denied free will,
the tragedy remained an exercise in aesthetics.

Compared with the classical German drama, the French "problem
drama"[48] was in Lukács's view scarcely worth discussion. The work of
writers such as Alexandre Dumas, Émile Augier, Victorien Sardou, and
Edouard Pailleren centered around the presentation of a particular situation, with a view to dramatizing some moral lesson. The aim of the
entire trend was to strengthen and safeguard bourgeois life, in particular
family life, against every danger. Clearly, Lukács argued, the requirements of public morality could not give birth to true drama.

In section III, "The Heroic Age," Lukács identified the two dramatists whose work first reflected the declining fortunes of the bourgeoi-

sie: Hebbel and Ibsen. In "Hebbel and the Foundation of Modern Tragedy,"[49] he reminded his readers that tragic drama could be written only by those who possessed a tragic Weltanschauung. In Friedrich Hebbel's consciousness the tragic sense of life was a priori; he was a tragic poet before he ever conceived the idea of writing a drama. His most direct poetic experience was that of metaphysical necessity.

Hebbel recognized, according to Lukács, that the tragic drama alone could "mirror" life because, like life itself, tragedy was governed by destiny. The tragic drama was for him the ideal of life in the Platonic sense of its perfect form. "That is why [Hebbel] hates with such fanatical strength everything in life that is not dramatic, everything that is accidental, everything that is only an isolated occurrence and not a part of the great dance performed to the music of necessity" (*MD*, 1:359–60). Hebbel's characters bore witness to the futility of struggling against destiny; they denied by their ultimate defeat that man was the captain of his soul and the master of his fate.

Lukács was attracted to Hebbel's work above all because it gave artistic expression to his alienation from others. The characters in Hebbel's dramas lived in "complete isolation," unable to understand one another. More particularly, "man and woman can never understand each other, nor can the most passionate, the most ardent love bridge that gap which is produced by the physical and spiritual differences between them" (*MD*, 1:402). In the end the greatest tragedy was Lukács's own: "Everywhere the most profound tragedy is the tragedy of nonunderstanding. Its intuition that paths still do not lead from one person to another, that everything is in vain; those people who love each other the most, who are most knowing and possessed of the deepest understanding remain forever unknown to each other" (*MD*, 1:403).

If Hebbel was the father of the modern drama, Ibsen was, Lukács argued, its genius. In "Henrik Ibsen: The Attempt to Create Bourgeois Tragedy,"[50] he described Ibsen's spiritual odyssey from Romanticism to tragedy via anarchism and revolution. Whereas Hebbel had begun with tragedy, Ibsen had had to work his way through to tragic vision. Hence some of the earlier plays, even those that exhibited great talent, were marred by fundamental flaws. Of *A Doll's House*, for instance, Lukács wrote penetratingly: "Ethics interfered. It was necessary to judge, to take Helmer down a peg or two so that Nora should be absolutely right. But how much greater the drama would have been had Helmer been equal to Nora as a person and had the contrary modes of thinking and feeling peculiar to man and woman brought the conflict into being" (*MD*, 1:455). In this play, Ibsen *was* morally didactic; he stacked the cards in favor of Nora in such a way that all sense of tragedy was sacrificed on the altar of social enlightenment and reform. Surely Lukács was right here; one need only recall that the power of *Antigone* derives from the fact that, as opponents, Antigone and Creon are equally justified. Beginning with *Rosmersholm*, Ibsen abandoned his reforming zeal and began to write his finest plays.

In the second volume, Lukács grouped together three sections in which he analyzed alternative responses to the decline of the bourgeoisie: "Naturalism"; "Beyond Naturalism"; and "The Contemporary Situation." His lifelong distaste for naturalism found early expression in the first section;[51] yet here he was somewhat more temperate than he was later to become. He characterized naturalism as a necessary transitional stage between epigonic, empty drama and the modern tragic drama. In and of itself, it was nothing, but without it the evolution of the modern drama would have been obstructed.

Dramatic naturalism was introduced to the world in the 1880s on stages in Paris and Berlin, those of Antoine's Théâtre Libre and Brahm's Freie Bühne. To be sure, naturalism had found an earlier home in the novel, but as Ibsen began to replace Zola as a naturalist model (mistakenly in Lukács's view), the novel began to give place to the drama as a genre—particularly in Germany during the last two decades of the nineteenth century. Naturalism did bring new life and more sophisticated means of expression to the drama, but Lukács was suspicious of its primary goal—the creation of the social drama.

In Lukács's discussion of the relationship between naturalism and socialism, he outlined his early view of Marxism. He insisted that Hauptmann and his generation of naturalists were not Marxian socialists, any confusion in that regard being occasioned by the fact that both groups wanted to alleviate the misery of the poor and downtrodden. Indeed, he maintained, as he was to do throughout his life, that naturalism and socialism were inimical. Whereas the naturalists concentrated on the most immediate causes of human misery, Marxism's historical conception sought the causes of that misery at a far more profound level, quite beyond the immediate agent. Moreover, "'socialism's system and Weltanschauung—Marxism—constitutes a synthesis, perhaps the most savage and the most rigorous synthesis since medieval Catholicism" (*MD*, 2:156). That synthesis could be given artistic expression only by artists of the stature of Giotto or Dante. Even at this early date, then, Lukács insisted upon the *religious* character of revolutionary Marxism.

In "Beyond Naturalism,"[52] Lukács directed his critical attention to impressionism and symbolism as abortive efforts to transcend naturalism. Of the former he wrote: "Skepticism was the Weltanschauung at the base of this direction; disbelief in the possibility of every absolute value, every assessment, reaching all the way to nihilism" (*MD*, 2:185). Having no belief in absolutes of any kind, the impressionists sank into the most egocentric form of individualism. Unlike Hebbel and Ibsen, who arrived at tragedy, they became epicureans and relativists.

Because Lukács believed the impressionists to be the principal enemies of a tragic culture, he renewed his attack on them in essays he wrote in 1909–10 and republished in book form under the title *Aesthetic Culture* (1913). Obsessed as it was with individual moods and momentary impressions, Lukács charged, the "aesthetic culture" of impressionism locked individuals up in themselves and isolated them from that which could be shared with others and which could give birth to a true culture. "Culture once possessed a quality that transcended the merely individual and subjective (because it belongs to the essence of culture that it is the common treasure of men); now there is nothing that can transcend the discrete moments of solitary individuals. There were once relationships between people; now there is complete loneliness, the complete absence of relationships."[53]

If universals were abandoned in favor of a meaningless series of sensations and impressions, the artist was reduced to expressing those dimensions of his existence that were unique and private. But those dimensions were incommunicable and hence could not contribute anything to culture ("the common treasure of men"). Ultimately, the artist concentrated only on technique and "good writing," the essence of "l'art pour l'art." Lukács maintained that wherever this "aesthetic culture" was triumphant, there was "no architecture, no tragedy, no philosophy, no monumental painting, no authentic epic."[54]

In order for there to be a true culture, in Lukács's view, there had to be some essential reality beyond fleeting appearances that all men could recognize and share, and that is why he attached such importance to culture. In life men were eternally alienated, but at the level of culture, they could at least share a knowledge of the "essence" of things (the forms) beyond the formless appearances of life. They could recognize and *affirm* their fate and thus give meaning to their existence, or as one of Lukács's latter-day students has put it: "Art transcends the alienation of ordinary life without abolishing it."[55] Lukács wrote to encourage those artists, such as the Hungarian postimpressionist painters known as "The Eight," who sought the "essence" of things in their paintings.

Impressionism was the child of a skeptical, nihilistic world view, which in turn was the child of the experience of existential loneliness. Lukács, like Simmel, recognized the paradox that this loneliness was greatest when one was surrounded with large numbers of people—in cities. Of the great cities of Europe, he was most familiar with Vienna, and he came to regard Viennese culture as the quintessence of impressionism.[56] "The city called forth the aesthete as a type and it is clear that every city has its own type of aesthete. Here I mention only the type nearest us, the most conspicuous: that of the Vienna of Hofmannsthal and the Hofmannsthal Circle."[57]

Lukács viewed symbolism, which also wished to advance beyond naturalism, in a more positive light. Whereas the impressionists took for their theme contemporary life, the symbolists turned their attention to past ages or to the world of mythology, and by distancing themselves from everyday life, they increased dramatic possibilities. And yet, even the greatest of these dramatists—Maeterlinck, Wilde, and D'Annunzio —failed to create a new drama; for them, necessity was not based on a Weltanschauung rooted in experience, but on a stylistic device. "Their monumentality remained merely decorative; it was only pictorial, only ornamental, not truly dramatic and tragic" (*MD*, 2:329).

After a discussion of comedy and tragicomedy, in which he deplored the nihilism of writers such as Frank Wedekind and Gustav Wied and the antitragic socialist plays of George Bernard Shaw, Lukács turned to the concluding section of *Modern Drama*, "The Contemporary Situation."[58] Of the two chapters comprising this section, "Toward Great Drama" and "Hungarian Dramatic Literature," the first was the more important because it was there that Lukács identified "neoclassicism" as the most promising direction for the modern drama. This movement was associated with the now-forgotten names of Wilhelm von Scholz, Leo Greiner, Samuel Lublinski, and Paul Ernst. In search of necessity, these writers attempted to eliminate from the drama everything that was too real and too momentary. Nor was this merely an aesthetic problem, because they perceived necessity to be the form of everything. "These writers are all conservatives in a great and profound sense; they have understood and experienced the necessity of everything that governs and holds life together and that is manifest in every aspect of life" (*MD*, 2:424). Their characters wished to travel to the end of that road determined for them by fate. Of Ernst's *Brunhild*, Lukács concluded: "This is the most profound and the most powerful contemporary attempt to move in the direction of a modern and yet monumental tragedy" (*MD*, 2:435).

We know now that the neoclassical dramatists disappointed Lukács's hopes, for even Paul Ernst, whom he vastly overrated, has fallen into obscurity. And yet *Modern Drama* ought not to be dismissed because its would-be heroes did not prevail. It represented a remarkable achievement of learning and critical insight and deserves the attention of anyone who is seriously interested in the possibilities of a historical approach to literature. That its author was in his twenties served notice that this would not be his last word.

Béla Balázs

The final chapter of *Modern Drama*, "Hungarian Dramatic Literature," was more an addendum than an integral part of the study, because Hungarian drama had learned nothing, in Lukács's judgment, from the great traditions of European drama. Only the French problem plays had elicited a response in Hungary. The reasons for this backwardness were sociological; because of the undeveloped character, economic and cultural, of the Hungarian bourgeoisie, the tragic sense that accompanies a ruling class's decline could not be a factor.

The chapter was written before Lukács had discovered the work of Béla Balázs, the dramatist with whom he was soon to forge an intellectual-spiritual alliance that would endure until 1919. Balázs was born Herbert Bauer to a family of Jewish extraction in Szeged on 4 August 1884. His father, Simon Bauer, was a well-educated, thoroughly assimilated Jew who taught German language and literature at a city secondary school; his mother, Jenny Levy, was German by birth. The family included two other children, Ervin and Hilda, who were to play minor roles in the drama of Lukács's life.

Balázs's early years were passed in Lőcse, to which the family moved in 1890, and in Szeged, to which he returned eight years later, following the death of his father. It was during these formative years that his profound sense of alienation developed; in his case, it derived not from any felt distance from his family but from his Jewish origins. He had, from the beginning, a deep desire to identify with the Hungarian people. Not only did his father encourage this desire but the city of his birth, Szeged, was and is regarded as a truly Hungarian city, in contrast to Budapest, which has always been considered by Hungarians to be a foreign (German) city. Did not Szeged rest along the banks of the "Hungarian river" —the Tisza?

In Lőcse, where he lived during his earliest conscious years, Balázs attended the German evangelical school and church, and yet, as a Jew, he felt himself to be an outsider. In a remarkable passage of *Álmodó ifjúság (Dreaming Youth)*, the autobiographical novel he published in 1946, Balázs described how painful it was for him to be allowed to go home from school during the hours set aside for religious instruction. When asked by his fellow students why he sometimes went home by himself, he learned to reply: "Because I am a Jew."

It is true that no one taunted him; on the contrary, they envied him the free time. Nor could his parents understand why Balázs soon refused to leave the school grounds, waiting instead by the door to the class "with sad longing in my heart." When he could endure it no longer, he pleaded with the priest to allow him to remain in class, promising to be on his best behavior, but although permission was granted, he remained lonely and isolated because the priest never asked him any questions. The impact of this sense of not belonging on a young and sensitive boy can well be imagined: "That I was excluded from one community without belonging to another, that in my early childhood I stood outside of every denomination and every community as an isolated, lonely individual, this determined my conduct and my fate throughout my entire life."[59]

When Balázs was 13, his beloved father died, thus deepening his sense of loneliness. In response to this loss, he began to keep a diary, the symbol of his isolation. After returning to Szeged from Lőcse, "the friendless afternoons and evenings were long and I sat for extended periods of time in front of my diary."[60] Not only did writing in his diary help to assuage Balázs's loneliness, it helped inspire him to be a writer. He began to compose poems and soon aspired to a literary career. We know from *Dreaming Youth* that one of his teachers recognized his talent and encouraged him, but at the same time he warned the young man that if he wished to be an "authentic Hungarian writer" and not another Budapest journalist, he would have to master the Hungarian language. That did not mean, the teacher went on to say, the Hungarian of the Budapest Jews, but rather the ancient tongue of the Hungarian *Volk*.[61] Balázs devoted his every energy to this task in the hope of identifying completely with the Hungarian people, and throughout his early years he was extremely sensitive to literary attacks, the substance of which was that he was in fact a German (read Jewish) writer.

In 1902, Balázs completed his gymnasium studies, winning at the same time the coveted Széchenyi Prize, emblematic of the best final literary examination in the school district. This success coupled with assistance from friends of his deceased father (Bernát Alexander was one of them) made it possible for Balázs to enroll as a student in the liberal arts faculty at the University of Budapest. Moreover, he received a partial scholarship to become a member of the prestigious Eötvös Collegium, a teacher's training institute established in 1895 and named for József Eötvös. Patterned after the famous École Normale Superiore in Paris, the Eötvös Collegium sought, successfully, to support the education of a pedagogical elite, particular preference being given to those who, for financial reasons, might not otherwise be able to pursue advanced studies. Members were, however, chosen so that a majority was of "pure" Hungarian origin; there were few Jewish members. Unlike most Jewish students, then, Balázs was able to take advantage of directed independent research in addition to his classes at the University in German and Hungarian literature and philosophy. Just as important for the future, his roommate at the collegium, Zoltán Kodály, introduced him to another young composer—Béla Bartók.

Balázs and Kodály were among the students who founded the Thália Society, and Balázs acted in a few of the theater group's productions; it was then that he first met Lukács, but no closer association developed at the time. It was with Kodály that he shared his dreams of a Hungarian culture that would one day achieve European stature.[62] In 1906, when he received a grant to pursue his studies and research in other countries, Balázs offered half the money to Kodály so that they could travel together.[63] The two young men studied for a time in Vienna and in Paris, but they decided to pass the better part of their year in Berlin. Like Lukács, whom he met again in the German capital, Balázs succeeded in gaining admittance to Georg Simmel's seminar on the philosophy of culture. The seminar convened in Simmel's home and was by invitation only. The experience heightened his awareness of his native land's cultural backwardness, for the German students made little secret of their disdain for the Magyars. Balázs was therefore elated when an early version of his *Halálesztetika* (*Death Aesthetics*) was enthusiastically received: "I read 'Death Aesthetics' to Simmel and his students. I impressed the Germans. I am very glad of this, but not for myself. I impressed them as a Magyar. They were completely astounded that a Turanian Tatar can also do such work. I could dance with delight."[64]

Death Aesthetics appeared in 1907 and was dedicated to Simmel. The work was strongly influenced by Schopenhauer's conception of aesthetics, and some of its central ideas can be found in Lukács's *The Soul and the Forms* and in at least one essay by Simmel.[65] Beyond that, it has unmistakable affinities with that broad current of thought known as existentialism. In his aesthetics, Balázs illuminated the existential significance of human finitude in much the same way that Tolstoi did in *The Death of Ivan Ilyich*, Hofmannsthal in *Death and the Fool*,[66] and Heidegger in *Being and Time*.

Balázs's argument was straightforward. The artist, he claimed, was distinguished by his ability to penetrate behind the world of appearances and to catch sight of *the* life, "the *Ding an sich* life." Art was therefore consciousness of noumenal life, but that consciousness was possible only because of man's finitude, because of his awareness that his *phenomenal* life would end. "If we were immortal, we would not know that we were alive. In that case, neither the concept nor even the beautiful

György Lukács (left) and Béla Balázs about 1910
Courtesy Magyar Tudományos Akadémia Filozófiai Intézet
Lukács Archívum és Könyvtár
(Lukács Archives and Library, Institute of Philosophy,
Hungarian Academy of Sciences), Budapest

word 'life' would be conceivable. Only through death is the consciousness of life possible. Death makes it possible for us to recognize life as a
wonderful event. *'Der Tod ist der Musaget der Philosophie,'* Schopenhauer says. We can only catch sight of that which has boundaries.''[67] By
setting boundaries to life, death directed our attention away from quotidian existence toward our noumenal (essential) life, our life as *formed*.

If art is that consciousness of essential life made possible by human
finitude, the crown of art, according to Balázs, was tragedy, in which
life was given form not only by death but by fate—what Balázs called
the "unfathomable."[68] By excluding that which is merely accidental,
fate focused attention on that which was essential. Thus Balázs had
arrived at Lukács's conclusion: the tragic drama was the highest form
of art.

On 31 December 1906, while he was still in Berlin, Balázs completed
his first tragic drama—*Dr. Margit Szélpál*, in which he introduced the
great symbol of his early work: the wanderer. The wanderer is he who is
homeless in the world, without roots and without membership in a community of his fellowmen. Margit Szélpál is a young girl from a small
Hungarian village who goes to Berlin to study.[69] There she wins her
doctorate in biology and seems about to embark upon a successful career, when she stuns her colleagues by announcing her intention to
return home in an effort to discover her roots. "I want to be at home
someplace," she tells one of them, who replies: "Nonsense! There are
no homes in science. . . . There are no homes in infinity. . . . The
path of the mind and spirit is open and endless and he who travels it
is a wanderer."[70]

Precisely for that reason, Margit returns home to marry an uneducated
man with deep roots in the village. She bears him a child and attempts
to rejoin the village community as a simple wife and mother, but it is all
in vain, for she is miserable and restless. In the pivotal scene, Margit
encounters a wandering stranger and immediately recognizes in him a
fellow sufferer. In anguish, she asks: "People live and are at home
everywhere. Are only we not?" The wanderer's reply is the most important line in the drama: "They are not aware that they are alive."[71] Unlike those who have found their place in the world, the tragic wanderer
is conscious of his noumenal life because he is aware of his tragic fate,
of the "unfathomable" forces that isolate him from every community
but at the same time set limits and hence give form to his *metaphysical*
existence (his soul). In this way, *Dr. Margit Szélpál* gave creative expression to the theory Balázs had worked out in *Death Aesthetics*.

In the final act, Margit's former colleagues from Berlin come to per-
suade her to accompany them on a scientific journey; her husband,

knowing of her unhappiness, sets her at liberty, but she refuses to go and bids her friends farewell. After declaring her love to her husband, she leaves him to wander the world. In acknowledging to her Berlin friends that she was not at home in the village, she had added, "I am not at home anywhere. Not with you and not here."[72]

In two separate reviews, Lukács praised this drama, recognizing as he did a like-minded Hungarian writer of authentic talent. In one review, he called attention to the symbolic importance of two scenes involving books. In the first, Margit tells her teacher and colleague that she is perfectly well aware that a book they "co-authored" was in reality his alone, all the original ideas having been his. In the second scene, Margit is angry to discover that her husband, who had denounced books as useless to life, had begun to read in an effort to elevate himself to her intellectual level and in this way establish human contact with her. Both men failed in their attempts to draw closer to Margit. According to Lukács, "this quest for community is a symbol of the impossibility of community."[73]

In his verses, too, Balázs attempted to separate out everything "that stands in the path of the meeting of two human souls" or, more often, to demonstrate the "tragic impossibility" of destroying such barriers.[74] Indeed, Lukács recognized Balázs as a kindred spirit and potential ally on the appearance of the latter's poetry in the *Holnap* (*Tomorrow*) anthologies.[75] Reviewing *The Wanderer Sings*, Balázs's first collection of poems, he repeated what he had written earlier: Balázs remained a tragic dramatist even in his verses. "These verses are all in some way abbreviated dramas: in the English tradition they would be entitled 'dramatic lyrics.'" More specifically, Lukács argued that the content of these verses was the "tragedy of love," the inability of men and women to reach out to one another.[76] Balázs was flattered by Lukács's attention and praise, but more important, he was encouraged to know that Lukács shared his enthusiasms and general philosophic position. The two men soon formed their own "field of force"[77] in Hungarian life.

The Essay

Leó Popper and Irma Seidler

Before the *History of the Evolution of the Modern Drama* appeared, Lukács had published *The Soul and the Forms*, a book that was in many ways markedly different in character. To begin with, it was a collection of essays rather than an extended two-volume study. More important, it was a series of aesthetic-philosophic investigations rather than a literary history; the sociological analysis that was so prominent in *Modern Drama* was here completely absent. There is nothing so surprising about this[1] if one bears in mind that Lukács held aesthetics and literary history to be valid, but differing, enterprises. Most important, whereas *Modern Drama* was a scholarly work designed to serve as a qualifying credential for an academic position, the essay collection was a more direct reflection of Lukács's intimate personal experience of alienation. *The Soul and the Forms* is of particular importance to Lukács's intellectual biography not only because it mirrors his existential dilemmas, but also because it was the book, in the German edition, that first established his reputation beyond the borders of Hungary.

In order to understand the volume, it is necessary first to introduce the two persons who were closest spiritually to Lukács during these early years: Leó Popper and Irma Seidler. *The Soul and the Forms* evolved out of his friendship with the former and his romantic involvement with the latter. Indeed, this work (*Werk*) stands at the center of the first period of Lukács's life because it embodies his paradigmatic experience—his relationship with Irma Seidler.

Leó Popper was born in Budapest, the son of Dávid Popper, a well-known cellist and professor at the Academy of Music. As Mici Lukács's cello teacher, the elder Popper was a frequent visitor at the Lukács home; in due course, Lukács became acquainted with Leó Popper and the two became close friends. In fact, Popper was Lukács's only friend in the deepest sense of the word. Like some tragic hero, Popper contracted tuberculosis early in his life and, with his fiancée Beatrice de Waard, was compelled to travel from spa to spa and sanatorium to sanatorium in Switzerland until death overtook him.

Popper's illness thus aborted what promised to be a remarkable career. A gifted painter and composer, he was unable to develop his talents from the sick beds to which he was so often confined, but he did publish several essays on aesthetics in such German-language journals as *Kunst und Künstler* and Karl Kraus's *Die Fackel*. These essays and the informal conversations and correspondence he shared with Lukács exercised a decisive and lasting influence on the latter's ideas. In a work as late as the *Ästhetik*, Lukács praised Popper's work,[2] and a year before his death he was eager to support the plan of Charles de Tolnay, the distinguished Michelangelo scholar, to republish some of his friend's essays.[3]

"Every significant person has only one thought," Lukács wrote in his obituary for Popper. "Form is *the* thought of Leó Popper."[4] If Lukács learned from Simmel to understand works of art sociologically through an analysis of form, he learned from Popper to insist upon discriminations of aesthetic worth by means of formal, transhistorical judgment. In an interview he granted shortly before his death, he reaffirmed that Popper had taught him "that in art the perception of quality is the most important problem."[5] Tolnay has written of Popper that "the historical facts did not interest him, nor that one artist exercised a direct influence on another; modern historical science's empirical concept of place and time left him cold. He sought the essence: the interior attraction between two masters, the higher place-time order that draws those together who in physical place and time are often separated. Thus, he recognized and explained the kinship between Brueghel and Cézanne."[6] In Popper's view, even the most exotic forms of art could speak across cultures to human souls: "The effects of the primitives, the asiatics, and above all the tapestries all contain the same idea: that it is not those things that are alike that join hands, but often that which is most foreign to that which is most remote; that disregarding all obstacles, the form seeks its way to the soul."[7]

Tolnay goes on to point out that in Popper's judgment material and technique (that transcend place and time) must determine the constituent (informing) principle of every artistic genre. In the case of sculpture,

for example, "weight" is always the determining factor. The weight of
the block of stone imposes restrictions upon the sculptor; it defines for
him his possibilities. Popper's point here is worth considering. What
happens when a sculptor refuses to observe the limitations set by the
weight of the stone? Perhaps he wishes to provide the figure with limbs
that suggest freedom of movement—a symbol of infinity. Over the
course of time, according to Popper, weight will generally reassert its
prerogatives and destroy these limbs, making of the figure a torso. But
weight being the greater artist, the torso is often more beautiful than the
original work.[8] It follows that the task of the artist is to delineate the
form already present within his materials, to let it show itself. This
"form aesthetics" was the source of Popper's enthusiasm for Cézanne
and Maillol and his disapproval of the impressionistic aesthetics presupposed by the work of Monet and Rodin.

If Popper's "metaphysical" theory of form was his one thought, his
theory of "misunderstanding" was a corollary. According to this theory,
an artist's true intention was sometimes misperceived. Lukács cited as
examples of this phenomenon the influence of Shakespeare on the *Sturm
und Drang* and that of Ibsen on German naturalism.[9] Popper's insight
was to recognize that many such misunderstandings were conducive to
even greater achievement, a recognition that proceeded from his conviction that the form compelled the artist to follow a creative course not
consciously charted. On this view, there exists in the materials or language of the artist an inner imperative that he must obey, however
unconsciously.

But it was not only that Popper shared some of Lukács's central ideas.
He was, as I have suggested, Lukács's only close friend. In his letters to
Popper, Lukács discussed personal as well as intellectual problems,
particularly his relationship with Irma Seidler and his doubts concerning
his own abilities. He was able to *talk* to Popper in a way that he could
with no one else. So great was his allegiance to his friend that his father
cautioned him about self-disparagement: "Previously . . . it was Laczi
Bánóczi before whom you felt yourself to be an insignificant nobody.
. . . Now you raise Leó to such a holy pedestal far above you."[10] The
elder Lukács went on to encourage his son to preserve that almost cruel
objectivity toward his friends that he was capable of displaying toward
the rest of his surroundings. Like most of his father's advice, however,
this too went unheeded.

As Popper's confidant, Lukács became acquainted with the art critic's
other close friend—Karl Polanyi, a member of a remarkable Jewish-
Hungarian family. In addition to the active roles they played in fin de
siècle Hungarian intellectual life, Karl, Michael, and Laura Polanyi

were later to gain fame in the English-speaking world.[11] Their father, Mihály Pollacsek,[12] was a man of exemplary character; when, for example, a business venture of his failed around the year 1900, he insisted that every shareholder be paid to the last penny, even though to do so spelled his own financial ruin. Their Russian-born mother, Cecile Wohl, was a high-spirited, energetic woman with a great interest in Hungary's intellectual life. In the years preceding the outbreak of World War I, "Mama Cecile" presided over a salon that attracted men and women, young and old, who were eager to discuss new ideas from western Europe, and it was at her salon on 18 December 1907 that Lukács first met Irma Seidler, a cousin of the Polanyi children.

Like Dante's first meeting with Beatrice, Lukács's with Irma altered the course of his life. From this first encounter he viewed Irma as a symbol of "life," just as he saw himself as a symbol of "work," and in the year that followed, the two of them acted out the inevitable tragedy —the unbridgeable gulf between man and woman, work and life, as the paradigm of the universal tragedy of human alienation.

Because she was studying to be an artist, Irma traveled to Florence on 28 May 1908; Lukács and Popper accompanied her. Amid the treasures of Italian art, Lukács took time to jot down some notes: "At night on the boat. Two minutes alone. . . . Monday 1 June. . . . Leó returns home. . . . Saturday 6 June. S. Croce and S. Lorenzo with Irma. We take pictures. Bargello. Alone at night. A kiss in the dark. . . . Tuesday 9 June. To Ravenna. Evening Wednesday 10 June. Toward home." Back in Budapest he and Irma saw each other three more times. He was then writing an essay on Rudolf Kassner that would later be included in *The Soul and the Forms*. "I read from it to Irma on 28 June 1908 on German Hill. I saw her only twice after that."[13]

On 1 July, Irma left Budapest for Nagybánya where she planned to pursue her studies. At this time (1–3 July) Lukács committed some thoughts to paper: "Scruples: impossible nature of marriage. . . . Dread of the destructive influence of happiness, dread that it is beyond my capacity to get my bearings in a broader-based life."[14] It was this fear that happiness, entering "life," would make creative work impossible, that like Samson he would lose his powers if he permitted himself to succumb to the temptations of a woman, that determined the ultimate destiny of the relationship.

Between 1 July and 25 October, Lukács and Irma corresponded faithfully. In a letter of 3 July, she wrote of his fears and doubts, pointing out that two people could not expect to encounter each other in the profoundest sense without suffering.[15] Over the next few months—August, September, October—she continued her efforts to help Lukács overcome his "scruples," but all in vain. He was convinced that it was not given to him to *live*, in the ordinary sense of the word, anymore than it was to Tonio Kröger. Irma had forever to remain a symbol of that which he could never be a part, a symbol of that life and happiness that had to be sacrificed in order to be able to perform his work.

Finally, on 25 October, Irma wrote Lukács a long, painful letter of farewell:

> In life we can never join together inseparably. . . . You never told me, and I never knew for certain because I always had fundamental reasons for the opposite supposition as well, . . . whether or not you think that my life is *really* bound to yours. And despite the fact that you never said that you desire this, I am asking you today to return my freedom, which perhaps you did not take away, which you always hesitated and feared to lay hold of. Now I ask for its return. . . . You will now develop greatly, branch out, surpass yourself; you will be more conscious that you are sailing on an open sea. Exploit the immeasurable advantage of living for years only for your development; the opportunities are now there in perfection for you, in accord with your desire, to become at least as imposing a figure as Walter Pater. The stuff is there, the conditions as well, supposing, as you wrote, you are able to study for another three or four years. I must, however, bid you farewell and I part with a long, warm press of the hand. I part with those words which rang out in your beautiful article on [Stefan] George. God be with you Gyuri, I part because we cannot go on together any further. God be with you. Irma.[16]

Despite the unambiguous nature of this letter, Irma wrote again on 2 November, in the hope of a reconciliation. "My sweet darling Gyuri, I am packing and coming to Budapest. . . . I want to talk with you, to talk so that I can understand myself; if there is still a path to each other, I want us to travel it. . . . If we must part, [I want it] to happen not with bitterness, but with great and sweet feelings—gently."[17] Whether or not a meeting ever took place, we do not know, but a short time later, Irma married Károly Réthy, a Nagybánya artist.

Not long after he received Irma's letter of 25 October, Lukács drafted an extremely revealing reply, which, however, he never posted:

> Now I must write, now when you will receive these lines along with news of my death. . . . Once again the "ice age" has begun for me, complete loneliness, complete separation from life and

every human community. . . . The first evening in Florence I said
that everything slips out of my hands; . . . you replied by asking
whether I believed that it is that way now as well. . . . I never tied
you down because I wanted to wait until I became someone worthy
of you, [but] I will never be such a person. . . . On that Friday
evening in Florence (it was 5 June) I posed with complete resolution the question of my life: is it necessary that everyone slip from
my hands the instant that persons rather than intellects confront
one another? And 28 October (I received your letter then)
answered: yes, it must be thus.[18]

The idea that he lay under a curse that compelled him to alienate all
those who wished to draw near to him found moving expression in
Lukács's fairy tale, "The Legend of King Midas."[19] This story, which
was not intended for publication, was apparently written in one day—
18 November 1908—and it is vitally important for the light it sheds into
the deepest recesses of Lukács's soul. It centers on the young king's
loneliness and longings. Having given offense to a fairy, he receives the
golden touch, but is not, at first, terrified by this curse; on the contrary,
he is happy. He travels to many lands, one day meeting a girl singing by
the seashore. After several days and nights the girl leaves off singing,
rises, and opens her arms with desire, but when the king does not move,
she turns to leave. He runs after her, embraces her, and to his horror
witnesses her transformation into a gold statue. Nothing he does can
restore the girl and, weeping bitterly, he smashes the statue and scatters
the pieces in the sea.

King Midas continues to wander, no longer hoping for anything from
life, until he meets another girl. They speak to each other of their wanderings and sufferings (which turn out to have been similar); having
arrived at their place of encounter from different directions and having
both experienced much suffering, they conclude that they must seek a
new road. They speak, too, of their profound loneliness, yet now, for
the first time, they sense that there may be hope of human communion.
Their words, however, conceal the girl's longing and the king's fears;
he has not dared to speak of the terrible magic of his hands.

One night the king is again speaking of his loneliness, and he tells the
girl that his hands can "never take hold of anything. Life always slips
out of my hands. My hands can only touch lifeless things." In reply,
the girl asks him if he really believes that he is still alone, that he must
remain alone forever. He answers that he no longer believes that to be
his fate, but he still does not dare to embrace her. They continue to

be together but are never able to draw closer, and, as time passes, the distance between their souls increases. And yet, they cannot bear to live without each other.

One summer's day a shepherd's pipe is heard in the distance. The girl is curious and moves toward the shepherd in order to hear the music more clearly. Suddenly, the shepherd turns and embraces her; she resists but only weakly and timidly. She never returns to Midas. The story ends with the discovery by lonely wanderers of Midas's dead body, a white lily in his right hand. "And the white flower was only withered; it had not turned to gold in his hand."

Although he did not publish the story, Lukács did show it to some of his closer friends, including Leó Popper and Hilda Bauer. In a prophetic letter of 7 April 1909, Hilda wrote to him about the ultimate fate of the young girl. She "will not be able to endure her life when she awakens from the ecstasy and when the shepherd's kisses become weak and lifeless, and she will come to loath her life which is now just as one-sided as it was with King Midas; she will go in search of King Midas, who will be dead, and there next to him she will die."[20]

Though the break with Irma was final, Lukács and she continued to exchange letters, which though formal in style (in keeping with her marital status), were still mirrors into their souls. He was eager to make her understand the meaning and importance of their relationship. "There are people," he wrote in March 1910, "who understand and do not live and those who live and do not understand, and the former kind of person cannot truly reach the latter." According to Lukács, he and Irma were real-life counterparts of Tonio Kröger and Ingeborg Holm. Their relationship had removed the last lingering doubt concerning the necessary character of his existential loneliness. "Before I had the good fortune to know you," he told her, "I presumed, though I did not want to believe, that the entire mode of my life's ordering preordained that I be excluded from every human community. . . . In a moment of weakness you said that I was mistaken. . . . Now I not only know but I also firmly believe that [I was correct in the first place], and it is well that it be so (not that it is so, but that I have come to understand myself clearly). For that I have you to thank and I am grateful to you now as well."[21]

Out of the depth of his loneliness, Lukács, like Balázs, began to keep a diary, and in an entry dated 11 May 1910, he reflected upon his human failures and longings. "I believe that the cause of the débacle [the break with Irma] lies here: it is not as a 'scholar' that I am weaker than I thought—although that too is possible, even probable—but as a human being. I need something. I need people—indeed I need warmth. My 'warmth' is something achieved as a result of so difficult a thawing that it is almost impossible to give it this name, and I sense its absence. What I have been saying for years is not true—that I don't need anyone, that I can live anywhere. I don't believe I could."[22]

Lukács's depression grew deeper during the summer of 1910, when he was assailed by suicidal moods, yet by late September he had overcome his despair. He traveled to Florence once again and discovered that Giotto and Michelangelo meant just as much to him as they had when he had been accompanied by Irma. "Now is the time of the final farewell to Irma."[23] The coldness of which Lukács was capable was now particularly evident. He was, to be sure, still concerned about Irma, but she had become nothing other than an abstract symbol of "woman," of "life." Irma, on the other hand, continued to experience the anguish caused by the break, and her unhappiness began to manifest itself in her work. In a letter to Popper written in mid-October 1910, Lukács told of having seen one of her sketches for a fresco: "It was as if Nagybánya and Réthy had never existed, and this is for her . . . a bad sign—with respect to her marriage. It is symptomatic of this that she is coming to Budapest for the winter, while her husband remains in Nagybánya."[24]

But for his part, as Lukács saw it, the relationship with Irma had been the last temptation to enter life. Henceforth, he would devote himself entirely to his work, in full awareness that those devoted to the world of work (i.e., the world of the forms) were not permitted to unite with life. What for Lukács was most astonishing was that he could now accept this restriction with equanimity. "You know," he wrote to Popper in December 1910, "how much I needed people and human relationships in the past. In the final analysis, there were three who touched the center: Laczi [László Bánóczi], Irma, and you. For me the Irma-case was of decisive existential significance; that there was someone who found the core of my being, who was 'the' life for me, who was interwoven with my every thought and feeling. And she left (and *how* did she leave?!), and I live and move."

He no longer believed, Lukács continued, that anyone could help him come to understand his essential self; his work, he now concluded, opened the only possible road to himself. "And now I believe more deeply in the Platonic theory of knowledge: that all knowledge is only recollection, but the most exacting work is necessary if we are to be capable of recollecting. Even the realized work is not worth anything as a work (as such it is completely objective and become independent of me), but as an *act*, as *my* act, and as Fichte saw with uncommon depth, it is by my act only that I will become an 'I.' This is what work means to me today."[25] The search was not for his empirical, but his *metaphysical*, self—his soul.

What all of this meant was that Lukács was now persuaded that his loneliness was the inescapable price to be paid for self-understanding. "What I wish to do," he told Irma, "only a lonely person can accomplish. . . . 'Life,' for which so many sacrifice the true goals, matters not at all to [such a person]. . . . 'Life' and 'people' are shadows beside this isolated, genuine life; what can these give to someone who sees beyond them?" In what must have been a bitter pill for Irma, he went on to thank her again for revealing this truth to him.[26] After reading their correspondence, one cannot escape the conclusion that "György Lukács —against his will—used Irma Seidler as a means for his *Werk*, and *what* happened, and *how* it happened, happened *for the Werk, for the sake of the Werk.*"[27] That is why, in the most literal sense, *The Soul and the Forms* was Irma's book.

The Soul and the Forms, I

The Soul and the Forms was Irma's book. Published in Budapest in 1910, it comprised seven essays (five of which had originally appeared in the modernist literary journal *Nyugat* [*West*]), prefaced by an open letter to Leó Popper on the essay as a genre. The unifying themes of the book were human alienation, the paradigmatic form of which was the gulf that separated man from woman, and the tragic view of life that judged alienation to be an inescapable destiny.

Lukács conceived the idea of publishing his *Nyugat* essays, along with three new writings, early in 1909. "For a couple of days I have been occupied with one thought," he wrote to Popper. "How would it be if I were to publish my essays? It would be: Novalis, Kassner, George, Beer-Hofmann, and with them what I would do this summer and autumn—a long [Theodor] Storm essay and a short piece on the letters of the Brownings. The title would be: The Soul and the Forms: Essays. . . . And as an introduction, a letter, to you for example, on the form of the 'essay.'" Popper thought the plan worth pursuing.[28]

Having received his friend's endorsement, Lukács turned his attention to the problem of sequence, and five of the essays fell immediately into place. "Sequence. I think this must be the order. Novalis (death), Beer-Hofmann (death as foreignness and the symbol of separation), Kierkegaard (foreignness and separation in life), George (the poetry of foreignness and separation), [Laurence] Sterne (satire on both kinds of foreignness: in content and in form)."[29] The essays did appear in that order, and they constituted the core of the book.

"Novalis: Notes on the Romantic Philosophy of Life"[30] was a meditation on death, the definitive form of human separation. Beneath the Romantics' egoistic individualism, Lukács discerned with perception a longing to achieve a new sense of community. "They hoped that the most passionate display of individuality would in the end draw human beings closer to one another; in this way, they wanted to escape from loneliness and chaos." Beginning with their own small circle, they hoped to create a more encompassing community, but this dream was never translated into reality; even the circle of Romantics disintegrated as each member became increasingly unintelligible to the others. Once having become intoxicated by their membership in a community, however, they could no longer travel solitary paths, and many of them sought refuge in religion.[31]

Novalis was, in Lukács's view, the greatest of the Romantics because he alone possessed a tragic sense, an awareness that death was greater to be praised than life. After the death of the woman he loved, he too wished to die, until another woman's love summoned him back to life. Only then did death come for him; denied communion with his first love by her death and with his new love by his mortal illness, Novalis was yet serene, even on his deathbed. He achieved greatness because he was a willing slave of fate, the "unconquerable master."

In his study of the Austrian writer Richard Beer-Hofmann,[32] Lukács identified death as the symbol of human alienation. When someone died, he suggested, those left behind were confronted dramatically with the unanswerable question of "the eternal distance, the unbridgeable void between human beings," because the separation resulting from death was but the final form of the alienation that characterized everyday life. Because Beer-Hofmann confronted the question of death and possessed a sense of tragedy, he transcended the world of the Viennese aesthetes. In a transvaluation of values, he transformed the accidental into the necessary. In his stories and dramas everything that occurred was accidental, but, as Lukács saw clearly, if everything was accidental, nothing was, there being no such thing as an accident in a lawless world. And it was this necessity that gave form to the lives of Beer-Hofmann's characters and thus elevated his works beyond impressionism.

From the alienation caused or symbolized by death, Lukács turned, in "Sören Kierkegaard and Regine Olsen,"[33] to alienation in life. Following Rudolf Kassner's lead, he was one of the first European thinkers to concern himself with this John the Baptist of modern existentialism. His interest in the story of Kierkegaard's engagement to and subsequent separation from Regine Olsen stemmed from his own break with Irma; of all the essays in the volume, this was undoubtedly the most intensely personal. What he had written in his diary about his own fears that happiness and immersion in life would destroy his creative powers, he here attributed to Kierkegaard. To be sure, Kierkegaard wished to spare Regine the unhappiness and melancholy that was his, yet with great perception Lukács pointed out that melancholy was essential to his life. "Did he not abandon the struggle against his great melancholy, a struggle that might have been successful, because he loved this melancholy, loved it more than anything else, and could not have lived without it?" (*IM*, 292) He saw in Kierkegaard someone resembling himself; both were among those "for whom—for the sake of their existential greatness—everything remotely resembling happiness and sunshine must forever be prohibited" (*IM*, 293).

Kierkegaard recognized in time that to marry, and thus to end his isolation, would be to be drawn into life, the world of appearances. A woman was an obstacle in the path that led to the metaphysical world of the forms. "The real woman, the mother, is the most profound antithesis to every longing for the infinite" (*IM*, 295). This was a particularly revealing judgment because it suggested that for Lukács marriage was not only a surrender to life, it was also symbolic of a reconciliation with his mother, a reconciliation he could not accept.

In "Stefan George," [34] Lukács examined the poetry of loneliness and isolation. For the Hungarian, George was the great poet of the fin de siècle, because his songs were "wandering songs," songs of loneliness and solitary journeying. "And all the wanderings . . . lead from loneliness to loneliness, past human companionship, through the evanescence of great loves, back to loneliness" (*IM*, 163). It is "The Legend of King Midas" all over again. George helped men to understand how they long to escape their loneliness, but he showed them also "the refined pleasures of eternal solitude." In sum, George's poems, like those of Béla Balázs, were lyric tragedies. The man of George's poems, Lukács wrote, was "a lonely man, free from every social bond." The message of every one of his verses was the same: "Two people can never really become one." But, for all that, there was in these verses no complaint; life was confronted, as Lukács wished to confront it, with resignation and with courage.

The final essay in the book, "Conversation on Laurence Sterne," [35] was the most remarkable because it constituted a satire on all that had preceded it. It was, in fact, a defense of life against work. As was his custom, Lukács had sent the essay to Popper for criticism, but his friend failed to understand it. "This is a satire on Beer-Hofmann and George,"

Lukács explained. "You wrote after Beer-Hofmann that I should say no more concerning the foreignness of human beings. . . . Do you understand why this is more profound than every one of my writings? Because of its form: criticism of every one of my writings, of my entire life's form. . . . I am changing the sequence of the book and placing it at the *end*, because it satirizes the book."[36]

The conversation takes place in the room of an attractive young woman, a university student. Two of her male friends come—separately —for a visit and become engaged in a lengthy argument concerning the merits and weaknesses of Sterne's work. In the main, the argument focuses on the problem of human alienation; Lukács contrived to restate many of the points he had made in the preceding essays. While all the talk, some of it manifestly empty, is going on, the girl sits quietly to one side, ignored by both young men during the heat of the argument. Still, both are partially aware that the argument is but an elaborate attempt to win the girl's affection. The trouble is that the more deeply they become embroiled in their discussion, the further they move away from the girl; ironically, the discussion of alienation itself serves to alienate each from the other and both from the girl. When, at last, one young man departs, the other, having by this time comprehended the situation, kisses the girl. At this, her face shows relief "that that for which this long argument was such a superfluous preparation had happened at last, and she returns Vince's kiss." The satire was thus complete. Here work is not only one of the powers of alienation, it merely disguises a more primal lust for life. What is more, life here seems to be far more important than work—Sterne's books and the entire long-winded discussion; the girl, not the men, seems to be vindicated, and indeed, from the point of view of life, Lukács believed that she *was* vindicated.

The essays we have examined thus far constituted the core of *The Soul and the Forms*, but they were preceded by the introductory letter to Popper and essays on Kassner and Storm.[37] Because the Storm essay recapitulates the themes pursued in the essays already discussed, it need not detain us here, but in the letter and the Kassner essay Lukács attempted to define what he, as an essayist, was trying to achieve. He began by arguing that criticism was an art rather than a science. Unlike science, which interests us because of its contents, criticism, like art, does so because of its form; "science gives us things and the nature of things, art gives us souls and destinies, and things only through the prisms of souls and destinies." As an art, criticism concerns the essence of things; it alone perceives form (Being) behind the chaos (Becoming) of life.

Lukács went on to distinguish between creative writers ("poets") and critics ("Platonists"). Whether a man chose to be one or the other, the choice was never arbitrary but was dictated by the deepest promptings of his soul. To be sure, both the poet and the Platonist stood outside of ordinary life; for both, life was nothing and work everything. Both were compelled to create in order to disclose the metaphysical world of the forms, thereby transcending the accidental world of life. In the final analysis, both the poet and the Platonist spoke of and sought their own destiny, but whereas the former was able to do so directly, the latter could do so only through the media of the destinies of others—the subjects of his essays. In the act of uncovering the form, the destiny of his subject's soul as revealed in his work, the essayist discovered and revealed, however indirectly, his own soul's form. His subject was thus but an occasion, a *means* by which he could discuss the ultimate questions of his own spiritual quest. Plato, whom Lukács identified as the greatest of all essayists, "met Socrates and was able to give form to the Socrates legend; through Socrates's destiny he was able to address to life his questions about destiny" (*IM*, 318). This was what Lukács attempted to do in his essays. Like Socrates, he lived always "in the ultimate questions, and every living reality was as little alive for him as his questions were for ordinary men" (*IM*, 318). Lukács's view, in sum, was that to be an essayist was to be a philosopher.

In conclusion, Lukács reiterated what he had argued in *Modern Drama*—"not individual great men, but the necessities of the age bring forms into existence" (*IM*, 320). As both *Modern Drama* and *The Soul and the Forms* demonstrated, he believed the emerging form or world view of his own age to be tragic in essence. Moreover, he suggested that in his time critics (philosophers, essayists, Platonists—the terms are used interchangeably), men such as Pater, Kierkegaard, Otto Weininger, Schopenhauer, and Nietzsche, seemed more capable than creative writers of giving expression to the shattered, tragic contemporary world. Lukács conceived of *The Soul and the Forms*, then, as a work of philosophic art that, in lieu of significant tragic dramas, celebrated the tragic sense of life.

The Counterculture and the Field of Force

Unlike *History of the Evolution of the Modern Drama*, which though reviewed, and not unfavorably,[38] did not occasion much of a stir in Hungarian intellectual circles, *The Soul and the Forms* was widely discussed. As a result of this discussion, Lukács became far more aware of his isolated place in Hungarian intellectual life. Leó Popper wrote a sophisticated and complimentary review for the *Magyar Hírlap* (*Hungarian News*) and Emma Ritoók, who was soon to become a friend, published an admiring appraisal in *Huszadik Század* (*Twentieth Century*).[39] More typical, however, was Elemér Kutasi's attack in the same journal.[40] One would never have thought, Kutasi wrote, "that in our Hungarian language, the language made for concrete tangibility, the unambiguous, crystal-clear language of János Arany,[41] it was possible to write a book so lost in obscure incomprehensibility, so inflated with tortuous, bloodless abstractions as that of György Lukács." The distinguished literary critic János Horváth saluted Lukács as "a serious thinker" but deplored his style: "This is the most sloppy, the most un-Hungarian literary work to come into my hands of late."[42]

The most important review was that written by Mihály Babits for *Nyugat*.[43] Perhaps twentieth-century Hungary's grandest man of letters, Babits was poet, novelist, essayist, critic, and editor; his literary judgments were authoritative and influential. Babits's review was thoughtful and far from unsympathetic, yet, like Kutasi, he complained of Lukács's obscurity, which he attributed to the German, even the Viennese, character of his ideas. It was no accident, according to Babits, that Lukács chose to discuss Viennese writers or writers who were then fashionable in the imperial city.

To be identified with the Viennese aesthetes was almost more than Lukács could politely bear, and in a letter to Babits, he took up his own defense. He wished first, he wrote, to call attention to an error of fact. "You place me in Vienna, but not only are those whom I discuss not Viennese (Storm was a Holsteiner, Novalis a Saxon, George a Rhinelander, to say nothing of Kierkegaard and Sterne), but even Kassner and Beer-Hofmann, who were born in Vienna, are not 'fashionable' today in Vienna as you wrote . . . ; nor is my method Viennese."[44] More important, according to Lukács, was the question of German metaphysics, concerning which he expressed his eagerness to enter into debate. This debate was initiated in a formal reply to Babits that appeared first in *Nyugat* and later as the introduction to *Aesthetic Culture*: "On a Certain Obscurity: Reply to Mihály Babits."[45] Lukács did not deny that his work was obscure, but he insisted that "the popular, the clear, the easily understood philosophy is false." In particular, he thought it necessary to defend "obscurity" in his homeland, a country without a philosophic culture, and he even offered a critical explanation for this cultural poverty: "I believe . . . that not least among the reasons for the lack of a Hungarian philosophic culture is the dread of the efforts necessary for great philosophy. This is the reason that the most shallow and soulless materialists impress us as great philosophers, while the greatest thinkers are shunned as 'unintelligible' " (*IM*, 783). In personal letters of reply, Babits took pains to praise Lukács's "Notes toward a Theory of Literary History," and he agreed that a certain obscurity was integral to profound thought, but he suggested that the opacity of Lukács's writings was more a matter of expression than of philosophic profundity.[46]

Lukács's protestations notwithstanding, Babits was uncomfortably close to the mark. For all its learning and insight, *The Soul and the Forms* was a self-indulgent work, overwritten and affected. Though informed by a tragic vision of life, it exhibited a fascination with death all too reminiscent of Viennese impressionism.[47] Moreover, by elevating "man" and "woman" to the status of irreconcilable principles, Lukács betrayed his affinity with Otto Weininger, the haunted Viennese-Jewish writer who killed himself in 1903. Perhaps he knew that Weininger had also been alienated from his mother; certainly he admired greatly *Geschlecht und Charakter*, with its "powerful new conception of Eros."[48] Hungarian critics were therefore quite right to regard Lukács's collection of essays as the product of a foreign sensibility.

In any event, the critical reception accorded *The Soul and the Forms* alienated Lukács even further from Hungarian cultural life. From the first, he had set himself in opposition to the semi-official culture; now he knew that he could never be at home in either of the two leading journals of the emerging counterculture: *Nyugat* and *Huszadik Század*. Established in 1908, *Nyugat* was to become Hungary's most important literary review. Edited by Ignotus, Ernő Osvát, and Miksa Fenyő, it presided over a general cultural as well as a literary revival. Every one of Hungary's outstanding twentieth-century writers contributed to the journal—including Lukács and Balázs. Because of its existence, Hungarian writers were free to experiment with new forms and new subjects as never before.

And yet for Lukács it was ultimately an unsatisfactory forum. *Nyugat* did not, to be sure, adhere to any single Western tradition or movement. "In *Nyugat*," according to one former contributor, "naturalism, symbolism, impressionism, and other isms which stood in opposition to each other in foreign lands, lived together harmoniously."[49] Still, the literary renascence presided over by *Nyugat*, like Hungarian culture in general, was notably unphilosophic, and Lukács always identified the review with impressionism, so much so that one of the essays in *Aesthetic Culture* was directed against its editors.[50]

On a more personal level, too, Lukács was alienated from *Nyugat*. Although he was on reasonably good terms with Ignotus, he knew few of the major *Nyugat* writers and disliked Osvát, the working editor, intensely. "It would be possible," he recalled in later years, "to apply the German expression, Liebe auf dem ersten Blick, i.e. gegenseitige Antipathie auf dem ersten Blick, to my relationship with Osvát."[51]

Lukács's relationship with the circle around *Huszadik Század* was not much more friendly, the journal being positivist in inspiration. At a time when western Europe was witnessing a revolt against positivism, *Huszadik Század*'s contributors were deploying it against the defenders of official Hungary. Positivism had come to Hungary by means of translated literature in the 1860s and 1870s and had entered the University of Budapest with Ágost Pulszky, who taught the philosophy of law. It was, however, Pulszky's student, Gyula Pikler, who made of positivism a rallying cry. Following in the footsteps of his mentor, Pikler taught the philosophy of law at the university, where he was regarded by his students as an apostle, the herald of a new Weltanschauung.

Among these students was Oszkár Jászi, who, after taking his degree, began publishing a new journal, which was devoted to the "scientific" study of society. The appearance of *Huszadik Század* on 1 January 1900 inaugurated a new era in Hungarian intellectual history, for the journal introduced the Hungarian intelligentsia to the scholarly investigation of the entire range of Hungary's social, economic, and political problems. Contributors examined such issues as the failure to achieve political democracy, the plight of the peasantry and the industrial working class, the nationalities question, and the problem of cultural backwardness. In addition to these studies, selected translations and a comprehensive book-review section familiarized Hungarian readers with the latest theories and findings of Western sociology. The journal's general orientation, however, was never in doubt; beginning with the publication, in the first number, of a letter of greeting from Herbert Spencer, Jászi and his co-workers identified themselves with English and French positivism, at the same time that they rejected German metaphysics.

Faute de mieux, Lukács contributed to *Huszadik Század*, but he never entered the journal's inner circle. For one thing, he was irritated because the editors had seen fit to ignore his *Modern Drama*: "In vain did my drama history raise numerous social questions; it did not arouse interest in the vicinity of the positivistic outlook of the Hungarian sociologists."[52] For another, he had no use for Jászi, whom he always regarded "as a very muddled man, of very little ability theoretically."[53] In fairness to Jászi, it should be said that Lukács was easily offended. In 1909, for example, Jászi received an angry letter after having edited one of Lukács's essays. Jászi wrote back explaining that the deletions were made for reasons of space alone; because of the nature of the journal, he had to reserve most of the available space for sociological and political matters. In an attempt to heal bruised feelings, he insisted that Lukács

was a valued contributor and that "every well-meaning dissenting opinion that rests, as yours does, on a thorough knowledge, is congenial to
us."[54] Lukács was unappeased, and if it is true that he entertained a
higher opinion of other members of the circle (he continued to admire
Bódog Somló, for example), he was manifestly an outsider.

In its efforts to challenge official Hungary, of course, Lukács supported *Huszadik Század*. In 1901, Jászi, Pikler, Pulszky, and their
friends founded the Sociological Society, which arranged lectures and
sponsored the translation of major works of Western sociology. In 1906,
the Free School of the Sociological Society began offering classes for
Hungarian workers and university students, the subjects ranging from
elementary hygiene and working-class history to modern science, modern literature, and aesthetic appreciation. Lukács offered a course entitled "The History of the Social Drama" during the 1907–8 school
year.[55]

In the latter year, radicalized university students formed their own
antiestablishment organization—the "Galileo Circle"—the aim of
which was the "defense and propagation of unprejudiced science,"
natural and social.[56] Karl Polanyi, the circle's first president, often invited Lukács to attend meetings. On at least one occasion, he addressed
the Galileoists and he spoke highly of Polanyi in letters to Popper. Still,
it was clear both to Polanyi and to Lukács that they were traveling
separate paths, for the young Polanyi was opposed to any suggestion of
metaphysics.[57]

Although he was alienated from the official culture and from the
major journals of the counterculture, Lukács did identify with the central figure in fin de siècle Hungarian intellectual life—the poet Endre
Ady. Lukács and his generation acknowledged Ady's authority because
he succeeded so completely in identifying himself with Hungary's historical experience. His personal joys and sorrows, his successes and
failures, his strengths and weaknesses—all were those of Hungary,
refracted through the prism of a poetic sensibility.

"I am the son of Gog and Magog," Ady declared in the first of his
New Verses (1906), and as heir of the Magyars' legendary forebears, he
claimed the right to speak for his people: "I came on Verecke's famous
path, / Strains of ancient Magyar songs ringing in my ears, / May I at
Dévény break the spell / With new songs for new times?"[58] Such "new
songs," Ady contended, would also be ancient songs, for the courage
and spirit of the proto-Magyars would invigorate the progressive Western ideas of which he sang. With this assertion, Ady boldly challenged
the Hungarian gentry on its own ideological ground. He, not its members, was the true Magyar, the incarnation of that conquering people's

noble traditions. The scion of a family of the impoverished nobility, he insisted that *he* possessed the authentic national consciousness.

Ady was a major contributor and sometime-editor of *Nyugat* from its inception, and his name came to be closely associated with the journal, yet, as Miksa Fenyő later recalled, Ady "did not feel that *Nyugat* was an adequate expression of his character."[59] Unlike most contributors, the poet championed radical political and social change. An admirer of Jászi's reform proposals, his poetry achieved such apocalyptic heights that revolutionaries also laid claim to him. He was not, after all, a politician or a sociologist but a poet and a prophet of a Hungary transformed politically, socially, culturally, and morally. Rather than a concrete program, he offered his countrymen a poetic vision of a regenerated Hungary.

The appearance of Ady's *New Verses* electrified the members of the counterculture, and Lukács was no exception. "The *New Verses* exerted an absolutely transforming influence on me," he recalled later. "To express myself poorly, this [book] was the first Hungarian literary creation in which I found my way back home and which I regarded as my own. . . . At this time, I must confess, I had no inner concern for classical Hungarian literature. . . . One might say that for me at this time, Ady's poems were Hungary."[60] For his part, Ady praised Thália and thought highly of Lukács's 1909 study of his work,[61] but the two men never maintained personal contact, and because of Ady's independence, innocence of philosophy, and enthusiasm for French culture, neither Lukács nor Balázs regarded him as a possible ally.

Both men recognized that the most immediate problem confronting their alliance was the lack of an appropriate forum, and their hopes soared when a new journal, *Renaissance*, began to appear in 1910. "Have you seen the new journal *Renaissance*," Lukács asked a friend. "It is not yet good, but there are more good sentiments and respect for seriousness in it than in *Nyugat*. For the time being . . . this is my forum."[62] Balázs was even more enthusiastic and attempted, without success, to lure Mihály Babits away from *Nyugat*. "György Lukács and I have taken over the intellectual direction and editorship of the review *Renaissance*. . . . Flippancy, the feuilleton style, playful anarchism, revolution for the sake of revolution, compromising popularity, superficiality for the sake of fluency . . . —none of these will find space in our journal. We want a serious, distinguished review that moves among the great forms, one in which the content and not the pleasantness of the style will be the primary aspect."[63]

Renaissance did publish many excellent articles, including Lukács's "Aesthetic Culture" and Ady's "Petőfi Does Not Compromise," but within a few months, Lukács and Balázs had decided to abandon the journal because of the unreceptive atmosphere in Budapest and because they were preparing to launch a new journal of philosophy, to be edited in Italy. In a letter to Popper of October 1910, Lukács confided that "Herbert [Balázs] and I have parted company with *Renaissance*. It is not yet possible for us to create a good journal—in no case is it possible here [in Budapest]."[64]

The idea for *A Szellem* (*Spirit* or *Mind*) originated with Lajos Fülep in 1910. Born in Budapest in 1885, Fülep worked as a newspaper writer from 1904 to 1906, specializing in literary, drama, and art criticism. During this time, he frequented the Baross coffeehouse, where Sándor Hevesi held court at a table reserved for him, Lukács, Bánóczi, and Benedek. Just as these men had sought the renewal of the Budapest theater, Fülep determined to awaken Hungarian art. After conducting a series of controversial interviews with leading establishment artists, he was sent to Paris, where he visited the Salon d'Autumne and viewed paintings by Cézanne and Gauguin.[65] Stunned by what he saw, Fülep compared Cézanne to Giotto, Michelangelo, and Rembrandt. Cézanne "is a primitive man," he wrote, "as are Gauguin and Van Gogh; the three of them are the most primitive primitives since Giotto and Memling. The error of classifying Cézanne among the impressionists will be corrected. We see today already that he—with Gauguin—represented an express reaction against the impressionism of the Monets and Pissarros."[66]

In 1907, Fülep received a grant to study in Florence, where he was to remain until 1913. In search of a Hungarian philosophic forum, and dissatisfied with *Athenaeum*, the academy journal of philosophy, he wrote to Lukács in the spring of 1910, proposing the creation of a counterculture journal. Initially, Lukács was cool toward the idea, in part because he did not wish to offend Bernát Alexander and other professors who edited *Athenaeum* and whose support he would need if he were to gain a university appointment. He was also pessimistic about the chances a journal of philosophy in Hungarian might have of success. Nonetheless, he traveled to Florence that autumn to discuss the plan with Fülep and in December he advised Popper that a journal would be published and that it might become the Hungarian *Logos*, an "international journal for the philosophy of culture" edited in Germany.[67] *Logos* could boast of such contributors as Rudolf Euchen, Otto von Gierke, Edmund Husserl, Friedrich Meinecke, Heinrich Rickert, Georg Simmel, Ernst Troeltsch, Max Weber, and Heinrich Wölfflin. In the end, however, Fülep rejected the idea because the *Logos* editors (Richard Kroner and Georg Mehlis) insisted that he publish in each number two or three articles from their journal. Financial restrictions made too large a publication impossible; hence the number of original Hungarian contributions and/or translations of classic authors would be very small. If it came to it, he told Lukács, he would rather exclude Simmel than Meister Eckhart.[68]

The financial backing *Logos* might have provided remained a major problem. According to Fülep's original estimate, two hundred subscriptions would be needed to make of the journal a going concern; subsequently, he judged this number to be insufficient, and the plan would have been abandoned had Lukács's father not taken up the financial slack, paying the printing and incidental costs. In February 1911, Fülep made public announcement of *A Szellem*, a journal of metaphysics, ethics, aesthetics, and the philosophy of religion. "In March 1911, several of us will launch the journal *A Szellem*; we are as one in our concern about questions that touch on the essence of culture, even if we move toward their solutions along different paths."[69]

For the first number (March 1911) of *A Szellem*, Fülep and Lukács chose as their motto a quotation from Kant's *Prolegomena*: "That the mind of man will one day abandon metaphysical inquiries is as little to be expected as that we, to avoid inhaling impure air, will stop breathing altogether." In this way, *A Szellem* served notice that it stood in opposition to the positivism of *Huszadik Század* and the impressionism of *Nyugat*. In the spirit of this motto, Fülep and Lukács published translations of "*La nature et l'esprit*" by Émile Boutroux, "The Three Initial Hypostases" from the fifth *Ennead* of Plotinus, and "The Paradoxes of Christianity" from G. K. Chesterton's *Orthodoxy*. In addition, they included three original contributions: Sándor Hevesi (who assisted with the editing of the journal) wrote "On Human Happiness"; Fülep, "Remembrance in Artistic Creation"; and Lukács, "The Metaphysics of Tragedy." In the second number, which appeared in December of the same year, Hungarians could read translations of four of Meister Eckhart's sermons entitled "The Eternal Birth," two brief essays by Hegel, and Leopold Ziegler's "Kant and Metaphysics as the Doctrine of the Transcendental Categories." There were original contributions from Hevesi ("Shakespeare and the Middle Ages"), Lukács ("On Poverty of Spirit"), and a brilliant young philosopher named Béla Zalai ("The Problem of Philosophic Systematization"). At Hevesi's suggestion, a book review section was added.

No further numbers of *A Szellem* were, however, ever issued; the journal died for want of interest in Hungary.[70] Yet, its efforts were not all in vain. Because of its existence, the "field of force" surrounding Lukács and Balázs (who did translations for the journal) had attracted a remarkable group of Hungarian thinkers. To begin with, there was Fülep, a perceptive philosopher of art who shared Lukács's distaste for impressionism and his enthusiasm for Cézanne and Gauguin. In his *A Szellem* essay—"Remembrance in Artistic Creation"[71]—he returned to the same theme. Originally given as a lecture at the *Biblioteca Filosofica* in Florence, the essay took as its point of departure a critique of Croce's aesthetics of intuition, which Fülep castigated as the "belated epilogue of an artistic movement that flowered thirty years earlier: impressionism." True art and a true aesthetics, according to the Hungarian, would have to return to the concept of timeless form, the "Idea" that constituted the "essence of things."

It was as an idealist philosopher of art that Fülep was encouraged by the postimpressionist work of Cézanne and Gauguin. Nor did he despair of the situation in Hungary, for, during a stay in Paris, he had met and exercised a decisive influence on those Hungarian artists who later called themselves "The Eight." The Eight stood in opposition not only to the representational art preferred by the academy but also to the "Circle of Hungarian Impressionists and Naturalists" that had been organized in 1906 by Pál Szinyei-Merse and József Rippl-Rónai. Like Fülep and Lukács, the members of The Eight[72] recognized the greatness and historic importance of Cézanne. More specifically, they admired the French master's profound sense of harmony and his ability to express the essence of his subject. Their predilection for still lifes and nudes was a consequence of their own desire to express concretely the essence of nature and of human life.[73]

In addition to reinforcing Lukács's convictions with regard to modern art, Fülep contributed to his growing interest in mysticism. Not only did *A Szellem* publish translations of Plotinus and Meister Eckhart, it also took notice of new editions of mystical works. The publication in Germany of an edition of Heinrich Suso's works, for example, inspired Fülep to reflect on the philosophic significance of Suso's teacher, Meister Eckhart. "Eckhart has played and doubtless will continue to play an important role in the fertilization of modern metaphysical speculation. We may assert with perfect confidence that every future metaphysics that does not wish to give up the struggle for the principal philosophic values must take account of those pregnant forms of truths to be found in every mysticism."[74]

Béla Zalai was another *A Szellem* contributor whom Lukács recognized as an intellectual brother in arms. As late as the 1960s, he could say that "in the period prior to 1918, he [Zalai] was the only original Hungarian thinker."[75] Born in 1882, Zalai studied mathematics, physics, and philosophy in Kolozsvár, Paris, and Budapest, taking his doctorate in philosophy under Bernát Alexander. Subsequently he taught at a business school and did translation work, but he also published a small number of philosophic essays, one of which, written in German, Lukács read and admired. In a letter of 9 November 1910, he suggested to Fülep that *A Szellem* publish a translation. "Zalai is one of us: anti-psychological, anti-positivist, a metaphysician, etc. An intelligent and cultured person, he stands outside of every Hungarian group. I believe that it would be worthwhile to give him a chance."[76]

Zalai esteemed Lukács highly and was eager to contribute to *A Szellem*, but rather than republish his article, he submitted a new essay entitled "The Problem of Philosophic Systematization." Much to Lukács's surprise, Fülep believed the concluding sections to be incomprehensible.[77] The essay was published only because of Lukács's support and insistence, but it exercised a profound influence on several young Hungarians who were later to gain fame beyond the borders of Hungary: Karl Mannheim, Arnold Hauser, and Wilhelm Szilasi.

Karl Mannheim translated Hegel's "Who Thinks Abstractly?" and "On the Essence of Philosophic Criticism in General and Especially Its Relationship to the Present State of Philosophy" for the second number of *A Szellem*. The translations were commissioned by Lukács, with whom Mannheim had corresponded since the summer of 1910, and they signaled Mannheim's formal entry into Lukács's and Balázs's "field of force." Even after *A Szellem* ceased publication, Mannheim continued to correspond with Lukács in an effort to work out his own philosophic position, and on the evidence of these letters, he formulated his earliest philosophic problems in the language of German mysticism and metaphysics.[78]

Wilhelm Szilasi[79] translated "The Three Initial Hypostases" from the fifth *Ennead* of Plotinus for the first number of *A Szellem*. Fülep was not excessively pleased with this translation, but he published it because neither he nor Lukács wished to offend Bernát Alexander, with whom Szilasi was on good terms. Lukács was irritated with Szilasi for another reason—he believed that the young philosopher had appropriated some of his ideas without acknowledgment. Szilasi defended the ultimate originality of his work,[80] but he conceded that he should have made formal acknowledgment of Lukács's influence. He reminded Lukács, however, that he had "emphasized continually to you and everyone else (perhaps a bit excessively) how very much I have learned from you" and he concluded by saying that "I view you as the goal and ideal toward which I must strive."[81]

Two women were also drawn into the "field of force." Emma Ritoók, who had praised *The Soul and the Forms*, translated Leopold Ziegler's

"Kant and Metaphysics as the Doctrine of the Transcendental Categories" for the second number of *A Szellem*. Anna Lesznai, the pen
name of Amália Moskovits (Mrs. Oszkár Jászi), was a poet and painter;
she did not contribute to *A Szellem*, but it was at this time that she became a close friend of both Balázs and Lukács. Thus, even though the *A
Szellem* experiment had failed, the "field of force" had attracted some
of Hungary's finest young thinkers, and Balázs was convinced that they
would constitute the nucleus for an even larger group. In a letter to
Anna Lesznai, he speculated "that we will soon found a religion. (I
didn't smile when I wrote this.)"[82]

The Soul and the Forms, II

Lukács was far less optimistic. He had become convinced that if he
were to find a larger and more sympathetic readership, he would have to
publish in German.[83] Moreover, he would have to seek like-minded
thinkers in Germany rather than in Hungary. To that end, he sought
the advice of Franz Baumgarten, who though Hungarian by birth, had
settled in Germany in 1909 and had succeeded in establishing contact
with many leading German intellectuals.[84] Over the next few years,
Baumgarten introduced Lukács to numerous German writers and editors
and provided him with information concerning publishing possibilities.

To set his German career in motion, Lukács hoped to publish an
abbreviated version of his *Modern Drama* in German translation, but
when this plan failed to materialize, he concentrated his efforts on
finding a publisher for a German edition of *The Soul and the Forms*. To
increase his chances, he added two essays that had not appeared in the
Hungarian edition: "Longing and Form: Charles-Louis Philippe" and
"The Metaphysics of Tragedy: Paul Ernst." The essay on Philippe[85] was
an extraordinary piece of writing that Lukács described as "the last
'Soul and the Forms' essay";[86] in other words, it was the last Irma essay. Here Lukács's reading of Philippe was clearly determined by his
break with Irma and its existential significance. Philippe's works, he
argued, exemplified Socrates's "philosophy of longing," a philosophy
rooted in Eros. As that which both possessed and did not possess, Eros
had forever to long for its object. "Eros is in the middle: longing unites
those who are unlike, but at the same time destroys every hope of their
becoming one."

Lukács's discussion of Philippe's *Marie Donadieu* was a personal
confession. When the promiscuous Marie returns to Jean, the truest of
her lovers, it is too late, for his love, according to Lukács, had already

been transformed into longing. Jean no longer needs Marie in *life*; he has idolized her to such an extent that she could be meaningful to him only insofar as they are separated in the world of appearances. "But every word and every act in his life will be an implicit song to that which she has given him." She had taken away his loneliness and then returned it to him, and yet he is happy in the same way that Dante was when Beatrice refused to return his greeting. He possessed a new strength and joy that was purchased at the price of her pain and unhappiness, just as Lukács's contentment was purchased with Irma's pain. Lukács perceived in Philippe's work a transvaluation of all values: an existential sorrow that gave pleasure; Christian renunciation transformed into joy; a celebration of the tragic; *amor fati*.

The essay on Paul Ernst, "The Metaphysics of Tragedy,"[87] appeared first in *A Szellem* and in *Logos*, and it was to become the most famous essay in the book. Ernst was a great favorite of Lukács's. In *Modern Drama*, he had exaggerated the importance of the German writer's *Brunhild*, and when the two men first met, on 3 June 1910 in Weimar,[88] each immediately recognized the other as a kindred spirit. Like Lukács, Ernst had a tragic view of life. But it had not always been so; born in 1866, he began his career as a journalist and publicist for German social democracy. His studies of history and his experience of life soon, however, led him to reject both socialism and democracy. As a dramatist, he allied himself initially with naturalism, but it soon became clear to him "that the important matters, namely moral struggles, could not be represented in too close proximity to nature." What was needed, he concluded, was the consciousness of "necessity," and he began therefore to espouse neoclassical tragedy.[89] Like Lukács, too, he identified form as the highest principle of art: "Every man is a slave of his time save one: that artist who is a servant of form."[90] Such an artist occupied a position beyond history and his work could therefore achieve a timeless, universal validity.

It was precisely this timeless quality, according to Lukács, that distinguished tragic drama. Tragedy unveiled for us that characteristic of human existence that was most universal—its form or limits. It uncovered not only those limits imposed by individual destinies but also those defined by our common finitude. For tragedy, death—the boundary as such—was an ever present reality, inextricably intertwined with every event. To give form to the soul was to delineate its limits, it was to deny that its possibilities were infinite. Without the awareness of limits imparted by form, the soul could not awaken to self-consciousness. The soul "is because it is limited; is only because and insofar as it is limited." The argument is that if the soul were immortal, it could never be conscious of its existence, because that consciousness depended on an awareness of the possibility of nonexistence. An awareness of death, then, was necessary if the soul's essence were to be exposed.

It is this argument that has led some critics, Lucien Goldmann above all, to suggest that the Ernst essay prefigured twentieth-century existentialism.[91] Goldmann maintained that Lukács had distinguished "authentic" from "inauthentic" existence on the basis of the former's consciousness of the boundaries of human life and especially of the absolute boundary set by death. Authentic being was what Heidegger would later call being-toward-death. Further evidence has recently been adduced to support Goldmann's claim.[92] The argument has merit, if not pushed too far; for both the young Lukács and Heidegger (with whom the comparison is usually made) consciousness of our finitude was a prerequisite for understanding the meaning of human existence.

In any event, Lukács believed that Ernst's plays closely approximated the drama of necessity perfected by the Greeks and revived by Hebbel. They were made possible by the death of God. "Only when we have become completely godless," Ernst had argued, "will we again have tragedy,"[93] for in a world without God, grace, the transcendence of tragedy, was no longer possible. Aware that God had forsaken men, Ernst's characters did more than recognize their destinies, they saluted and affirmed them. They exhibited what Nietzsche called "the will to power," the willing of fate; therein lay their greatness. As Ernst put it, tragedy "arises out of the deepest suffering and still affirms life with the greatest rejoicing."[94]

In addition to the new essays, Lukács made a number of small but important changes in the introductory letter to Popper, indicating his desire to go beyond essays to some more systematic philosophic work. He now characterized the essayist as a Schopenhauer, who wrote his *Parerga* in anticipation of his own, or another's, *The World as Will and Representation*—a John the Baptist who heralded the coming of someone greater.[95]

Before *The Soul and the Forms* could be published in German, the essays comprising it had to be translated, a task that was undertaken by Popper, Ottó Mandl, and Ernő Lórsy.[96] In February 1911, Lukács signed a contract with the publishing house of Egon Fleischel and Company in Berlin. There remained the all-important question of the dedication. In May 1910, he told Popper that he wished to dedicate the German edition to Irma. "If it is not possible to do so openly, then something else must be devised. Inner integrity, to return that which one has received to the giver." He asked his friend what he thought of the following wordings: "This should be placed in the hands of she who gave it to me"; "In memoriam 18. XII. 1907."[97] In his diary, he had already jotted down another idea: "In memory of my first Florentine days."[98]

The diary also reveals precisely what individual essays in the collection signified to him personally: "The Philippe essay matures in a strange manner. It seems that this will be the most authentic Irma essay. . . . The truly great lyrical series will therefore be: George, Beer-Hofmann, Kierkegaard, Philippe, because the connection with the others is much looser. Novalis: the mood of the [first] meeting; Kassner: Florence, Ravenna;[99] Storm: Nagybánya letters. Even more remote: Sterne: futility, the 'frivolous' moods of the winter following the break. Ernst: the hours of reckoning. But in the [first] four will be the entire history."[100]

In the spring of 1911, Lukács wrote to Irma:

> If you read through it [The Soul and the Forms], really read through it, . . . you know everything about me, the best part of my life, more and better than I would be able to relate in any other manner. You also know . . . from whom I received the tones granted to me, around whose figure, a figure ceaselessly varying before me, every question centered. . . . You know, I repeat, why these papers were written—because I am unable to write verses. And you know, too, I repeat, to whom these "verses" speak and who spoke them within me. Hence, perhaps I do not need to voice my request. These writings are to appear in German (complemented by two pieces long planned and recently written)—permit me to return them to the one from whom I received them, permit me to dedicate this book to you, to inscribe on the first page: "Irma von Réthy-Seidler, in dankbarer Erinnerung."[101]

Irma signaled her approval. "I am proud that I have some part, or that you believe I have some part, in the genesis of a book such as this."[102]

With the completion of this book, Lukács believed the period of his youth and innocence to be at an end, personally and with respect to his work—the two, as always, being interrelated. To Popper he had written that Philippe was the last "Soul and the Forms" essay; "now comes 'science' [in the German sense of Wissenschaft]. Slowly. And perhaps by way of compensation for the poetic lyricism left behind—true metaphysics will come."[103] To Irma he wrote: "I have the feeling that the time has finally come to end that great period (at least for me it was indescribably great) with a friendly clasp of the hand. . . . I have been ready for it for a long time now, perhaps ever since the break. Perhaps for you, too, this time has already arrived; I believe and I hope that it has."[104]

From Tragedy to Utopia

When *Die Seele und die Formen* appeared, the dedication read: "*Dem Andenken Irma Seidlers*," for on 18 May 1911 Irma jumped to her death from one of the bridges that span the Danube between Buda and Pest. According to a newspaper account, "only temporary insanity could have occasioned the unexpected catastrophe. . . . They [Irma and her husband] were free of material care, and they had a happy marriage. Everywhere this attractive, arresting, witty, and temperamental woman was loved."[105] The truth was otherwise. Unknown to Lukács, it was the ending of a brief affair with Balázs that prompted the suicide. "This is my first sin," Balázs wrote in his diary. "In the most weighty sense of the word. Strange that because of it I felt the purity of my life and heart for the first time. I came to know what sin was and also that it hadn't been there before. I realized recently what Weininger meant when he said that it was the broken sinners that became saints, and that temptation is there at the source of every religion. . . . Since Irma's death I have been beset by religious questions and by a compelling thirst to find my God."[106]

And yet Irma knew that her affair with Balázs was nothing more than that. Her reasons for taking her own life went deeper. Her marriage to Réthy had gone from bad to worse, and her paintings had failed to generate any interest.[107] Above all, she had been driven to despair by the break with Lukács; his letter of 22 March had been the final blow. In a letter dated 8 May 1911, Mici Lukács wrote to her brother of a meeting she and their father had had with "Mama Cecile" Polányi at an exhibition of paintings by The Eight. Mrs. Polányi spoke to the elder Lukács "about you and Irma—about how much Irma loves you and wants to divorce her husband." This had to be discouraged, Mrs. Polányi warned, because it would mean only trouble for both Irma and Lukács.[108] Certainly Lukács never doubted his ultimate responsibility, and in a letter to Popper, he bared his soul: "The solitude that I wanted now rushes upon me like the judgment of life. If anyone could have saved her, I could have . . . and I did not want to and was incapable of it. I was a 'good friend' of hers, I know, but that was not what she needed. Something else. More. And the actions appropriate for that were not in me. And with this the judgment is pronounced."[109]

As if Irma's death were not enough, Lukács received word in October that Popper had succumbed to tuberculosis. The man to whom, as Balázs put it, he was so "mystically alike,"[110] was now gone. "How infinitely alone I have always been," Lukács confided to his diary. Of

Irma and Leó, he wrote self-pityingly: "I was never for them what they were for me."[111] During the month of November, he contemplated suicide, a traditional way out in the Austro-Hungarian monarchy, but by the middle of December, he had emerged from his personal slough of despond: "The crisis appears to be at an end. I have taken refuge in the theory of knowledge and in frivolity."[112]

Lukács had chosen to live; the existential crisis was over, but it had transformed his life. He was now determined to live beyond tragedy and hence beyond the irresolvable conflicts that defined the tragic condition. Against his own injunctions, he now challenged fate and began to argue that it was at least possible for men to enter the realm of freedom. No longer would he believe that the path from soul to soul was eternally blocked; no longer would he regard alienation as the *condition humaine*. To Margarete Susman, who had reviewed *The Soul and the Forms* favorably, Lukács now wrote that the book and its form had "become altogether alien to me."[113]

Lukács's turn from tragedy to utopia was given initial expression in a dialogue entitled "On Poverty of Spirit" that he published, after some initial hesitation, in German and in Hungarian.[114] This dialogue is the indispensable introduction to all of his subsequent work, pre-Marxist and Marxist, for although he did not identify himself or Irma by name, Lukács described his spiritual and intellectual crisis in the wake of the suicide. The story begins as a man learns of the tragic suicide of a close female friend. Longing to talk with someone, he sends a note to the dead girl's sister, telling her that he is working and has no need of people. She, sensing that human contact is precisely what he *does* need, goes to the man's dwelling and finds him seated at his desk. He comes straight to the point: he holds himself responsible for the death of his friend. "She had to die, so that my work could be completed, so that nothing in the world should remain for me other than my work" (*IM*, 545). The sister protests that he could not have known her intention, but he insists that his actions had been governed by a barren ethics of duty, rather than by that unconditional identification with another that he calls "goodness," the *unio mystica* of the mystics. To be sure, he acknowledges that for most people duty is enough. "These people, you see, can do with duties and their fulfillment. Indeed, for them the fulfillment of duty is the only way in which their lives can be raised to a higher level. This is so because every ethic is formal, the postulate of duty or of form— and the more perfect the form, the more it lives its own life, the further removed it is from every immediacy. Form is that kind of bridge that dissociates, a bridge on which we come and go and always return to ourselves without ever meeting one another" (*IM*, 539–40). Ethics in the traditional sense was by its very nature foreign to men; it was among the powers of alienation.

It was here that Lukács posited a life ("the living life") that transcended the alienation of man from woman, work from everyday life: "Living life lies beyond the forms, everyday life on the near side; goodness is the grace that enables us to break through these forms." Were men to receive this grace, paradise (a place free of alienation) would become reality. So transformed would men be that they would no longer truly be human: "We are human beings simply because we are able to create only works, because we are able to conjure up only happy islands in the midst of unhappy disquiet and the squalid flux of life. If art [work] could form life, if goodness could be transformed into action—then we would be gods. 'Why callest thou me good? There is none good but one, that is, God,' Christ said."

Lukács identified several of Dostoevski's characters—Sonia, Prince Myshkin, Alyosha and Alexei Karamazov—as examples of good people. Theirs was a godly world that lay beyond the God-forsaken world of the forms—beyond tragedy. Indifferent to every theoretical impossibility and caring nothing for "realism," these "mad, unreasonable" utopians *acted*; unlike the detached observers of the tragic world, they were "Gnostics of the world of deeds." By their work-conscious acts, their identification with others was made complete; "subject and object become one." For this reason, "goodness is a miracle. Miracle and grace and redemption. The descent of the heavens to earth" (*IM*, 541).

Nor was Dostoevski alone in his understanding of goodness, for Kierkegaard shared his insights. Instructed by *Fear and Trembling*, Lukács argued that Abraham, too, was good, though not ethical; with his sacrifice, the father of the Hebrews had quit the world of tragic conflicts (those based upon the irreconcilability of two, equally valid, moral duties) and tragic heroes—the ethical world of Agamemnon and his sacrifice. Here Lukács came to a critical point in his argument. Abraham was "good" *because* he sinned, *because* he was willing to kill the innocent Isaac. The story of Abraham was the classic example of what Kierkegaard called "the teleological suspension of the ethical." That God stayed Abraham's hand was, as Lukács recognized clearly, quite irrelevant from the moral point of view; in his heart the patriarch had already killed his son. Goodness was thus beyond morality, and he who would be good could not expect to remain morally pure; he had in fact to be a sinner. The good man was a holy sinner whose purity was of another, a higher order; he sinned so that he might save others—the "work" of goodness—and thus please God in defiance of the moral law.

Those who received the terrifying grace of goodness belonged, according to Lukács, to a higher spiritual "caste" than either of the two castes he had recognized previously: those of life and of work.[115] Irma had belonged to the former, he to the latter, and between the two there was a tragic and unbridgeable gulf. Each of these castes had duties appropriate to it alone, and it would have been a sin for a person even to wish, as he had at times, to cross over from one caste to another in order to save someone. Ultimately, Lukács had resisted the temptation to surrender that detachment necessary for his creative work; thus he had remained pure with respect to the demands of the moral law (i.e., the duties of his spiritual caste). He had purchased his moral purity, however, with Irma's life. Too late he had discovered the highest caste, that which by granting life to work and work-like essence to life could have made it possible for him to reach out to her across the abyss.

Lukács decided against suicide because he believed that he had now received the gift of grace; in conformity with Kierkegaard's "stages along life's way," he had advanced from the ethical to the religious stage. And yet, Lukács conceived of religion as a metaethic.[116] Henceforth, he would take his place in the most dangerous of heretical traditions—that which equated religion with perfect justice and which therefore insisted that the Kingdom of God be established on earth. In the dialogue, the man shoots himself. On his desk, the Bible is open to the *Apocalypse*, and he had marked the words: "I know thy works, that thou art neither cold nor hot: I would thou wert cold or hot. So then because thou art lukewarm, and neither cold nor hot, I will spue thee out of my mouth" (Revelation 3:15–16). Having wanted to help (hence, not cold), he had been incapable of an act of goodness (not hot). This fictional suicide was Lukács's way of putting his previous detachment behind him, of passing judgment upon the tragic sense of life; it was a symbolic affirmation of the death of his former self. Intoxicated by millennial hope of the "second coming" and convinced that he had been redeemed, he stood on the threshold of a radically new life.

Ljena Grabenko: Utopia

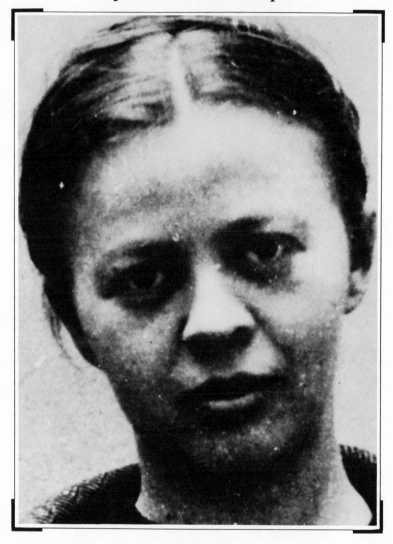

Ljena Grabenko about 1913
Courtesy Petőfi Irodalmi Múzeum (Petőfi Literary Museum), Budapest

C·H·A·P·T·E·R

3

Heidelberg

Ernst Bloch and Martin Buber

Irma's suicide impelled Lukács from tragedy to utopia, from heroic acceptance to apocalyptic hope, and yet the conversion did not come without some warning; there had always been a part of Lukács that rebelled against necessity, witness his admiration for Ady, whom he described as the poet of the "revolution-less Hungarian revolutionaries" who "never, even for one moment, reconciled himself to Hungarian reality."[1] Moreover, in 1910 Emma Ritoók had introduced him to Ernst Bloch, a remarkable utopian thinker who fairly radiated hope.

Born in Ludwigshafen am Rhein on 8 July 1885, Bloch was the son of assimilated Jews.[2] Upon completion of his gymnasium studies in 1905, he went to Munich, the cultural center of Bavaria, to study philosophy under Theodor Lipps. But neither Lipps nor Ernst Mach, with whom he had exchanged letters, were to be Bloch's true mentors: "The philosophers from whom I can learn something have been dead for nearly a century—I said at that time. I meant Hegel and his school, Schelling, and Fichte."[3]

From 1908 to 1911, Bloch lived in Berlin, where he sought out Georg Simmel, the only contemporary thinker from whom he believed he might have something to learn. It was at Simmel's private seminar that he first met Lukács. Simmel had asked him to be present when the Hungarian made his initial appearance, in order to take his measure as a thinker, but after the meeting Bloch was unable to express an opinion, having in the meantime forgotten Simmel's request.[4] Sometime later,

Bloch traveled to Budapest to visit Emma Ritoók, yet another member
of the Simmel seminar, and there she reintroduced the two men. "Up to
that time," Lukács recalled, "I inclined toward the Neo-Kantianism of
the day, but in Bloch, I saw someone who philosophized as if that philosophy did not exist. I saw that it was possible to philosophize in the
manner of Aristotle or Hegel."[5] With this recognition, Lukács's essay
period came to an end; in a letter of October 1910 he told Popper that
"Philippe" was the last "Soul and the Forms" essay and expressed his
desire to become a metaphysician.

According to Bloch, however, metaphysics was nowhere to be found
in contemporary Germany. Intrigued by his new friend's claim that one
could learn only from the great German idealists, Lukács took a closer
look at more recent German thought and did not like what he saw. He
told Paul Ernst that he was horrified by Germany's intellectual decline,[6]
and in A Szellem he called attention to the dilemma of contemporary
German philosophy. "It is confronted with an age . . . that has lost all
connection with the great ages of German intellectual life (I mean, of
course, those of Eckhart, Böhme, and Kant-Hegel) and is therefore
shallow and amorphous."[7]

When Dilthey died in 1911, Lukács published an obituary in A Szellem. Of this philosopher, who once so impressed him, he wrote that "it
would be hypocrisy to mourn his death as an irreparable loss. Those few
who believe in a philosophic renaissance long ago ceased to regard
Dilthey with expectant eyes."[8] He conceded that Dilthey had guarded
Germany's best cultural traditions and had perceived positivism's philosophic emptiness, but he insisted that the German had fallen victim to
the absurd belief that psychology could answer general philosophic
questions. Like the majority of his contemporaries, Dilthey feared metaphysics; unable to abandon his concept of psychological Erlebnis, he
became a mere "essayist," now a pejorative term in Lukács's vocabu-
lary. Compared to the great idealists, not even Simmel now seemed to
Lukács to be an authentic philosopher, and in a Nachruf of 1918, he
would describe his former teacher as an impressionist, "a Monet of
philosophy, whom as yet no Cézanne has succeeded."[9]

Having all but despaired of contemporary thinkers, Lukács looked
for inspiration to Kant, Fichte, Schelling, and, to a lesser degree, Hegel.
His reservations concerning Hegel derived from his rejection of the German's Versöhnung mit der Wirklichkeit (reconciliation with reality).[10]
In search of utopia, Lukács was attracted instead to the ethical idealism
of Kant and, even more, of Fichte, for he recognized that "if we wish to
find among the idealist philosophers something comparable to Marx's

missionary zeal, we have to turn to Fichte rather than to Hegel."[11] Indeed, the young Lukács maintained that Marx's philosophy issued from that of Fichte.[12]

Even more important to Lukács than philosophic idealism, but closely related to it, was religious mysticism, and in this case, it was he who instructed Bloch.[13] Still, Bloch's religious atheism, his belief in an immanent, *historical* eschatology, reinforced Lukács's initial fascination. Moreover, the Hungarian's study of the German idealists made him more aware of the mystics' philosophic significance. When Lajos Fülep wrote in *A Szellem* concerning Eckhart's importance to modern metaphysics, he echoed what Franz Pfeiffer, who published the first scholarly edition of Eckhart's German writings, wrote in 1845: "The German mystics are the patriarchs (*Erzväter*) of German speculation." Nor was his an idiosyncratic view; Dilthey, too, had emphasized the continuity of tradition represented by mysticism and idealism.[14]

Lukács was initially drawn to religious mysticism by Ady's poetry. In 1909, he described Ady as a revolutionary whose revolution was religious rather than economic in nature, adding that those who were familiar with the poet's work would understand what he meant. Nevertheless, Lukács did single out the concluding stanzas of "The Trumpet of God" in an effort to remind his readers of the eschatological power of Ady's verse:

> God, the primal Life, will come
> And He will sound His trumpet on this earth:
> "Ye quick, dead, and yet unborn,
> Behold, today I render justice,"
> And He will sound His trumpet on this earth.
>
> He who lived at the cost of others' tears
> Will come to a terrible, hideous end.
> He who is a tyrant in tomb, life, or womb,
> Will perish like a carrion in a flock:
> Will come to a terrible, hideous end.[15]

For Ady, Lukács concluded, poems possessed a significance that transcended the aesthetic; in them he was able to give form to his "mystical longings," his revolutionary hopes.

Lajos Fülep was interested in Jewish mysticism as early as 1910, in preparation, perhaps, for his subsequent entry into the Christian ministry after World War I. On 16 November 1910, he wrote to Lukács that he had read "Buber and found him to be fascinating."[16] So did Lukács, and with good reason. Martin Buber was to become a primary influence in Lukács's life.

In 1881, Buber had been taken at the age of three into his grandfather's home in the Galician capital of Lemberg, his parents having been divorced. He was not to see his mother again until he had a family of his own, and thus, although the circumstances differed, Buber, like Lukács, was estranged from his mother; we have it on his own authority that this separation made him particularly sensitive to the universal problem of human alienation, or to use the word he coined, "mismeeting" (*Vergegnung*).[17]

Although he attended a Polish gymnasium from 1892 to 1896, Buber identified himself with German culture early on and, after completing his studies in Lemberg, he matriculated at the University of Vienna. Sensitive to the alienating force of anti-Semitism, he joined the *Neue Gemeinschaft* (New Community) organized by the literary critics Heinrich and Julius Hart and frequented by the utopian socialist Gustav Landauer, whose translation of Meister Eckhart's writings he much admired. It was not long before he turned his attention to philosophy and religious mysticism; his doctoral dissertation (1904) was entitled "On the History of the Problem of Individuation: Nicholas of Cusa and Jakob Böhme." Because of these interests and the hope of community he invested in Zionism, he began his intensive studies of that form of Jewish mysticism called Hasidism.

The Hasidism to which Buber became a convert was the most recent in time. It was the Polish and Ukrainian Hasidism of the eighteenth and nineteenth centuries, founded by Israel Baal Shem, "Master of the Holy Name," who died in 1760. It may well be, as Gershom Scholem has argued persuasively,[18] that Buber's interpretation of Hasidism was more personal than historical, that it was based almost entirely on the legends, epigrams, and anecdotes of the Hasidic saints, to the exclusion of more theoretical writings, but whatever its idiosyncrasies, it was Buber's interpretation of precisely these tales that captivated Lukács. During the summer of 1911, he read Buber's versions of *Die Geschichte des Rabbi Nachman* and *Die Legende des Baalschem*.[19]

Lukács had introduced himself to Buber by sending him a manuscript copy of "Sören Kierkegaard and Regine Olsen," and in his letter of reply, Buber praised the essay because it treated "so well a theme [that of choice] so important to me."[20] Moreover, he sent complementary copies of the Baal Shem and Rabbi Nachman volumes. Lukács was immensely impressed; "in particular, Baal Shem was for me unforgettable!" He thought it a pity that there existed no complete edition of Hasidic tales and asked Buber if he planned to compile such an edition.

"One would gladly learn so much—for example, the ethical turn of metempsychosis—within the entire breadth of the tradition."[21]

It is not surprising that Lukács was so taken with these two books, and especially with *The Legend of the Baal Shem*, for in them he encountered messianic hope of a genuine *Gemeinschaft*. In "The Life of the Hasidim," the first section of *Baal Shem*, he read that every man was the abode of a wandering soul and that all souls had sprung from the same primeval soul. These wandering souls moved from man to man, from "form" to "form," each form being a prison. To be a redeemed soul was to cease wandering and to return home to the primeval soul; it was to be able to recognize itself as *identical* to all other souls. "And this," Buber wrote, "is the meaning and mission of *kavana* [intention]: that it is given to man to lift up the fallen and to free the imprisoned. Not only to wait, not only to watch for the Coming One: man can work toward the redemption of the world." Man could prepare "the final oneness of all things."[22]

In the subsection entitled "Shiflut" (humility), Lukács learned that those who wished to work toward redemption had to be humble, and "he is truly humble who feels the other as himself and himself in the other." Such humility—what Lukács called "poverty of spirit"—characterized only those who truly loved; to love more was fundamental to Hasidism and was the redemptive act. This requires emphasis; true love was active love. Those who loved ministered to the suffering of others, experiencing this suffering as their own, in contrast with those who merely showed pity for the suffering of others. He who pitied did not live with the suffering of the sufferers. Rather, he received "from the most external features of this suffering a sharp, quick pain, unbridgeably dissimilar to the original pain of the sufferer." He could not recognize, as could he who performed helpful acts consecrated by love, "the truth that all souls are one; for each is a spark from the original soul, and the whole of the original soul is in each."[23]

Nothing expressed better than these teachings Lukács's utopian dreams. Their similarity to the teachings to be found in "On Poverty of Spirit" can scarcely have been accidental; there, too, redemption was conceived of as the achievement of *Gemeinschaft* in this world—the temporal transcending of individuality (the "forms") and complete identification with others. Buber might with equal justice have written of Lukács what in fact he wrote of Rabbi Nachman and those Hasidim who resembled him: "Like the prophets of Israel, so too these, their late sons, were no reformers but revolutionaries; they demanded not the better, but the absolute; they wanted not to educate, but to redeem."[24] The ethical turn of metempsychosis, concerning which Lukács had written to Buber, referred to those loving acts of goodness, those metaethical deeds that served to release human souls from the prisons of successive individual forms and to lead them into the utopia of *Gemeinschaft*.

In a letter of 20 December 1911, Lukács informed Buber that he had called attention to his books in Hungary: "I have written a brief review of both volumes in the Hungarian philosophic journal *A Szellem* (similar to *Logos*). The editor of this journal, Mr. Ludwig Fülep, a distinguished expert on the Italian and Spanish mystics, is very interested in these [Buber's] books."[25] Lukács's review, entitled "Jewish Mysticism," appeared in the second number of *A Szellem*. The principal merit of the books, he wrote, was that they silenced criticism according to which the metaphysical source of Judaism had run dry. "The 'Hasidic' movement, of which Baal Shem was the first and Nachman the last great representative, was a mysticism of primitive power, the only truly great movement since the mysticism of the German Reformation and the Spanish Counter-Reformation and every bit the equal of these and preceding movements. What is most striking here is how unrelated mysticism is to religion—despite every profound inner religiosity. Baal Shem interprets the Old Testament just as freely as Eckhart does the New Testament. Both make use of these books only as a framework for their new symbols."[26]

Not long after the publication of this review, Béla Balázs made an important entry in his diary:

> Gyuri's new philosophy. Messianism. The homogeneous world
> [Lukács's term for *Gemeinschaft*] as the redemptive goal. Art the
> Luciferean "better made." The vision of the world become
> homogeneous before the actual process of transformation. The
> immorality of art. Gyuri's big turn toward ethics. This will be the
> center of his life and work. . . . Gyuri discovered and acknowl-
> edges the *Jew* in himself! Quest of the forefathers. The Hasidic
> sect's Baal Shem. Now he too has found his forefathers and his
> kind; only I stand alone and forsaken. . . . Gyuri's theory con-
> cerning the type of Jew now evolving or developing once again
> —the anti-rational ascetic; concerning that which is the opposite
> of everything that today is customarily called "Jewish."[27]

The last sentence is of particular importance. Lukács's enthusiasm for the antirational stemmed from his conviction that the rationalization of society increased the distance between people, rendering all relationships impersonal and reified. In the "irrationalism" of Hasidism, he perceived evidence that refuted the widely held belief that Jews were the rationalists par excellence and could thus be held responsible for the alienated world of the fin de siècle. A considerable burden was thereby lifted from his spiritual shoulders.

Lukács was willing, even eager, to accept his Jewishness if the Hasidim were quintessential Jews, but there was another sense in which he had discovered the Jew in himself; he was living proof that "there is no distinction in the Jewish consciousness between religion and morals."[28] Certainly the goodness of which he had written in "On Poverty of Spirit" was a category at once moral and religious. Thus Balázs was right when he maintained that art now had for Lukács a *moral* mission —that of providing a vision of a new, homogeneous world that could inspire the actualization of utopia. True art was Luciferean because it rebelled against the world God had made and created in its stead a better world; taking his cue from Buber's creatively altered Hasidic tales, Lukács now focused his attention on the fairy tale and its "counterpart" —the "romance," or "untragic drama."[29] Both were for him anticipations and microcosms of perfection; both were utopian in essence.

Fairy Tales and Romances

In an effort to increase his understanding of the fairy tale as a genre, Lukács turned for guidance to Anna Lesznai, who was born to a landowning family of assimilated Jews and became a contributor to *Nyugat* when her cousin Lajos Hatvany, a contributor and financial backer, carried her first poems to the journal's editorial offices. Like Lukács and Balázs, she experienced life as loneliness and alienation. That her poetry was replete with fairy tale motifs was a result of her determined efforts to escape her sense of isolation; in her work she created an "imaginary community" that was "not only a form of escape from loneliness, but at the same time the embryo of a utopian-messianic striving after the creation of a more human, more authentic community."[30] In 1912, she confided to her diary that "the fairy tale is religious because it is the boundless, or rather the *flawlessly proper* world."[31]

Instructed by Lesznai, Lukács persuaded himself that fairy tales delineated a redeemed world, one in which ultimate reality was magical rather than empirical or metaphysical. This magical reality could be understood only as a primal unity in which the empirical/metaphysical distinction was meaningless. It taught men that their reality, whether empirical or metaphysical, was but one of many imaginable realities. Recognizing this, they needed no longer to regard their reality as an inescapable prison; they could understand that it was the result of their own *choices*. All great literature, Lukács now believed, treated a given reality as the result of man's free choice, not as something forced upon him by some transcendent necessity.[32]

Just as he had attempted to identify the reasons for the great ages of the tragic drama in *Modern Drama*, Lukács endeavored to ascertain what ages were most receptive to fairy tales, and he concluded that they made their greatest appeal to those ages that stood at a crossroads, those for which reality seemed increasingly problematic. The age of the fin de siècle was just such an age, for in his own time, he argued, even the soul's reality had become problematic, contributing to a new loneliness and sense of alienation.[33] In the quest for new realities of the soul, the fairy tale was of particular relevance. Encouraged by Lukács, Balázs wrote fairy tales that attempted "to discover the road from soul to soul, to relieve the isolating loneliness, to merge with another world."[34]

The utopian possibilities of the fairy tale were matched, in Lukács's judgment, by those of the untragic drama, or romance. Once the champion of the tragic drama, he now admired those dramatic works that were situated beyond tragedy, and in a brief essay entitled "The Problem of the Untragic Drama" that appeared in *Die Schaubühne* (1911),[35] he denied that fate and the tragic protagonist constituted the zenith of human existence. For him, Sophocles's *Oedipus* was no longer the paradigm of great drama; nor did the Greeks represent the alpha and omega of dramatic achievement. He now identified the later Shakespeare, the author of *The Tempest*, as the greatest dramatist; the age of Shakespeare, the age of the romance, was the ideal toward which he now hoped his own age would strive.

The world of the romance was far removed from that of the tragic drama. Whereas the principle of the latter was human alienation, that of the former was the obliteration "of the border line between the I and others and between the I and the world" (*IM*, 521). Shades of the Hasidim. Quite naturally, the heroes of the two forms of drama were also worlds apart; the tragic hero "struggles with fate, the [hero of a romance] struggles against fate" (*IM*, 522). In conclusion, Lukács described the untragic drama as democratic in form because it did not, like tragedy, give birth to castes that isolated human beings from one another.

This article was to have served as an initial exploration of the theme, and Lukács also prepared the first part of what was to have been a major work (in German) on "The Aesthetics of the 'Romance': An Attempt at a Metaphysical Foundation of the Form of the Untragic Drama."[36] Never completed and left unpublished, this work constituted Lukács's reply to the author of the *History of the Evolution of the Modern Drama* and of "The Metaphysics of Tragedy." Although he acknowledged that great drama had often been closely associated with tragedy and the tragic sense of life, he pointed out that tragedy, rooted as it was in the world of the pagan Greeks, could never be reconciled with that other main pillar of Western civilization and culture—Christianity. Christian philosophers spoke of "grace" and of "redemption" rather than of fate and destiny, and as he wrote to Paul Ernst in September 1911, "my work on the untragic drama has directed me very much to the question of the boundary between religion and art."[37]

Among the romances that Lukács admired most were the plays of Euripides (an atypical Greek), Calderón, and Shakespeare, certain of the works of Corneille and Racine, and several modern dramas (*Faust, Peer Gynt*, Hebbel's *Genoveva*, and Hauptmann's postnaturalist plays). In common with fairy tales, these untragic dramas ended happily; just as the tragic hero had to experience defeat, so the hero of a romance had to prevail. In the utopia of the untragic drama, man's hope was always rewarded. Lukács was pleased to discover that this promise had been claimed by the contemporary dramatist he esteemed above all others— Paul Ernst.

In the festschrift honoring Ernst's fiftieth birthday (1916), he praised his friend's ability to transcend the tragic drama and to reach the drama of grace (*Gnadendrama*). Ernst had once written that great drama (tragedy) could only be written when the world had become completely godless—a view that Lukács had shared. In such a world, there could be no redemption, no ultimate mercy; tragic destiny was inexorable. But, Lukács maintained, Ernst began to ask himself whether it might not be the case that only *one* god had died and that modern man's purposelessness was but the darkness that preceded the coming of another. If that were so, would not the tragic hero be the bearer of the antigod principle? Was the god-forsaken world of tragedy the final reality? Ernst could not ultimately accept this, and thus after *Brunhild* (tragedy) came *Ariadne auf Naxos* (drama of grace).[38]

Inspired by the utopian world of fairy tales and romances, Lukács believed that he was finally prepared to become a philosopher. Following Ernst Bloch, he would construct a philosophic system that took its point of departure from the works of German idealism and was rooted in a profound religious sensibility. This abrupt change in the direction of his life and work did not go unnoticed by his family and friends, most of whom disliked Bloch. Lukács's father and sister both regarded the German utopian as a bad influence and Béla Balázs commented in his diary that Bloch's "hypnotic" influence on Lukács was disturbing.[39] Bloch's most relentless critic, however, was his former friend and lover Emma Ritoók.[40] Admittedly bitter, this astute writer and philosopher repeatedly cautioned Lukács to beware of the German thinker and his ideas, and it was precisely the religious tone of his philosophy to which she objected: "Once I asked Ernst whether he believed in God or only needed Him for his philosophy. He did not reply. The religious question concerns a man's, not a philosophy's, relation to God."[41] The theological dress of Bloch's thought was not, in her judgment, appropriate to Lukács's mode of thinking, and she encouraged him to write a philosophy for the twentieth century, adding that Bloch would certainly not do so.

Lukács would have done well to heed this advice, but instead, he began to discuss with Bloch the possibility of settling somewhere outside of Hungary where both of them could pursue their philosophic investigations. He had passed much of 1911 in Florence, but because both men planned to write in German, a German-speaking area seemed preferable; thus the choice was narrowed to Austria and Germany. In the fall of 1911, Bloch traveled to Austria; "I don't believe," he wrote to Lukács, "that I can live among these uncivil, poisonously embittered, impossibly susceptible, eternally race-theorizing German-Austrians."[42] Thus Germany was selected, and in 1912, they traveled to Heidelberg, then a major center of German intellectual life. Without doubt, their decision was influenced heavily by the fact that Heidelberg was the home of Max Weber.

Max Weber and His Circle

Lukács's decision to leave his homeland for Germany was prompted by several considerations. To begin with, Hungary lacked a philosophic culture; surrounded at best by impressionists (*Nyugat*) and positivists (*Huszadik Század*), one who longed to be a philosopher could scarcely hope to feel at home. Nor was the situation likely to change for the better; *A Szellem* had been obliged to cease publication after two numbers and Lukács did not think it could be resuscitated. This failure and his numerically small "field of force" in Hungary persuaded him to look for a home where his work would meet with more sympathy and understanding, a land with a more fertile philosophic soil.[43]

There was also the matter of an academic career. At his father's insistence, Lukács had attempted to habilitate (qualify for a university appointment) in Budapest and had failed. In a letter of 23 August 1910, Bernát Alexander had warned him to expect trouble from Gedeon Petz, a philologist who as president of the habilitation committee would have the deciding vote with regard to formal requirements.[44] Lukács was in

Florence on 4 May 1911, when his application for appointment as a *Privatdozent* in "literary aesthetics" came up for review. Later that same day, his father wrote to him concerning the result: "Dear Gyuri, it is with embarrassment and profound outrage that I give you the news that according to the afternoon report given me by Professor Alexander your *Privatdozent* petition has been rejected by a vote of 23 to 15. Gedeon Petz spoke against you and with his great influence voted you down. He spoke against your subject matter, explaining that it was by no means defined and—though Beöthy came strongly to your defense— not useful; the majority voted against you. Alexander will also write to you soon."[45]

Faithful to his word, Alexander composed his letter the same day, providing Lukács with details of the academic proceedings.[46] It was, in fact, Petz who had been primarily responsible for the defeat, though Frigyes Medveczky, professor of philosophy, also spoke in opposition, questioning the wisdom of appointing someone who had held his doctorate for only two years. This objection might have been set aside had not Petz mentioned that Lukács also held a doctorate in law—the implication being that he was something of a dilettante. With that, Lukács's fate was sealed. The official reason given to him by the dean of the faculty was that the required three years had not elapsed since he took his doctorate on 27 November 1909.

However serious the official reasons for Lukács's rejection, there was another, unspoken reason—his Jewish origins. In a subsequent conversation with the elder Lukács, Alexander admitted as much, and completely taken aback, the older man replied, "Why Gyuri is no longer a Jew!"[47] In a letter to Lukács of 24 June 1912, Alexander told him that "in every denominational matter, the faculty is very nervous." The appointment of the Jewish mathematician Lipót Fejér had created in many the fear that Jews were taking over the universities, particularly in view of the fact that at the same time, two Jewish mathematicians had been named to the faculty at the University of Kolozsvár.[48]

That this was not simply a "denominational matter" is clear, for in 1907, Lukács had been baptized in a Lutheran church. Moreover, his friend Béla Zalai (also of Jewish extraction) had been born in the Reformed faith—and he, too, Alexander reported, had been rejected by the Budapest faculty. Lukács had already learned of Zalai's fate: "I think you are aware, via Emma [Ritoók]," the young philosopher wrote to Lukács on 23 June 1911, "of the refusal of my habilitation; likewise, I know from Emma of Bloch's case. *Tres facimus collegium*; but on the other hand, it scarcely matters, except for the material consequences."[49]

The fact that both Lukács and Zalai were denied academic positions, in part at least because of their Jewish background, reflected the growth of anti-Semitism in Hungary. Times were changing. In the 1880s, when the University of Budapest appointed Alexander, Samu Szemere, and József Bánóczi to the faculty of philosophy, no problem existed. All three were Jews. But from about 1900, the "Jewish Question" came increasingly to the fore, and although no de jure quota was ever established, one was set de facto.[50] And despite Zalai's feigned indifference, such exclusion could not but hurt and embitter men of ability.

József Lukács refused to accept defeat, and he and Alexander discussed the possibility of a position at the University of Pozsony (Bratislava). Literature and aesthetics still seemed the best field, despite the fact that Lukács now preferred an appointment in philosophy. Beöthy would support him strongly, but Medveczky was liable to be less enthusiastic; in addition, Ákos Pauler, a philosopher of some distinction, was then teaching at Pozsony. Even after Lukács had settled in Heidelberg, his father continued to project the possibility of a Pozsony professorship. In a letter of 24 July 1912, he informed his son that Pauler had accepted a position at Kolozsvár, leaving open a professorship in philosophy. By return mail, Lukács advised his father that he did not wish to pursue the matter further, because he had decided to seek an academic career in Germany.[51]

Lukács was fortunate to have in Franz Baumgarten a cicerone to guide him through the corridors of German intellectual and academic life. Aware of Simmel's reputation in Freiburg and Heidelberg, Baumgarten suggested that Lukács obtain a letter of introduction from him to present to Wilhelm Windelband, Emil Lask, and Max Weber.[52] With Simmel's assistance secured, Baumgarten was optimistic. He told Lukács that although Heinrich Rickert judged "The Metaphysics of Tragedy" to be "too feuilletonish," he was eager to meet the author. Moreover, the pompous philosopher could always be won over by a recommendation from his "idol"—Max Weber.[53] Armed with this good counsel, Lukács and Bloch traveled to Weber's city—Heidelberg.

At that time, the city on the Neckar was one of the greatest centers of learning in Germany, indeed in all of Europe. Its university was liberal and cosmopolitan; students came from all corners of Europe and the faculty could boast of such well-known scholars as Windelband, Ernst Troeltsch, and Alfred Weber. The presence of Windelband and of Rickert's brilliant student Emil Lask identified Heidelberg as a major center of Neo-Kantianism. Lukács knew, too, that the sociologist Emil Lederer also lived in Heidelberg, and Lederer's wife Emmy was Irma Seidler's sister. Most important, however, Heidelberg was the home of Max Weber.

Weber was already something of a legend by the time Lukács arrived in Heidelberg. So many visitors came to seek his wisdom that the great sociologist had little time or strength to devote to his own studies. Finally, in order to accommodate everyone, he decided to hold regular Sunday-afternoon gatherings. Among frequent visitors at these gatherings were Friedrich Naumann, Theodor Heuss, Troeltsch (who lived in a room on the second floor of the Weber home), Friedrich Gundolf (a member of the inner circle around Stefan George), and Karl Jaspers. As Simmel's friends and former students, Lukács and Bloch found a ready welcome at Ziegelhäuser Landstrasse 17, the Webers' home on the south side of the Neckar, opposite the castle.

Lukács made an immediate and enormous impression on Weber, with whom he engaged in intense conversation. Paul Honigsheim, another regular visitor at the Weber home, reported that Weber once told him that whenever he spoke to Lukács, he thought about their discussion for days.[54] We know, too, that Weber was very much taken with "On Poverty of Spirit."[55] So was Marianne Weber: "What is expressed there," she wrote to Lukács, "has moved me very deeply. . . . I *thank* you for this gift from soul to soul, that you can no longer take back."[56] Only a week before (22 July 1912), she had addressed these warm words to the Hungarian: "I am obliged to express to you yet another word of gratitude for the beautiful hours that you have given me. Out of the wealth of your soul, you know how, as very few do, to communicate that one is not stifled by the shame of one's own poverty, and you will certainly sense that the conversations with you were more to me than the mere amusement of some social hours."[57]

Because of the strength of his personality and the high standard of his work, Lukács captivated most of the Germans. Both Troeltsch and Alfred Weber, for example, thought well of *Die Seele und die Formen*.[58] Yet only one person in Heidelberg, with the exception of Max Weber, exercised any lasting influence on the direction of Lukács's thought— Emil Lask, a solitary man who "ached to be less alone."[59] He seems to have enjoyed Lukács's company and to have been flattered by the Hungarian's friendly overtures: "You have been so kindly disposed toward me," he wrote to Lukács, "that I am impatient to see you and to speak with you."[60] The two men often took walks together, and although we do not have any record of their conversations, it is not too much to suppose that they exchanged views concerning German idealism, in particular the philosophy of Fichte. Aware that Lask had written his dissertation on Fichte, Lukács later characterized Lask's lifework as an attempt to clarify a philosophy of value that was rooted in the thought of Kant and Fichte.[61] The two Jewish thinkers from Austria-Hungary may also have discussed the philosophic problem of irrationalism, because "Lask appeared to him [Lukács] as the author in whom modern irrationalism was most pronounced methodologically."[62] Indeed, Lask was greatly influenced by Neoplatonism, having prefaced his major work, *Die Logik der Philosophie und die Kategorienlehre* (1911), with a motto taken from Plotinus's sixth *Ennead*.

Max Weber was also engaged in the study of rationalism and irrationalism. The fate of his times, he wrote in "Science as a Vocation," was "characterized by rationalization and intellectualization and, above all, by the 'disenchantment of the world.'"[63] He spoke of Western civilization, the uniqueness of which he had come to understand only after brilliant and extensive explorations of Chinese and Indian civilizations, studies that are valuable in and of themselves. Only in the West, he was convinced, did the process of rationalization come to define every mode of human existence. There, all actions were directed toward specific goals—all were *zweckrational*. Capitalism was the economic expression of rationalization, calculation for profit.

Important as a capitalist economic system was, however, it was not the only example of rationalization. Law, too, was rational, a logical system derived from general principles. Bureaucratic government was perhaps the most obvious example of the triumph of rational procedures; indeed, Weber was the great prophet of our age of bureaucracy. The purpose of bureaucracies, the establishment of regular, nonarbitrary rules of procedure had once seemed desirable and progressive, but as Simmel had warned, objective culture invariably cut loose from the subjective spirit that it was designed to express and took on a life of its own. Even religion, insofar as it systematized dogma in a theology, fell victim to the rationalization process; it, too, contributed to the *Entzauberung der Welt*.

Despite Weber's famous determination to separate fact from value, he believed that rationalization condemned Western men to a life of alienation; enslaved by bureaucratic structures of their own making and unable to view their fellows as anything but *means* to some *end*, they had locked the door on their "iron cage." Such an analysis of the times could not but impress Lukács, but what he could not accept was Weber's resignation. For the German, rationalization was inescapable, the fate of Western man. Even his own scientific researches, the researches that had given him such profound insight and understanding, constituted an example of rational procedure. Precisely this recognition lay behind Weber's determination to keep fact (established by rational investigation) distinct from value (a privileged realm of irrational decision). Not that such a realm could ever conquer the rationalized world; it was but the last redoubt of a genuine individuality.

Although no evidence can be adduced to prove that Lukács discussed his interest in fairy tales with Weber, the latter was certainly well disposed toward any "enchantment" of a world so utterly disenchanted. Like Lukács, he believed that under the conditions imposed by the rationalization of life, art possessed a redemptive character: "Art takes over the function of a this-worldly salvation, no matter how this may be interpreted. It provides a *salvation* from the routines of everyday life, and especially from the increasing pressures of theoretical and practical rationalism."[64]

We do know, on the other hand, that Weber shared Lukács's enthusiasm for mysticism, and for much the same reason: mysticism too was beyond rationality. Paul Honigsheim testified that Weber "had a feeling for mysticism. He listened with interest when [the Russian scholar] Nikolai von Bubnoff reported his studies in the area of mysticism."[65] Weber once asked his wife whether she thought of herself as a mystic. She did not, but what of him? "It could be," he said, "that I *am* one. Just as I have 'dreamt' more in my life than one really ought to be allowed, I am not really *quite* securely at home anywhere."[66]

Having concluded that Western civilization was distinguished by its rationalized world, Weber searched for the cause of this unique and determining condition, finding it in religious asceticism, which was, according to Weber, the very antithesis of mysticism; whereas the latter was irrational, the former was, despite appearances, rational to the core. In what is one of the great products of the modern mind, *The Protestant Ethic and the Spirit of Capitalism* (1904–5), Weber suggested that there was an elective affinity between capitalism (economic rationalism) and Calvinism. The argument is so well known that it does not require detailed examination. In essence, what Weber said was this: Calvin's relentless emphasis upon predestination allowed no room for good works, or so it seemed. In fact, as part of a desperate search for proof of their election, Calvinists came to regard good works, actions that glorified God, as essential. Good works were "the technical means, not of purchasing salvation, but of getting rid of the fear of damnation."[67] Further, because for the elect *all* pursuits were sanctified, there was no distinction between sacred and secular callings. The hardworking, upright businessman might also glorify God by his work. Finally, success in one's "calling" was taken to be a sign of God's favor, the assumption being that He would not bless the efforts of the damned.

It was, to be sure, important that one not employ the fruits of one's success in the pursuit of worldly pleasures, because superfluities and ostentation reflected an irrational attitude devoid of objective purpose. One was a steward and as such was always to be ready to give an account to one's Master. What this attitude led to in practice was the "accumulation of capital through ascetic compulsion to save." Out of all this "one of the fundamental elements of the spirit of modern capitalism, and not only of that but of all modern culture: rational conduct on the basis of the idea of the calling, was born . . . from the spirit of Christian asceticism."[68]

Weber searched in other civilizations for something comparable to this "protestant ethic," and his authoritative studies are lasting monuments to that quest. In his view, they offered evidence to support the claim that the ascetic rationalism of Calvinism was the variable that made the crucial difference in the development of Western civilization. Lukács was delighted with the thesis, for it quite consciously shifted responsibility for the spirit of capitalism from the Jews to the Puritans.[69] It was not the Jews but the Puritans who were responsible for the rationalized, alienated world against which Lukács purposed to do battle.

But it was not only Weber's thesis that attracted Lukács, it was his interest in things Russian.[70] He had learned the Russian language in great haste at the time of the 1905 revolution and had followed events avidly in several Russian newspapers. He was acquainted with many Russian emigrés, among whom were Nikolai von Bubnoff and Fedor Stepun, who helped plan the Russian-language edition of *Logos*. He intended to write a book on Tolstoi and was so profoundly impressed by Dostoevski that Honigsheim could not remember any Sunday-afternoon conversation in the course of which the Russian writer was not at least mentioned.[71]

Dostoevski's *The Brothers Karamazov* was among Weber's favorite works of literature. In particular, "The Grand Inquisitor" helped to convince him that in this "irrational world of undeserved suffering, unpunished injustice, and hopeless stupidity," men had to choose between two problematic ethics: an ethic of ultimate ends (*Gesinnungsethik*) and an ethic of responsibility (*Verantwortungsethik*). Those who lived by the former attempted to do that which was right without regard for the consequences, foreseeable or otherwise, of their actions. In an effort to maintain the purity of their souls, however, they collaborated in the perpetuation of the world's ills. Those who lived by the ethic of responsibility, on the other hand, recognized that good ends could often be purchased only at the price of "morally dubious means," especially violence.

In Weber's judgment, there was no escaping this tragic dilemma.

Each man was obliged to seek *either* his soul's salvation *or* the fulfillment of desirable political goals. Under no circumstances, therefore,
should anyone seek his and others' salvation in politics. In words that
would soon describe Lukács, Weber registered his disapproval of those
adherents of the ethic of ultimate ends who suddenly turned into chili-
astic prophets. "Those, for example, who have just preached 'love
against violence' now call for the use of force for the *last* violent deed,
which would then lead to a state of affairs in which *all* violence is
annihilated."[72]

Weber's fascination with Dostoevski and with Russia in general was
but one instance of the cult of things Russian that was so much a part
of central European intellectual history from about 1880 to 1918. In an
increasingly bureaucratic and homogenized West, the East became a
symbol of hope. In Russian mysticism and the otherworldly traditions
of Orthodoxy, Weber thought that he had caught sight of a potentially
viable alternative to the rationalized West. Thus for him, Russians were
not to be regarded as backward, ultraconservative obscurantists but
rather as the bearers of a revolutionary alternative to a West dying of
slow strangulation. Lukács could not have agreed more.

Ljena Grabenko

Lukács's interest in Russia and Dostoevski increased immeasurably
after he met Ljena Andrejevna Grabenko, who was to his utopian period
what Irma Seidler had been to his tragic years. The daughter of Andrei
Mihailovitch Grabenko, the Zemstvo secretary in Cherson,[73] she had
served a term in a czarist prison because of her association with the
terrorist wing of the Socialist Revolutionary party. During the Russian
Revolution of 1905 "she carried a baby in her arms, a little child whom
she had borrowed from someone, and beneath the baby's blanket she
had hidden some bombs."[74] When Béla Balázs met her in Paris late in
1911, he was immediately attracted to her.

> We became friends the first day [he wrote in his diary]. She
> is a wondrous example of a Dostoevski character. Every one of her
> experiences, ideas, and feelings could have been lifted out of
> Dostoevski's most fantastic chapters. She was a terrorist, in prison
> for years. In this terrible work she destroyed her nerves, stomach,
> and lungs. Now she is sick and tired. She fears death and wants
> something for herself: to study, to be educated. So occupied was
> she with the education of the Russian peasants that she was unable

to find time to study something herself. A sad, beautiful, profound, intelligent person, and she has wondrous stories.[75]

Intrigued by Balázs's discovery, Lukács asked his friend's sister Hilda
for details. In a letter of 4 July 1912, she reported that Ljena wanted to
be a painter but that she possessed neither the talent nor the necessary
discipline. "She is a strange person and disquieting, but this is because
she is abnormally nervous."[76] It was the summer of 1913 before Lukács
and Ljena met, but she made an enormous and instant impression on
him. According to Balázs, she became for Lukács "an experimental
station, a human realization of his problems and ethical imperatives."[77]
Like his relationship with Irma, that with Ljena transcended the formal and approximated the essential communion that he believed was
frustrated by the social world. Having heard from her brother of this
remarkable woman, Mici Lukács told him that she was destined to
transform his life.[78] These were prophetic words, for this new Beatrice
was to be Lukács's guide through the terrifying netherworld of Russian
spirituality, a journey that would reach its end with his entrance into the
Hungarian Communist party.

For her part, Ljena "needed Gyuri in the spiritual sense: *'Il est ma
salvation,'*" she said.[79] The Russian woman hoped to draw so close
to Lukács that for them words would become superfluous. "If I could
express myself not only with words but by direct transmission of the
feelings, I do not believe that I would have to take refuge beneath
words. For you, truth is always somewhere among words, because you
are not sufficiently strong."[80] The words are harsh, but it was precisely
Ljena's complete indifference to formal niceties, her willingness to strip
him and herself spiritually naked, that so attracted Lukács.

This woman—neurasthenic, physically unattractive, and unable to
make sense of his work—held Lukács in human bondage, in the prison
of her soul; he began to speak of marriage. In reply, she spoke to him of
a more complete union: "Forgive me, my dear. I wanted to write that I
love you, but it is no longer that. It is not love that I begin to feel for
you; it is already something more profound."[81] Lukács persisted, although he too hoped to achieve a oneness with Ljena that he had failed
to achieve with Irma. As Marianne Weber put it in her letter to him of
15 November 1913: "How great and wonderful it will be for you to
unite with a woman whom you perceive as the completion of your self
in the deepest sense."[82]

But although he was willing to discuss his hopes with his closest
friends, Lukács was not inclined to seek the approval of the members of
his family. They did not learn of the seriousness of the relationship until

he announced his marriage plans in December 1913. His father was deeply hurt and disturbed by the thought that Ljena differed from them in background, religion, and nationality. She belonged to a "race" that was very foreign to theirs. His sister Mici, too, was taken by surprise and was upset because Lukács had not confided in her. In her letter of 17 December, she described to him how distraught their father was that he had not seen fit to say anything about such an important matter, and she begged him to return home to smooth things over, vowing her help and love. Finally, she emphasized how much she and their father wanted him to be happy.[83]

The elder Lukács attempted to maintain his dignity despite the deep wound he had received. He told his son that he must introduce his fiancée to the family before she could be formally accepted, but Lukács refused to comply even with this request; four months later (April 1914), his father wrote to ask where and when he would be wed. In late May or early June 1914, Lukács and Ljena were married in Heidelberg; the Lukács family was notified only after the fact.[84] Mici Lukács wrote to her brother a scathing letter of remonstrance. He had always preached the necessity of protecting their father from upset and disturbance. And why? So that he could continue to work for their benefit. "Let us be frank, that was the original motive." She praised her father for his understanding, love, and selfless devotion to their welfare. He, her brother, had been his father's pride and joy, and when he had asked only that Lukács wait a couple of months before marrying, his request had been callously disregarded. The cash nexus alone, she concluded, connected her brother to his family. Her view of life was, she conceded, very petit bourgeois, but she believed nonetheless that even an independent person had obligations, and in her judgment, Lukács had now one binding moral duty—to make his father happy by becoming a *Privatdozent*.[85]

Though harsh, this remonstrance was by no means unjustified. József Lukács may well have seemed to his son the very embodiment of the "protestant ethic and the spirit of capitalism," but he was selflessly concerned about his children. His letters to his son reveal a love and kindness that was undeterred by indifference and even open insult. Moreover, in the wake of Lukács's rejection by the University of Budapest, he had made financial provision for him such that he would not have to worry about living expenses, and he promised to do even better. "I must continue to gather capital for you. If I am able to maintain my health and capacity for work for long enough, I hope I shall assure for you a yearly annuity that, assuming modest desires, will provide complete independence with respect to your scholarly aims."[86]

In response to his son's marriage, József Lukács raised an issue that went to the very heart of their disagreements: "The forms of relations between people exist so that with their help we may try to understand one another. No one, particularly one who enters a family bond, has the right rudely to disregard these forms. However alien your woman is to respect for family bonds, the least she must do with respect to your mother is to try to approach her. If this too is in part convention, it is nonetheless indispensable, for it is impossible always to operate with feelings one hundred per cent."[87] But this measured wisdom was *precisely* what Lukács could not accept. He wished to live beyond the forms of "society" in a "community" where human relationships were direct and unmediated—a community of naked souls.

Through Ljena, Ernst Bloch later recalled, "Lukács married Dostoevski, so to speak; he married his Russia, his Dostoevskian Russia which didn't exist in reality."[88] Indeed, after his marriage, Lukács came increasingly to see in Russia and in Russian thought the hope of the future, and he began to plan a book on Dostoevski and the Dostoevskian world in which "new, concrete relationships linking soul to soul come to the fore."[89] Something, however, still stood in his path: his quest for a university appointment and the qualifying work he had begun to prepare when he arrived in Heidelberg in 1912—*The Philosophy of Art*. He was working on that study when war broke out shortly after his marriage to Ljena Grabenko.

The Philosophy of Art

In the foreword to a work of his later years, *Die Eigenart des Ästhetischen*, Lukács informed his readers that he had first conceived a plan to write a systematic aesthetics in Florence during the winter of 1911–12 and that he had worked on it in Heidelberg from 1912 to the outbreak of war in 1914. "I still remember," he continued, "the kindly-critical interest that Ernst Bloch, Emil Lask, and above all Max Weber displayed in my endeavor."[90] Marianne Weber had also testified to her husband's great respect for the work that "was to pave the way to an academic career for him [Lukács],"[91] and in his famous lecture, "Science as a Vocation," Weber had called attention to Lukács's ongoing enterprise.[92] The essential worth of the project was, then, well attested.

Be that as it may, Lukács never completed the work, and for more than fifty years it did not, for all practical purposes, exist. Then, during the 1960s, Arnold Hauser returned sections of the manuscript that

Lukács had entrusted to him in 1919; after Lukács's death in 1971, more of the manuscript was discovered among his second wife's papers. Still other material turned up in the "Heidelberg valise" and in the possession of Professor Charles de Tolnay. Thanks to the informed and skillful work of György Márkus and other members of the "Budapest School" of Marxism—Lukács's friends and students—the manuscripts, all in German, were transcribed and arranged in what is very likely their proper order.[93] According to Márkus's brilliant reconstruction, Lukács wrote three chapters between 1912 and 1914 and five between 1916 and 1918; the former have now been published as *Heidelberger Philosophie der Kunst, 1912–1914*, the latter as *Heidelberger Ästhetik, 1916–1918*. For now, I shall be concerned only with Lukács's work of 1912–14, the *Heidelberg Philosophy of Art*.

In order to understand this uncompleted work, one must bear in mind that for Lukács art was the Luciferean "better made"; it created a utopian world that stood in sharp contrast to the alienated world created by God. The philosophy of art that he was working on in Heidelberg on the eve of World War I represents an attempt to give systematic expression to this idea. Despite, therefore, its academic language and apparatus, this is not a dispassionate treatise. It is an exploration of its author's existential concerns and spiritual longings. It is utopian romanticism in scholarly dress.

The first of the three chapters that comprise the *Philosophy of Art* is entitled "Art as 'Expression' and the Forms of Communication of the World of Experience (*Erlebniswirklichkeit*)." Lukács began by posing, in Kantian terms, what he regarded as the fundamental question of aesthetics—"Works of art exist—how are they possible?" In this way, he attempted to serve notice to his readers that the existence of the work of art (*Kunstwerk*) was the fact that was central to any aesthetics worthy of the name.[94] Neither the creator nor the beholder, but the work itself, would be the object of Lukács's philosophic investigations. In chapter 1 and chapter 2, "Phenomenological Outline of the Creative and Receptive Attitudes," he attempted to make clear why this was so.

The origins of the work of art, according to Lukács, could be traced to man's longing to discover a better world than that of experience. More precisely, man sought to find in art an adequate means of communication with other men, a search that was emblematic of a "more profound longing for community and unity with one another."[95] The search was necessitated by the alienation that defined the world of experience.[96] Because the world of the work of art transcended the world of experience, men hoped to be able to free themselves from their isolated particularity and to communicate with each other across time and space. According to this view, art was the one vehicle of communication truly open to alienated men.

But, said Lukács, such was not the case. The meaning embodied in a work of art did not necessarily correspond with the intention of the creator. No more did the objective meaning of the work coincide with that read into it by the receptor. The relationship of both creator and receptor to the work of art was, in fact, characterized by profound misunderstanding, and this misunderstanding "that in the world of experience was only a *vérité de fait*, here becomes a *vérité éternalle*."[97] As Lukács acknowledged, that was Leó Popper's great insight;[98] thus the whole of the *Philosophy of Art* takes its point of departure from Popper's theory.

Because the meaning of a work of art was independent of both creative intention and receptive understanding, it could not be viewed as a privileged mode of communication between men. In one sense, of course, this was a tragedy, but understood aright, this autonomy was crucial to Lukács's design. If the work did reflect accurately the intention of the creator or the understanding of the receptor, it would, in some sense, be related to the world of experience—indeed, ultimately it would be governed by it. In that case, it would partake of the alienation that defined that world. The theory of misunderstanding made it possible for Lukács to defend the autonomy of the world of art: "This paradoxical and unique position of the work of art as eternal misunderstanding," he wrote, "first makes possible the independence and immanence of aesthetics. Through the eternity, universality, and objectivity of its central value, it is sharply separated from the world of experience."[99]

Why was it so important to Lukács to establish the autonomy of aesthetics, the world of art? The answer, I think, had little to do with abstract theory and can be found only with reference to Lukács's utopian hopes. Indeed, if the world of experience was, for him, defined by the reality of alienation, the world of the art work was characterized by utopian reality. In the work of art men caught sight of a world perfectly harmonic, corresponding to their longings, and self-contained—a "blissful totality."[100] In sum, the work of art was for Lukács a utopian totality separated from the world of experience, our world, by a great gulf. Between the alienated world God created and the Luciferean world of the work of art there was no connecting bridge.

It might seem at first glance that Lukács's insistence upon a radical separation between the world of experience and the world of art represented a reversion to his tragic period, but on closer inspection we can see that that was not the case. True, no steady, evolutionary progress toward utopia is here envisioned. What Lukács posited was an apocalyptic confrontation between the alienated and the utopian worlds. For him, as Marianne Weber put it, "the final struggle between God and Lucifer is still to come and depends on the decision of mankind. The ultimate goal is salvation *from* the world [of experience], not, as for [Stefan] George and his circle, fulfillment *in* it."[101]

There was, to be sure, no easy road from is (*Sein*) to ought (*Sollen*). Lukács was well aware of this, having watched the Neo-Kantians struggle with the problem. A great leap across the abyss, the radical destruction of the world of experience alone could make the utopian totality of the world of art an experiential totality. Precisely *how* this would come about, Lukács did not then know, but *that* it would eventuate he believed with all the fervor of the true believer.

Lukács did not complete the *Philosophy of Art*, and one wonders whether he could have, because the contradiction between formal, academic prose and the utopian spirit that informed it could not easily be reconciled. As we shall see, he was only too eager to abandon the project for a book more appropriate to his existential, as opposed to professional, interests. In any event, he had another reason to set the manuscript aside—the guns of August that signaled the beginning of World War I. By the time the guns again fell silent, Lukács had lived through yet another major existential crisis, and his life had taken a new and fateful turn.

The Great War

War and the Intellectuals

More than any other event, World War I has shaped the spiritual history of our age. In its wake, the decline of the West has often seemed not merely inevitable but desirable. In retrospect, it is particularly ironic, therefore, that in 1914 so many welcomed the war with exuberant enthusiasm; that was true not only of a handful of militarists but of entire populations of Europeans. The overwhelming majority of European intellectuals also greeted the outbreak of hostilities with outspoken approval. From England to Russia, the list of those who defended the war included almost every thinker of consequence: Bergson, Durkheim, Péguy, Apollinaire, Toynbee, Freud, Mann.

Among the reasons for the European intelligentsia's fascination with war were the lure of adventure, a distaste for bourgeois life, and the mysticism of violence.[1] But, above all, Europe's intellectuals perceived in the war the possibility of ending their alienation from their fellows. This was particularly true of the Germans, or so Lukács argued in an unpublished essay entitled "The German Intelligentsia and the War."[2] The isolation that weighed so heavily on German intellectuals before the war had to end, he maintained; a path to "a new, fraternal community" had to be opened. By compelling men to become comrades in the face of danger, the war became for the intellectuals the catalyst for a return from society to community. This analysis is certainly consistent with what we know about the members of the Weber Circle. Marianne Weber remembered that the coming of war signified "an hour of the greatest solemnity—the hour of *depersonalization* (*Entselbstung*), of integration into the community. An ardent love of community spread among people, and they felt powerfully united with one another."[3] Her husband was proud to serve as a reserve officer and Emil Lask, having volunteered, was sent to the front.

Hungarian intellectuals were every bit as enthusiastic about the war, and for many of the same reasons.[4] Anti-Russian since the czar's intervention in the 1848–49 War of Independence, they also persuaded themselves that the Austro-Hungarian monarchy was conducting a defensive war. Even writers on the political left such as Ignotus, novelist Zsigmond Móricz, and poet Gyula Juhász supported the national effort, but more important from Lukács's point of view, Béla Balázs decided to volunteer. From one angle, Balázs viewed the hostilities as a struggle between Germany and France for European cultural hegemony. French culture was so stagnant, he argued in a *Nyugat* essay, that young French intellectuals were themselves turning to their Frankish heritage. Men such as André Gide and Romain Rolland looked for inspiration to Balzac and Cézanne, who, though French, did not embody the Latin spirit. They attempted to demonstrate, Balázs wrote, "that Mallarmé's sanguinary obscurity and Claudel's primitive profundity are more truly French because they are not Roman but Frank—of German origin!"[5]

Nor was this all, for Balázs believed that the war would foster a spirit of internationalism. In the published version of his wartime diaries, *Soul in War* (1916), he pointed out that nationalism was the product of the nineteenth century "and just as it did not exist in the eighteenth, so it will cease to exist in the twentieth."[6] The future belonged to internationalism, and as a citizen of Austria-Hungary, he was a part of that future because the multinational monarchy was in the forefront of the battle against the nationalist past. And if his Jewishness made it possible for him to perceive the importance of the new internationalism, "then *this* is the great, proclaimed mission reserved for the Jews."[7] Finally, Balázs longed for community. "Forty million men have now walked into the shadow of death," he told Anna Lesznai. "I want to declare my solidarity with ten million Russians and Serbs and I don't know how many Frenchmen when I share with them a mutual suffering on a common battlefield."[8]

Not every Hungarian intellectual shared Balázs's dreams and aspirations. Oszkár Jászi described the war as a catastrophe and Endre Ady was in despair, but it was Lukács who opposed the struggle most vehemently. Far from drawing closer to a community of men, therefore, he was even more isolated. When his confidante Marianne Weber related to him acts of heroism, he snapped back "the better the worse!"[9]

The war, he insisted, was nothing but the quintessential expression of an "age of absolute sinfulness" (Fichte). Badly shaken by news of Béla Zalai's death in an Omsk hospital on 2 February 1915,[10] he was further aggrieved by Lask's death in battle. Hence, it was against a background of historical crisis and personal loss that he set aside the *Philosophy of Art* and began work on a study of Dostoevski in which he planned to elucidate his ethics and philosophy of history.[11]

Lukács had before him a previous attempt to approach the fundamental questions of the times through a study of Dostoevski: Thomas G. Masaryk's *Russland und Europa. Studien über die geistige Strömungen in Russland. Zur russischen Geschichts- und Religionsphilosophie* (1913, published in English as *The Spirit of Russia*). As he pointed out in his review of this work,[12] it was designed to serve as an introduction to Masaryk's projected examination of the great Russian writer's work. As such, it constituted an excellent guide to nineteenth-century Russian thought. Yet for all his mastery of sources, Masaryk had been unable, in Lukács's judgment, to lend to his studies unity of expression, because he lacked a systematic or "historico-philosophic" point of view. Lukács hoped to make good this omission, but in a letter to Paul Ernst, dated 2 August 1915, he confessed that he had bitten off more than he could chew; the work had to be abandoned.[13] He had, however, completed the first section, which he published as *The Theory of the Novel: A Historico-Philosophic Essay on the Great Epic Forms* (1920). This extended essay was dedicated to his wife, Ljena Andrejevna Grabenko.

The Dostoevski Book

Like *The Soul and the Forms* (Irma's book), *The Theory of the Novel* (Ljena's book) was an intensely personal work and a study of alienation, but whereas the former witnessed to a tragic sense of life, the latter projected utopian hope. In a 1962 preface to a new edition, Lukács explained that he had originally intended to cast the book in the form of a series of dialogues between young people who had withdrawn from the terrible world of the Great War. "They attempt to achieve self-understanding by means of conversations that lead by degrees to the problems treated in the book—to the outlook on a Dostoevskian world."[14] Though Lukács ultimately chose a less dramatic form of presentation, the search for a new world on the Dostoevskian model remained at the center of the work.

In essence what Lukács did in *The Theory of the Novel* was to relate the forms of epic literature—the epic proper and the novel—to "integrated" and "problematic" civilizations respectively. As the principal example of an integrated civilization, he cited the Greek, or more precisely, the Homeric world. This world constituted a totality in which the soul was not conscious of any separation between itself and the world or between itself and others. Nor did it distinguish between is and ought, immanent and transcendent. The epic (integrated) world was a true *Gemeinschaft*, an "organic—and therefore intrinsically meaningful—concrete totality"[15] in which human alienation was unknown. In time, however, the soul became increasingly aware of itself as essence and as objectivization, and because "the concept of essence leads to transcendence simply by being posited,"[16] the immanent meaning of the Homeric world became the transcendent meaning of Plato's world and the gap between is and ought, life and transcendent form (or Idea) was *created*; alienation now defined the human condition. 224432

Because, therefore, civilization had become problematic, the epic slowly degenerated into the novel, "the epic of an age for which extensive totality of life is no longer manifestly given, for which the immanence of meaning in life has become a problem, yet which is disposed toward totality."[17] The world of the novel was that of *Gesellschaft*, in which convention and social forms imprisoned the soul. "The outer world," Lukács wrote, "has become so exclusively conventional that everything, positive as well as negative, humorous as well as poetic, can take place only within that sphere."[18]

Lukács then attempted a typology of the novel based upon the hero's responses to the social world that smothered his humanity. The first response he called "abstract idealism"—a quixotic rebellion against the world in the name of the ought. The second response, "the romanticism of disillusionment," substituted passivity and resignation for furious, but hopeless, rebellion; narcissism became the only retreat. Only in the important final chapter, "Tolstoi and the Projection Beyond the Social Forms of Life," did Lukács make it clear that in Russia alone there was hope for the renewal of the epic. Less of a *Gesellschaft* than the West, Russia had given birth to a literature that was close to the epic's utopian form. Tolstoi's work witnessed to his desire to portray a life of essential community closely bound to nature, and in certain rare moments—usually moments of death—his characters caught a glimpse of a life beyond sterile and alienating conventionality. Meaning flooded their souls and they transcended both social being and pure subjectivity. But these moments were the exception, not the rule, for in general, even in Tolstoi's works, "one lives once more in the world of convention, an aimless, inessential life."[19] In the final paragraph of the book, Lukács maintained that only Dostoevski had created imaginatively a utopian reality that truly transcended the world of experience. For that reason, his work did not fall within the purview of a theory of the novel; Dostoevski did not write novels. He was a new Homer: the epic creator of a utopian world beyond the social forms.

That *The Theory of the Novel* was but part of a broadly conceived study of Dostoevski, students of Lukács's work had long been convinced, but he himself denied having had any such intention. Perhaps that was because the Russian writer was not a subject for polite conversation in communist circles. In any event, after Lukács died, his friends discovered among his papers an outline for the Dostoevski book along with the manuscript copy of *The Theory of the Novel*. A year later, they found his notes for the book in the Heidelberg valise. He had written them on scraps of paper and placed them in envelopes according to general subject. With skill and dedication, Ferenc Fehér and Ágnes Heller deciphered them, and we now know a great deal about the most important project of Lukács's utopian years.

He planned three chapters, the first of which he entitled "Subjectivity and Adventure"; it was this chapter, in slightly altered form, that he published as *The Theory of the Novel*. Chapter 2, "The World Without God," was to constitute an extended analysis of the age of absolute sinfulness—the world of the novel. On the basis of Lukács's list of subtopics and notes, one can construct this chapter with accuracy. We must begin with one of the greatest moments in modern literature: "The Grand Inquisitor" in *The Brothers Karamazov*. In this powerful legend, set in Seville during the Spanish Inquisition, Dostoevski contrasted the Grand Inquisitor with Christ. The spokesman for the Church points an accusing finger at the Savior, charging that the freedom He offered men to choose between good and evil was unendurable to all but a few. For the vast majority of men, freedom was a curse, and the Church promised to relieve the weak and fearful of that awesome burden by allowing, even compelling, them to find peace in slavery.

For Lukács, the alienation that characterized the relationship between Christ and the Church was of paramount importance. Christ had abandoned the world, leaving behind only the "Objective Spirit"—the Church. Following Simmel, Lukács believed that the Church as an institution had taken on a life of its own, independent of Christ, who had given it birth. But because he regarded the triumph of Objective Spirit in human history as general, he employed the name "Jehovah" to signify both spiritual and secular institutions: that is, Church and State. "*Church* as the model for the modern state," we read in his notes.[20] "The Jehovah that built the Tower of Babel"[21] had alienated men from one another and from the true God, the realm of freedom and brotherhood. Lukács had discovered a fixed point of reference—"the *non-objectivized Christ*."[22]

Lukács's notes make it clear that it was the state that exercised him the most—not merely tyrannical states, but the state as such. In his hatred of the state, he discovered authoritative support in St. Augustine's writings: *"Augustine's condemnation of the State*: Man ought to rule over animals alone—the state is organized sin."[23] Unhappily, in Lukács's view, the Objective Spirit as the state had triumphed in Germany and in western Europe generally, and those who shared his utopian hope for the creation of a genuine community of men would, like him, have to look east—to Russia—for inspiration and example. Russia, particularly as interpreted by Dostoevski, represented "The Coming Light"—the title of the third and final chapter of Lukács's book.

Perhaps the best introduction to this concluding chapter is a letter that the new Mrs. Lukács wrote to her husband three days before the Bosnian terrorist Gavrilo Princip assassinated Franz Ferdinand in Sarajevo. In it she expressed her fervent wish to understand his ideas concerning the absence of God. "If God is dead, why is He needed; how and why is salvation perceived to come only in His presence? . . . Why will He not be able to come without the help of men? How is it possible then for Him to be absolute?"[24] Lukács proposed to answer questions such as those by proclaiming the good news of the second coming, the creation of a Dostoevskian world in which "naked, concrete souls" were set free from the "shackles" of *social* identity.[25] To that end, he would study Dostoevski's God-seekers, those atheists who were "profoundly suffering, profoundly seeking brothers of the new Christians"[26] because they longed to meet the nonobjectivized Christ, the spirit of love and brotherhood. The question posed by Dostoevski's atheists was, How could one live without God?[27] Lukács believed that they found two answers, exemplified by the fictional Ivan Karamazov and the flesh-and-blood terrorist Ivan Kaliayev.[28]

Of the Karamazovs, Ivan is the most rational and hence the most Western, and in his notes, Lukács wrote of him that "the extreme vacillation of the Ivan-type is between the existence and nonexistence of God (they are atheists who believe in God . . .); therefore, as a consequence of the nonexistence of God, [there is] no new morality, but on the contrary—everything is permitted."[29] How, then, is Ivan to live without God? The answer is, as we know, that he murders his father, the degenerate Fyodor Karamazov. Not that he deals the old man the fatal blow on the head; that is left to the bastard Smerdyakov, Ivan's half-brother. But it was Ivan who taught Smerdyakov that everything is permitted and who left his father's house, knowing in his heart that the murder would be accomplished in his absence. In his notebooks, Dostoevski refers to Ivan simply as "the murderer."

Lukács shared Dostoevski's condemnation of Ivan's nihilism and his atheism, for to deny the binding character of the moral law was, he recognized, to remove the grounds for objecting to injustice. For Lukács, the atheism represented by Ivan Kaliayev, of whom he had learned much from Ljena, was more impressive because it appeared to be moral rather than nihilistic. Far from proclaiming that everything is permitted, Kaliayev believed murder to be morally wrong, however necessary, and in his book, Lukács intended to depict not only "the new, silent God" (who requires man's help), but also "his believers (Kaliayev) who consider themselves to be atheists."[30]

Ivan Kaliayev was the most fascinating and idealistic member of the Terrorist Brigade (or combat organization) of the Russian Socialist Revolutionary party. Born in Warsaw on 24 June 1877, he studied in Moscow and St. Petersburg. Like many of his fellow-students, he hated the czarist regime and, despite literary interests (his comrades called him "The Poet"), was drawn into antigovernment activity. With the inevitable arrests, he became ever more radical and, at the urging of his friend Boris Savinkov, joined the Terrorist Brigade in 1903.

Founded soon after the turn of the century, the brigade was heir to the traditions of *Narodnaya Volya* (The People's Will), the nineteenth-century terrorist brotherhood responsible for the murder on 1 March 1881 of the "Czar Liberator" Alexander II. Its leader was Yevgeny Azev, who was, incredibly enough, an agent of the czar's police. In common with those of many double agents, Azev's loyalties were not always unambiguous, and it was he who masterminded the assassination of Minister of the Interior V. K. von Plehve (1904) and of the Grand Duke Sergei (1905).[31] Boris Savinkov was second in command and under him was an extraordinary group of young men and women who, like Ljena Grabenko, were eager to lay down their lives for what they believed to be the cause of Russia and mankind. United by their "holy" mission, they constituted the kind of *Gemeinschaft* for which Lukács longed. "We were one fraternity," Savinkov recalled, "living by one idea, by one aim. Sazonov [von Plehve's assassin] was right when later, in a letter written to me from his Siberian prison, he said: 'Our band, our knightly order was animated by a spirit in which the word "brother" expressed but inadequately the reality of our relations.'"[32] These sensitive young people plotted and carried out murder in cold blood.

What impressed Lukács about these young killers was their moral and religious earnestness. Concerning Kaliayev, Savinkov later observed that "his love of art and the revolution was illumined by the same fire that animated his soul—his furtive, unconscious but strong and deep religious instinct."[33] This religious sensibility manifested itself in the profound sense of responsibility that Kaliayev shared with his new comrades. When, for example, he raised his hand to throw a bomb into the Grand Duke Sergei's carriage on 2 February 1905, he saw at that instant that the Grand Duchess Elizabeth and the children of the Grand Duke Paul had accompanied the intended victim. Risking arrest and endangering the safety of his comrades, he lowered his hand and fled. On reporting to Savinkov, he asked: "How can one kill children?"[34] Two days later he killed the Grand Duke and on 10 May 1905 he was hanged, having delivered a defiant speech at his trial.

But it was not simply that Kaliayev refused to kill people he believed to be innocent. He and his friends never claimed that the end justified the means. The end—the destruction of the czarist system—was, to be sure, a noble one in their eyes, but the means employed—murder— could never be justified morally. They were determined to pay for their crimes with their lives, for by doing so they would affirm not only their actions but also their responsibility; more than their lives, they were prepared to sacrifice their moral purity for their fellowmen.

Kaliayev's death and Azev's treason demoralized the brigade but inspired a powerful roman à clef in which Savinkov—signing himself "Ropshin"—posed the moral problem of terrorism and of revolution. Under the influence of the "new religious consciousness" propagated by Dmitri Merezhkovski and Zinaida Hippius, the terrorist chieftain published in January 1909 the first installment of The Pale Horse in the journal Russian Thought. The title was suggested by Hippius and refers to the fourth horse of the apocalypse. "And I looked, and behold a pale horse: and his name that sat on him was Death, and Hell followed with him. And power was given unto them over the fourth part of the earth, to kill with sword, and with hunger, and with death, and with the beasts of the earth" (Revelation 6:8).

The Pale Horse is the story, told in diary form, of a group of five terrorists who plot the assassination of a provincial governor. Unlike the self-assured killers of more recent vintage, however, these young conspirators are assailed by doubt and guilt. Two characters personify most fully the moral dilemmas of terrorism: George (the diarist) and Vania. George is Savinkov's version of Ivan Karamazov; a rationalist who is convinced that everything is permitted, he kills in order to witness to the consistency of his logic. "Why shouldn't one kill? And why is murder justified in one case and not in another? People do find reasons, but I don't know why one should not kill; and I cannot understand why to kill in the name of this or that is considered right, while to kill in the name

of something else is wrong."[35] He does not believe in socialism or anything else. He is, in a word, a nihilist. But like Ivan's, George's nihilism
ravages his soul. Empty and alienated even from his comrades, he
resolves to take his own life.

George's co-conspirator Vania is modeled after Kaliayev.[36] Religious
to the core of his being, he too is prepared to kill—but with a difference;
he does not shrink from "the conscious acceptance of guilt in the necessary murder."[37] He will not assuage his conscience by means of any
rationalistic sleight of hand. "To kill is a great sin. Just remember:
'Greater love hath no man than this, that a man lay down his life for his
friends.' And he must lay down more than his life—his soul."[38] It is he
who kills the governor and he who mounts the gallows, and because of
this supreme act of love for mankind, Savinkov treats Vania as a saint;
in contrast to the nihilist George who dies in his sin, Vania dies in a state
of grace.

The Pale Horse was written in the spirit of Dostoevski. Indeed, Savinkov referred repeatedly to Smerdyakov and included a horse-beating
scene reminiscent of Raskolnikov's terrifying dream. Thus the book
acquired a special significance for the young Lukács. Ljena read it to
him, translating from the Russian into German, and she also made written translations of several key passages.[39] When Lukács discovered
that the *Berliner Tageblatt* had serialized the novel, he tried without
success to obtain copies, finally turning to Paul Ernst for help. Shortly
thereafter, he explained to his skeptical friend what it was that attracted
him to Ropshin-Savinkov:

> I perceive in Ropshin—considered as a document, not as a work
> of art—no symptom of disease, but rather a new manifestation of
> the old conflict between the first ethic (duties vis à vis institutions)
> and the second ethic (imperative of the soul). The order of rank
> always preserves characteristic dialectical complications when the
> soul is directed not toward itself but toward humanity—as among
> politicians and revolutionaries. Here precisely the soul must be
> sacrificed in order to save the soul: one must, out of a mystical
> ethic, become a cruel political realist and violate the absolute
> commandment, which is *not* a duty to institutions, but "Thou
> shalt not kill!"[40]

It was by the "second ethic" that Savinkov and Kaliayev lived and it
was to have been central to Lukács's Dostoevski book. The aim of the
second ethic was the realization of human solidarity, in the Russian
sense: "*Types of Solidarity*: (a) Orient: thou art the other (the others,
also the enemy), for I and thou are illusions . . . (b) Europe: abstract

fraternity, way out of loneliness. The other is my 'fellow citizen,' my 'colleague,' my 'compatriot.' Race and class hatred etc. are not excluded. Even require it. (c) Russia: the other is my brother; when I discover myself, as I discover myself, I have discovered him."[41] The path that led from soul to soul could, however, be broken only by the "criminal" who violated the formal law, and the terrorist was the paradigmatic criminal: "Terrorist as hero whose essence is expressed as 'rebellion' against *this* Jehovah. . . . (System of law as Jehovah)."[42]

These Russian terrorists converted Lukács to what he called the "metaphysics of socialism." As the guardian of the second ethic, socialism surpassed what he denigrated as western Europe's "ethical democracy: metaphysics of the state."[43] Under the latter, politics was practiced within the limits set by Kantian ethics; the institutions that together comprised the state were accepted as given. Under socialism, the possibility of a new "polis" became real. Because of its opposition to individualism and dedication to the ideals of community, Lukács had always taken some interest in socialism, but the Second International left him cold, its ideology being too positivist and its politics too parliamentary. As early as 1910 he had spoken of socialism's promise, but he had concluded that it lacked the "religious strength possessed by primitive Christianity."[44] There was, however, one socialist he admired— Endre Ady. "Endre Ady's socialism: religion (for lesser figures only a narcotic)," he wrote in 1909. "The voice of one crying in the wilderness, a shout for help from one who is suffocating, an obstinate clinging to the only possibility that yet remains."[45]

In Hungary, Ady's religious socialism was idiosyncratic, the Socialist party being a copy of the German original. Indeed, the poet never joined the party. In Russia, however, Lukács discovered a socialist movement far more messianic than that of the West, a movement that was as much religious as it was political. In *The Brothers Karamazov* he read that "socialism is not only the labour question, or the question of the so-called fourth estate, but above all an atheistic question, the question of the modern integration of atheism, the question of the Tower of Babel which is deliberately being erected without God, not for the sake of reaching heaven from earth, but for the sake of bringing heaven down to earth."[46] If, as he and Ljena fervently hoped, the Russian socialists were successful in overthrowing the czar, all of Russia, and eventually all the world, might be peopled by "new Christians" of the sort Dostoevski depicted so powerfully: Alyosha Karamazov, Prince Myshkin, and Sonia.[47] It was his misunderstanding of these famous characters that led Lukács from Christianity to heresy and from Christian love to hatred of his fellowmen.

The son of Fyodor Karamazov by his second wife, Alyosha believes in God, but is assailed by doubts. His faith derives from his love of humanity and his dream of a time when "all will be holy, and will love each other, and there will be no more rich nor poor, exalted nor humbled, but all men will be as the children of God and the real kingdom of Christ will come."[48] From his teacher, the elder Zossima, Alyosha learns that "every man is responsible for everyone, only people don't know it. If they knew—it would be paradise at once!" This teaching runs through *The Brothers Karamazov* like a silver thread. Zossima hears it confirmed by a guilt-ridden murderer whose crime had never been discovered. "It is indeed true," the man says out of the depths of spiritual agony, "that when people grasp this idea the Kingdom of Heaven will become a reality to them and not just a dream." The Kingdom will not, however, be the *result* of scientific advances or the enactment of new laws or property regulations, but rather their cause. For the present, isolation defines the human condition; men separate themselves into "self-contained units" independent of the whole. They are unable to understand the necessity of human solidarity, and until that great day when all men recognize one another as brothers, "a man has to set an example at least once and draw his soul out of its isolation and work for some great act of human intercourse based on brotherly love, even if he is to be regarded as a saintly fool for his pains. He has to do so that the great idea may not die."[49]

Alyosha protects this truth in his heart and being, and although he is unable to pass it on to Ivan, he does succeed in communicating it to Dmitry. The truth, it seems, can only be appropriated by those who suffer, and it is only after being falsely accused of the murder of his father that Dmitry dreams his strange dream. He is on the great Russian steppe on a cold November day. His cart, driven by a peasant, nears a town and he sees a mother holding her crying baby. He asks his driver why the baby is crying and is told that it is starving and almost frozen, because the mother is very poor. Dmitry senses in his heart strange and never-before experienced emotions: "He wanted to cry, he wanted to do something for everyone so that the babby [sic] should cry no more, that no one should shed tears from that moment."[50]

On the eve of his trial, at which he knows he will be condemned and sent to Siberia, Dmitry tells Alyosha that "a new man" had arisen in him because of his dream. No longer does he fear his banishment: "It's for the 'babby' that I'm going. For we are all responsible for all. For all the 'babbies,' for there are little children and big children. All of us are 'babbies.' And I'll go for all, for someone has to go for all. I did not kill my father, but I have to go. I accept it!"[51] In his notes, Lukács wrote:

"*Way out of sin*. Make yourself responsible for the sins of men. Mitya [Dmitry] (little child)."[52]

But Dostoevski's point was not, as Lukács believed, that men must sin in order to redeem "mankind"—Christ had already been made sin for us. Rather, he taught men to recognize themselves as responsible, guilty beings *capable* of the heinous acts others committed. By becoming aware of their kinship with criminals, they might receive the grace necessary to love their fellows *as they are*, to perceive beauty in human existence despite moral failure. This, however, was precisely what Lukács could never accept, for like Kaliayev *and* Ivan Karamazov, he rejected God's world, a world in which injustice exists. He could not, as Dostoevski's saints can, forgive his fellowmen, because to forgive is to suspend the requirements of the moral law, to be, in a very real sense, unjust. Lukács's profound love of justice was at once his strength and his weakness. He was *too* moral, too hungry for justice. Because he viewed the world strictly in moral terms and eschewed nihilistic despair, he was driven inexorably to proclaim utopian demands for total justice.

Contrary to what Lukács believed, Dostoevski was not a utopian writer. If no one was more sensitive to this world's corruption, no one so loved corrupt men. Consider Prince Myshkin, "the idiot" whom Lukács rightly identified as one of Dostoevski's most remarkable saints. An epileptic, Myshkin had gone to Switzerland to seek a cure, there to remain for four years. For anyone familiar with Dostoevski's love of children, there can be no doubt that the prince's Swiss village is *his* paradise: "There were always children there," he tells the Yepanchin family, "and I was with children all the time I was there, only with children."[53]

As the novel opens, the prince is returning to Russia, which for Dostoevski is "the world." Judged by worldly standards, he is indeed an "idiot" because he is truly good. He will not, for example, act in his own interest, and his compassion for sinners is so great that he loves and forgives Rogozhin, even after the latter, having once made an attempt on his life, kills Nastassya Filippovna, a child-like and beautiful creature whom the prince loved dearly but platonically. It is this loving forgiveness that elevates the prince beyond morality. He does not condemn even those who by any ethical measure are deserving of condemnation—liars, cheats, the cruel, the bitter, the homicidal. Though never approving of their vile actions, he accepts *them* just as they are, even if some are unable to endure the forgiveness he so freely bestows and hate him for it. Indeed, there is not a single character, even among his friends, those who love him, who does not harbor some deep resentment for him, and at the end, having suffered because of the sins of others in Russia, he returns to Switzerland, broken in spirit and health.

According to Ernst Bloch, Lukács identified Ljena with Sonia in *Crime and Punishment*,[54] but the resemblance is more apparent than real. To be sure, Sonia *is* made sin for others. Only eighteen years of age and pure in heart, she becomes a prostitute in order to provide desperately needed money for her stepmother, brother, and sisters, all of whom have been left destitute because of her father's alcoholism. Unlike Raskolnikov, who refuses to admit that his murder of the moneylender and her sister is a "crime," Sonia accepts responsibility for her harlotry: "I'm a great, great sinner!," she tells the young murderer. But Sonia sacrifices herself for specific human beings, *not* for "mankind" in the abstract, and although she deplores her father's drunkenness and Raskolnikov's crime, she loves and forgives both of them. In the end, it is her Christ-like love that redeems Raskolnikov by reestablishing his ability to love and *to be loved* and thus ending his terrible alienation from other men. As Lukács recognized, "Sonia leads Raskolnikov out of the labyrinth of the abstract sin that had isolated him from every human community and made impossible for him life among men."[55] Lukács's tragedy was that he and Ljena, unlike Sonia, hated injustice more than they loved human beings.

War and Apocalypse

The Russians, Berdyaev often observed, are either nihilists or apocalyptists, and in practice the distinction is not always very sharp. Both rejected the doctrine of progress that informed so much of nineteenth-century thought. Both deplored the human condition and both, for different reasons, were prepared to kill. But whereas the nihilist counseled despair, the apocalyptist proclaimed eschatological hope, a hope that derived from his conviction that the end of history as we know it represented at the same time the beginning of a radically new epoch, so free of history's contagion that it could only be the result of a great leap forward.

Staggered by the seemingly meaningless slaughter that was the Great War, the greater number of European intellectuals became spiritual Russians, abandoning the doctrine of progress and embracing either nihilism or apocalypticism. Lukács chose the latter, convinced with Yeats that "some revelation is at hand; / Surely the Second Coming is at hand" and eager to learn precisely "what rough beast, its hour come round at last, / Slouches towards Bethlehem to be born?" It was no accident that he was captivated by a book, the title of which (*The Pale Horse*) was taken from the *Apocalypse* of St. John; among his notes on the second ethic, we read "Age of the Apocalypse."[56]

Apocalyptic hope and belief had had a long history, originating in postexilic Judaism and reinforced by Zoroastrianism and Christianity; thus it was very much a part of Western intellectual history. Yet it had not long remained central to either orthodox Judaism or orthodox Christianity, neither of which rejects the world so totally or focuses so single-mindedly upon eschatology. Since St. Augustine's *City of God* at the latest, apocalypticism had always constituted a heresy, the greatest of all heretical temptations. First elaborated into a coherent system of historical interpretation by Joachim of Floris (1131–1202), apocalyptic speculation and expectation excited such heretics as the Cathars, Waldensians, and Taborites. "For medieval people," Norman Cohn has written, "the stupendous drama of the Last Days was not a phantasy about some remote and indefinite future but a prophecy which was infallible and which at almost any given moment was felt to be on the point of fulfilment."[57] The oppositional schools of the Middle Ages exercised a strong influence on Lukács,[58] who perceived a more sophisticated version of apocalypse in Fichte's work. Indeed, though it is Hegelian in structure, *The Theory of the Novel*, and the Dostoevski book as a whole, is Fichtean in spirit, because at the time of writing, Hegel was still associated in Lukács's mind with "Jehovah," the state.[59]

Lukács was especially fascinated by the philosophy of history that Fichte outlined in a series of public lectures entitled "Grundzüge des gegenwärtigen Zeitalters" (Characteristics of the Present Age). In these lectures, delivered in 1804–5, the German philosopher identified five ages in world history; the third, his own, he characterized as that of "absolute sinfulness" (*vollendeten Sündhaftigkeit*). And yet, according to Fichte, all was by no means lost, for the worst had first to be lived through before history could advance to the final ages, those of "incipient vindication" and of "absolute vindication and sanctification."[60] As he put it in a letter to Friedrich Jacobi dated 31 March 1804: "I believe that I have understood our age as that of the absolute corruption of all ideas. Nevertheless, I am of good cheer; for I know that new life can come only from complete decay."[61] During the war years, Lukács often spoke of Fichte, "who said that humanity had to pass through the age of absolute sinfulness on the way to justification. Today this age has arrived and whoever fails to execute the age's command does not repudiate sin, but rather the only road that leads out of sin."[62]

As a result of the war, his reading of Dostoevski and Savinkov, and his marriage to Ljena Grabenko, Lukács became a Russian in mind and spirit, and the uncompleted Dostoevski book was a monument to his spiritual adoption. Had he completed it, he would have been proud to place it alongside two contemporary apocalyptic volumes: Ady's selected poems and Bloch's *Geist der Utopie* (*Spirit of Utopia*). Having declared himself to be "the son of Gog and Magog,"[63] Ady also believed that the war signaled the coming of an apocalyptic age. His "Remembrance of a Summer's Night," one of the greatest poems inspired by that epochal event in any language, is replete with allusions to St. John's *Apocalypse*.[64] One might easily summon many other lyrical witnesses, such as "Man in Inhumanity,"[65] but for present purposes it is enough to point out that, if he was more pessimistic, Ady, like Lukács, was convinced that he was living in an age that could end only with the victory of Satan or of God.

The third volume of the wartime apocalyptic trilogy would have been Bloch's *Spirit of Utopia* (1918), a book he originally entitled *Eschatological Man*.[66] Begun in April 1915 and completed in May 1917, the *Spirit of Utopia* bears the unmistakable imprint of the Lukács-Bloch brotherhood of longing, for like Lukács, Bloch sought a utopian community of men, an identification with others unmediated by the forms of individualization. In his concluding chapter, "Karl Marx, Death, and the Apocalypse," he revived that Hasidic belief concerning which Lukács had written with such interest to Buber: metempsychosis (*Seelenwanderung*). Bloch perceived that death is not simply a disagreeable biological fact but an event of overwhelming philosophic significance. Unlike Heidegger, for whom finitude was that which gave meaning to human existence, he held that transcendence alone promised a way out of nihilism and despair. Death directed our attention away from our bodies and toward our souls, with regard to which one could suppose either that they would be annihilated or that they would be quickened again and again. To suppose the former, Bloch maintained, was to abandon hope and to succumb to a tragic view of existence, but to embrace the latter was to postulate hope and to make possible the transcendence of our finitude. "The doctrine of metempsychosis," he advised his readers, "had to be recommended conclusively as the most powerful antidote to the metaphysical impermanence of corporeal and social destinies." Hope of transcending the "meaningless necessity of social destiny" was grounded in the infinite possibilities vouchsafed to the soul by ever new incarnations. Because of these possibilities, "nothing accidental is irrevocable." Our intermittent existences took us beyond the tragic limits set by time and place: "Everything could pass away, but the house of mankind must be preserved in full strength and stand illuminated, so that at some future time, when destruction rages outside,

God can dwell within it and help us—and it is this [idea] that proceeds from metempsychosis to the apprehension of a genuine social,
historical, and cultural ideology."[67]

Bloch's language paralleled his hopes. Biblical images, verbal tor-
rents, apocalyptic expectations—all were declarations of independence
not only from traditional philosophy but also from orthodox Marxist
literature. Though agreeing with Marx that economic and institutional
change was necessary, he insisted that man did not live by bread alone.
"What is to come economically is determined, but the ethical itself is
here not yet allotted its desired autonomy in the final social order."[68]
In the end, Bloch was convinced, men made history, not history men;
moreover, something more powerful, more utopian was required if
Marxism were to provide men with a vision worthy of the name. What
he missed in Marx's writings was any music—the "profoundly utopian
art"—in the "mechanism of the economy and of social life,"[69] and
in one of the most famous passages of the book, he concluded: "One
can say therefore that it is precisely the strong emphasis on everything
economic and present at hand and also the still arcane latency of all
transcendental moments that brings Marxism near to a Critique of Pure
Reason, for which no Critique of Practical Reason has yet been written."[70] Bloch intended to provide that second critique.

Even the most casual reader will perceive in the *Spirit of Utopia* the
presence of Weber and Dostoevski. In Bloch's view, Marxism was too
enamored of the doctrine of economic rationality, too confident of the
virtues of organization. It had to be invested with "the superior (from
the point of view of utopia) world of love of Weitling, Baader, and
Tolstoi, the new power of Dostoevskian human encounters, and the
adventism of heretical history."[71] The goal of socialism was something
far greater than economic well-being; it was "life in the Dostoevskian
sense."[72] Despite differences of temperament and artistic inclination
that were soon to become manifest, it was apocalyptic hope and the
Weberian-Dostoevskian heritage that made of Bloch an intellectual-
spiritual comrade of the young Lukács, whom he was pleased to char-
acterize as "the absolute genius of morality."[73]

The Heidelberg Aesthetics

Lukács first published *The Theory of the Novel* in Max Dessoir's *Zeitschrift für Ästhetik und allgemeine Kunstwissenschaft* (1916), and it
was well received. Bloch, who evinced little sympathy for the *Philosophy of Art*,[74] was very much impressed: "I have read your work in its

entirety once again and find it for the most part excellent and indescribably well-aimed."[75] Though he had read only the first few pages, Alfred
Weber described the essay as a "fine work" and Ernst Troeltsch wrote
that he had "gained a great deal" from it.[76] For Balázs, the work constituted a revelation: "I discovered . . . how extremely *important*, more
important than a new Weltanschauung . . . is the first appearance of
new men. The book of the soul, but not in the manner of Niels Lhyne or
Knut Hamsun—the soul's escape, its isolation, and its kingdom of
dreams. On the contrary, its release into the world, victorious rebellion.
Evidence and example that *it is possible* to live in the world!"[77]

Lukács was gratified by such praise and attention, but he was all too
aware that the voice of Max Weber could not be heard in the chorus.
Weber believed that the essay and Lukács's Dostoevski studies in general had diverted him from his "Aesthetics," without which he had
little hope of securing a university appointment, and in a long letter of
14 August 1916, he spoke candidly to his Hungarian friend about his
future. There was, to begin with, the possibility of habilitating as a
sociologist, which at that time meant as a political economist. Lukács
had published in the prestigious *Archiv für Sozialwissenschaft und Sozialpolitik* a chapter of his *Modern Drama* and an essay on the essence
and method of the sociology of culture. But Weber opposed this plan
because he was convinced that Lukács's true interests were philosophic
and that the plan represented an effort to outmaneuver Heinrich Rickert,
who was less enthusiastic about Lukács's work and for whom Lukács
had little regard personally or professionally. Weber warned Lukács that
he would not be permitted to give philosophic lectures as a "political
economist" and he assured him that Rickert, who had succeeded Windelband at Heidelberg in 1915, held him in high regard. But on one
point, Weber was insistent—the "Aesthetics" would have to be completed:

> A very good friend of yours—Lask—expressed this opinion:
> "He [Lukács] was born an essayist, and he will not stick with
> a systematic (professional) work. That is why he *should not*
> habilitate. Of course, the essayist is not a whit less important than
> a professional/systematic thinker—perhaps the very opposite! But
> he does not belong at a university and he intends his works above
> all for 'his own salvation.'" I strongly opposed this view on the
> strength of the excellent fragments of your Aesthetics that you
> once read to us. Because your sudden turn toward Dostoevski
> seemed to lend *support* to Lask's view, I hated this work of yours

and I hate it still. Basically I [now] share this view. If to finish a systematic work without in the meanwhile taking up something else is for you truly an unendurable torment and interruption, then with heavy heart I would advise you to forget about the habilitation. Not because you "don't deserve it," but because in the final analysis it will benefit *neither* you nor the students. Then your road is different.[78]

Although he must have known that Lask and Weber were right, Lukács decided to turn his attention once again to his "Aesthetics," and the never-completed result of this final effort was what today is known as the *Heidelberg Aesthetics*.[79]

If he were to habilitate, Lukács knew that he would have to win Rickert's approval. The necessity of impressing the rather difficult philosopher was one of the reasons for Lukács's decision to begin his work anew rather than return to the *Philosophy of Art*. The five chapters of the *Aesthetics* that he completed by the spring of 1918 (only one of which was taken over from the *Philosophy of Art*)[80] were far more strongly Neo-Kantian in character. In the curriculum vitae that he submitted with his *Aesthetics* to the University of Heidelberg in May 1918, he recalled that his early philosophic studies had focused on classical German philosophy but that "the ever clearer comprehension of the conception of value [*Geltung*] soon led me to modern German philosophy, above all to that of Windelband, Rickert, and Lask."[81] He mentioned also the methodological stimulus of Husserl's writings, to which Lask had introduced him.

This is not to suggest that Lukács adopted a more Neo-Kantian approach for purely opportunistic reasons. He may not have thought much of Rickert, but he had long admired Lask, whose philosophy of value owed much to Rickert, Windelband, and Hermann Lotze, as well as to Kant. Of particular importance to Lukács's philosophic strategy was the South-West School's distinction between value (*Geltung*) and being (*Sein*). "Gyuri often says," Balázs wrote in his diary early in 1916, "that his great metaphysical discovery is that metaphysical facts are not in the *Geltung* sphere. That is '*Sein*.' This reality is complete and sufficient as *Geltung* sphere (as with every sphere, because I cannot step out of it, not even into another sphere). But as '*Sein*,' it is *insignificant*."[82] In his *Nachruf* for Lask, Lukács was even more precise: "For the new philosophy, the difference between *Sein* and *Gelten* is given as irremovable, as qualitative difference, and as the essential result of this state of affairs, it must accomplish a radical break with methodological monism of every sort."[83] Following Lask, he embraced an extreme form of dualism, according to which the theoretical and the value spheres were wholly distinct; aesthetics was in the latter sphere.[84]

This dualism was important to Lukács because the burden of his *Aesthetics* was the same as that of his *Philosophy of Art:* the *Kunstwerk* represented the Luciferean "better made," a utopian world that contrasted sharply with the alienated world created by God. Once again, the academic trappings of Lukács's work are deceptive. The *Aesthetics* may be cast in the form of a *Habilitationsschrift*, but it is informed by the same utopianism that defined *The Theory of the Novel*.[85] That utopianism discovered an ally in Neo-Kantian dualism. Because the *Kunstwerk* was in the sphere of value, the issue of the *existence* of its "utopian reality" could not properly arise. Following the Neo-Kantians, Lukács could argue that "the values (*die Werte*) do not exist, but they possess worth (*sie Gelten*)."[86] Questions concerning existence or being (*Sein*) could arise *only* in the theoretical sphere; epistemology or metaphysics could investigate only *Sein*, the world of reality and of alienation. In sum, the absolute dualism of value and being made possible that of the utopian and alienated worlds.

Lukács began the first chapter of the *Aesthetics*, "The Essence of Aesthetic Constitution," with a question framed in the Kantian manner: "Works of art exist—how are they possible?" Inspired by his Neo-Kantian friends, he had gone "back to Kant," particularly to the master's third *Critique*.[87] In a note to the only chapter of the *Aesthetics* to be published during his lifetime, he wrote that "the *Critique of Judgment* contains the nucleus to the solution to every problem of the structure of the aesthetic sphere."[88] Lukács's attempt to work out the solution, however, owed more to the value theory he discovered in the writings of Rickert and Lask.

He began by insisting upon the absolute autonomy of that form of value known as aesthetics; it constituted a "sphere" that was distinct from all others. Moreover, this sphere was completely divorced from "reality" (the *Sein* sphere), whether that of nature, of cognition ("objective reality"), or of metaphysics ("true reality"). Between *Kunstwerk*, the object of any true aesthetics, and "reality" there could be no connection whatever.[89] There is nothing new here. To preserve the independence of the *Kunstwerk* uncontaminated by alienated reality had also been crucial to Lukács's design in the *Philosophy of Art*. In keeping with this dichotomy, he went on to distinguish between two forms of *Erlebnis* (experience). The experience of the world of reality (*Erlebniswirklichkeit*) constituted a facticity, but that of aesthetics was normative, "an *Erlebnis* that has become pure and homogeneous." In aesthetics we

discover "the meaning of *Erlebnis* as *Erlebnis*." Between the meaningless experience of the world of reality and the meaningful experience of
aesthetics, therefore, there could be no common ground; they were
separated by an "abyss."[90] The same abyss divided the factical "wholly
human" (*ganzer Mensch*) of the world of reality from the normative,
meaningful "human as a whole" (*Mensch ganz*) of the world of aesthetics.[91]

The aesthetic sphere was, then, a primal reality open to a philosophy
of value, but "bracketed off" (Lukács used Husserl's phrase) from *Sein*
and hence closed to theoretical reason. That is why Lukács preferred
Kant to Hegel, a monist who had attempted to defend a panlogism
that aimed at reducing all spheres to aspects or moments of an all-
encompassing logical (metaphysical) system.[92] The establishment of an
autonomous sphere of value (*Wertsphäre*) was possible only if one employed Kantian categories. His *Aesthetics* would be "sphere-immanent"
and "oriented around the *Kunstwerk*," which "carries its worth immanent in itself; it is value and value realization at the same time. Its
individuality, its singularity cannot therefore subsist in mere relation to
value, but must itself be value that has become form."[93]

Lukács entitled chapter 3 of his *Aesthetics* "The Idea of the *Werk* in
Itself," and although he completed only the first half, he published it in
Logos as "The Subject-Object-Relation in Aesthetics." Only in aesthetics, Lukács argued, did a true subject-object relation obtain; in the
aesthetic sphere alone alienation was overcome. In the logical (theoretical) sphere, the distinction between subject and object, self and world,
was presupposed. Indeed it was our consciousness of this "alienation"
that first directed our attention to the objective world that was living a
life of its own, independent of the subject that created it. In the ethical
sphere too a distinction was presupposed, that between ought (*Sollen*)
and is (*Sein*). Our consciousness of the imperfection of the world directed us to the subject's prescription—the *Sollen*. In both spheres, the
problem was the same—the world of reality and alienation. In *that*
world the divorce between subject and object could never be overcome.
Only in the aesthetic sphere, more precisely in the *Kunstwerk*, was there
perfect identity of subject and object, of content and form; "its meaning
consists precisely in rendering this antithesis meaningless."[94] This was
possible because the *Kunstwerk* resided in a sphere that was completely
divorced from the world of experiential reality. It was a microcosm of
utopia, "a self-contained, perfect, and self-sufficient totality."[95] In it
alone a "utopian reality" (of value, not of being) obtained that was
appropriate, indeed identical to the pure (unalienated, transcendental)
experience and will of the "human as a whole." This identity of sub-

ject and object was made possible by the fact that the creator of the *Kunstwerk*—*as creator*—was "transformed" into pure subjectivity, completely isolated from himself as "wholly human," as man of the world of experiential reality (*Mensch der Erlebniswirklichkeit*).[96]

Once again then Lukács had described an unbridgeable gulf between the worlds of alienated and utopian reality and had thus ruled out any gradual transformation or progress. Only an apocalyptic event, a Kierkegaardian leap across the abyss from one reality to the other could leave the world of absolute sinfulness behind and make of human existence a *Kunstwerk*.

The final two chapters of the *Aesthetics* are historical and critical, and in them Lukács sought to discredit Plato and Hegel. Although the attack on Hegel is worthy of notice, it is not clear, as György Márkus has pointed out, how these final chapters were to be incorporated into Lukács's overall strategy. More important, when Lukács submitted the *Aesthetics* as a *Habilitationsschrift*, Rickert read it and he, too, was at a loss to understand the systematic relevance of the last chapters.[97] Because of events in Hungary, however, Rickert's judgment no longer mattered.

That Lukács was able to write as much of his *Aesthetics* as he did was nothing short of miraculous because his marriage and his Heidelberg home had by this time become a "terrible and unimaginable hell."[98] Ljena had become enamored of Bruno Steinbach, a neurotic pianist of Viennese birth who soon joined the Lukács household. Paul Ernst's wife Else has described the domestic scene: "Our friend [Lukács] made the beds and washed the dishes. Bruno swept up, did the dusting, and saw to the marketing, because domestic servants were at that time no longer to be found in Heidelberg. Ljena, a woman rather strange to the European eye, carried out color experiments in her artist's workshop, solved difficult mathematical problems, and practiced on the piano. She mastered handicraft in all three areas, but she was not a housewife in the German sense."[99]

Bruno's nervous condition worsened every time he was faced with possible conscription, and in the spring of 1915, Ljena wrote a letter to Karl Jaspers, who acted as a psychiatric counselor for the entire household, in an effort to enlist his professional aid in Bruno's behalf. Her account of the latter's hallucinations may be exaggerated, but it does nevertheless convey something of the atmosphere in which Lukács lived and worked. "For four days and nights, he cried out horribly and when I came into his room, he was standing in the middle of it with a hammer, but did not want to tell me why he had screamed (I think because he still felt rather uneasy). Only on the following day did he tell me that he had

seen an old man who had laughed at him. He wanted to strike him, but
suddenly he felt terrified and for that reason began to scream."[100]

Why did Lukács permit Bruno's continued presence in his home? The
answer can be found in a letter to Jaspers. "My impression is that my
wife will neither wish nor be able to give up the relationship (*Zusam-
mensein*) with Br. St. (and in my view, with profound subjective reason)
so long as she is convinced that her presence can be of some benefit, if
not objectively, at least in Br. St.'s consciousness. I believe at present,
again with full awareness of my incompetence, that one must make this
difficult task as easy for her as possible."[101]

If Bruno was hopeless, Ljena was scarcely better. Her nerves had
suffered during her years as a terrorist and were unable to withstand this
new assault. Balázs recorded in his diary this incredible scene:

> Edith received a letter from Ljena in Heidelberg: "*Komm
> heraus, wenn du kannst. Ich bin in grösster Gefahr.*" Naturally,
> Edith made the journey through hedges and trenches, consulates
> and military authorities. . . . She did not find Gyuri there, but she
> did encounter Ljena—neurotic and close to a complete breakdown
> —together with the demented Bruno, who takes her money, beats
> and strangles her, and whose attacks she must fear every night.
> Hence, she does not sleep. Gyuri lived and "worked" with them in
> a small dwelling. . . . And meanwhile Gyuri still wrote three long
> chapters of his *Aesthetics*. Some 300 pages! Unbelievable![102]

To his credit, Lukács was determined to remain with Ljena, and when
he could stand it no longer, he did not leave in disgust or hatred. "This
is the way [Lukács] puts it," Balázs reported; "he feels himself to have
the *deepest* relationship with Ljena, so deep that this superficial incarnation of theirs can only disqualify that profound affinity of which
they are conscious. . . . That is why they cannot remain together."[103]

Thus, in the fall of 1917, Lukács decided to leave Ljena and Bruno
and to settle for a time in Budapest. Although he hoped later to return to
the city on the Neckar, this departure signaled the end of his Heidelberg
years. Before he left, he gathered together his correspondence, notes,
and various manuscripts, packed them in a valise, and placed them
in the Deutsche Bank of Heidelberg, where they were to remain until
1972. The date of deposit was 7 November 1917, the day that Lenin and
the Bolsheviks seized power in Lukács's beloved Russia.

C·H·A·P·T·E·R

5

The Russian Revolution

The Sunday Circle

Although Lukács did not resolve to return home until 1917, he had made several trips to Budapest during the first years of the war. Not the least of the reasons for these journeys was the uncertainty surrounding his military status. Originally classified as unfit, he was reexamined in August 1915; he would soon learn, he told Paul Ernst, whether or not he was to be devoured by "the Moloch of Militarism."[1] Once again rejected for front-line duty, he was assigned auxiliary service, first in a military hospital and later in the office of mail censorship. Thus from October 1915 to July 1916, when he was discharged, Lukács was in Budapest. In December, he and a small group of intellectuals began to meet on Sunday afternoons for discussion; the meeting place was Balázs's Biedermeier apartment on the Buda side of the Danube.

It was Balázs, discharged from the army in the fall of 1915, who conceived the idea of organizing the "Sunday Circle," and after the first few meetings, he was brimming with enthusiasm: "It has begun in such a way that perhaps it can become a spiritual/ethical academy. Only *serious* people who are metaphysically disposed are invited. Every new guest is recommended in advance and every member of the group possesses the power of veto."[2] In addition to Balázs and Lukács, the circle included Balázs's first and second wives (Edith Hajós and Anna Schlamadinger), Béla Fogarasi, Karl Mannheim, Arnold Hauser, Frederick Antal, and Emma Ritoók. Anna Lesznai, Lajos Fülep, and Júlia Láng (later Mrs. Karl Mannheim) soon joined the founding members, and among less regular visitors were René Spitz, János Wilde, Zoltán Kodály, Béla Bartók, Michael Polanyi, and Géza Révész.[3]

As the unchallenged leader of the circle, Lukács always chose the subject for discussion. Anna Lesznai remembered that a great variety of themes were touched upon—"painting, folklore, history. Most often the conversation turned to love, the philosophy of love."[4] Arnold Hauser recalled that he and his friends never discussed politics and that they often explored Dostoevski's writings.[5] Lukács had only recently been working on his Dostoevski book and like those young people he had imagined for that purpose, he and the other members of the Sunday Circle withdrew from a world at war at least one day each week. They too attempted "to achieve self-understanding by means of conversations that lead by degrees to the . . . outlook on a Dostoevskian world." Above all, that is, they concerned themselves with the problem of alienation and the quest for a genuine human community.

After his discharge from the army, Lukács returned to Heidelberg to begin work on his *Aesthetics*, and in his absence, the circle's discussions and debates became increasingly sterile, prompting anguished letters from members. Edith Hajós reported that "Sunday has gone completely to the dogs since you left. The two young men [Mannheim and Hauser] still come, but the former standard is never reached."[6] Anna Schlamadinger agreed: "Since you left there has been a slow but steady intellectual and moral decline, and Herbert [Balázs] is not strong enough to check it. He is now the only one who speaks and though he is often very right, his big mistake is that he never listens to others and his demeanor does not command such authority that they listen and submit patiently to him. . . . Gyuri, we were all much better and more intelligent when you were among us."[7]

Early in 1917, the members of the Sunday Circle formulated plans to establish a "Free School of the Humanistic Sciences," somewhat in the manner of the Free School of the Sociological Society that Oszkár Jászi had organized in 1906. But unlike Jászi's school, which was informed by positivism, their school was to be inspired by spiritualism and neo-idealism. After Balázs secured classrooms on the premises of the National Pedagogical Institute, he scheduled the first lectures and seminars for the months of March to June 1917. According to the program announcement, the lectures would not be popular introductions, but serious engagements with the problems raised by the new idealism and new spiritual culture that was sweeping Europe in the wake of the decline of positivism, materialism, and impressionism.[8]

Lukács was in Heidelberg when the Free School opened, but his friends hoped to coax him back to Budapest, going so far as to list him as the lecturer on ethics during the month of May. Anna Schlamadinger wrote to explain: "I am enclosing the prospectus. Anticipating your approval and confident that you will be coming during the spring months, they [his friends] included your name. If you do not wish to lecture or you would prefer to lecture on something other than ethics (our choice), you may still arrange it."[9] Balázs also wrote, emphasizing Lukács's singular importance to the venture: "In our school, everyone is eagerly awaiting you. . . . It is extraordinary, but your followers' secret sect is spreading and is no longer secret. They clamor for you impatiently and suspect that we used your name only as 'advertising.' . . . Seventy enrolled and fifty attend regularly. Never have I seen in Budapest such a fine and engaging, attentive, reverential, grateful audience."[10]

According to the Free School's announcement, there were to be seven lecture series and two seminars during the first semester. These lectures suggest that despite common concerns, Lukács was unable to impose his utopian solutions on everyone. Some, to be sure, were disciples, but others were becoming increasingly skeptical, and still others had become openly hostile. Béla Balázs remained Lukács's most loyal comrade, dedicating his series of lectures on "Dramaturgy" to his friend. Originally published in 1918, these lectures, with an introductory chapter, appeared in Vienna (1922) under the title *The Theory of the Drama*. Here Balázs reformulated the major themes of his *Death Aesthetics* and of Lukács's "Metaphysics of Tragedy." Tragedy was the most perfect literary genre and human finitude the essence of man's tragic destiny, but there was now more than a hint of Lukács's new hope. Death was no longer merely the boundary of life; it was the *frontier* beyond which lay some form of transcendence. Tragedy and loneliness were, in Balázs's revised view, characteristic only of empirical life; behind every death, "we—tragedy's Dionysian chorus—hear the music of a victorious eternal reality, the *still* living life."[11]

Béla Fogarasi had initially come to Lukács's attention when he published a major philosophic essay entitled "The Voluntaristic Theory of Judgment." A man of varied interests, he worked closely with Bernát Alexander on *Athenaeum* (the official journal of the Hungarian Philosophic Society), lectured regularly to the Sociological Society, and maintained some contact with the Bolzano Circle around Jenő (Eugene) Varga. He shared, however, Lukács's enthusiasm for Zalai and Lask and after attending the Sunday afternoon gatherings began to think more consciously in Lukácsian categories. As his contribution to the Free School, Fogarasi offered a series of lectures (never published) entitled "The Theory of Philosophic Thought."

Karl Mannheim had pursued university studies in Budapest and Berlin and had been particularly impressed by Bernát Alexander and Georg Simmel. Alexander sponsored his election to membership in the Hungarian Philosophic Society (1917) and his participation on *Athenaeum*'s editorial board, and Simmel introduced him to the philosophic problem of alienation.[12] Neither Alexander nor Simmel was able, however, completely to capture Mannheim's mind and imagination. Instead, the young philosopher discovered his mentor in Lukács. "I was close to Mannheim when he was a student," Lukács later recalled. "One could say that he was my academically unofficial student."[13]

When Mannheim began to attend the Sunday afternoon gatherings at Balázs's apartment, he was preoccupied with the problem of alienation[14] and quickly became one of the circle's leading figures, even though his relations with Lukács had begun to cool. There had been, apparently, some personal misunderstanding; but whatever its occasion, the reasons for the increasing distance between them went much deeper. Although they continued to agree on the centricity of the alienation problem, they differed with respect to a solution. Mannheim never entertained any sympathy for utopianism; progress, he believed, could only come as a result of long, hard work.

The differences between Lukács and Mannheim were reflected in their assessments of others. Although, for example, Lukács's enthusiasm for Simmel's work had begun to wane, Mannheim praised his former teacher for his unparalleled ability to render intelligible the fate of culture,[15] and in contrast with Lukács's high opinion of Ernst Bloch, Mannheim was critical. In a review of *Geist der Utopie*, he charged Bloch with having written in the "inaccessible, esoteric, deformed language of our age's decadent mysticism." He deplored, moreover, Bloch's lack of system:

> The revelations of the truly great mystics are connected, systematic even if they cannot be justified with respect to an alien system wherein connections can be rationally determined. Their insights are homogeneous, leading to one another. In mysticism's decadent periods, the real stuff of experience gleams only occasionally and where it is exhausted it blends with pedantry, aesthetic impressions, ingenuity, and affectation. . . . The trouble with Bloch is that having renounced the logical vehicle, the style and the aesthetic symmetries are sacrificed; abandoning rigorous logical connection, he is incapable of attaining that characteristic homogeneous system that constitutes the self-fulfillment of experiences of this nature.[16]

Mannheim's attack on Bloch's failure to organize his insights into a logical system appropriate to his concerns reflected his allegiance to Béla Zalai's philosophic legacy. His Free School lectures, "Epistemological and Logical Problems," were indebted above all to Zalai's *A Szellem* essay, "The Problem of Philosophic Systematization." Based upon his doctoral dissertation, "The Structural Analysis of Epistemology," the lectures were ontological investigations designed to advance cultural criticism.

Arnold Hauser came to the Sunday gatherings with Mannheim. Born in Temesvár in 1892, he went to study in Budapest in 1910, earning money by reporting on cultural life in the capital for the *Temesvár News*. In various columns, he praised the work of Lukács, Balázs, and Fülep,[17] and he was so impressed by *The Theory of the Novel* that he proposed to devote a seminar to it at the Free School.[18] Although his lectures, "Post-Kantian Problems of Aesthetics," were never published, he outlined his general position in a study (originally his doctoral dissertation) entitled "The Problem of Aesthetic Systematization."[19]

As the title suggests, Hauser was also indebted to Zalai's work. In essence what he attempted to do was to apply the late philosopher's insights to Lukács's aesthetics. He argued that we can think only within the structure of some system and that, indeed, systematization was precisely the *source* of meaning; a system was that which rendered meaningful isolated data, every one of which was meaningless in and of itself, by arranging them in an orderly relationship. The system of aesthetics was, to be sure, one of value—autonomous, as Lukács maintained; but *individual* works of art could not be both autonomous and meaningful. Following Zalai, Hauser rejected Lukács's argument for the aesthetic priority of the *Kunstwerk*.

Lajos Fülep's paper was entitled "The National Factor in Hungarian Visual Arts." He maintained that in art, form reflected national character, and he pointed to the integral relationship between art and the Weltanschauung of an age.[20] These lectures witness even more unambiguously to the fact that those who taught at the Free School were not merely Lukács's epigones. Fülep was a talented, independent thinker with little sympathy for Lukács's utopian enthusiasms. What he continued to share with Lukács was a distaste for impressionism, positivism, and materialism: "The possibilities latent in Cézanne's art can develop only on the basis of an appropriate new Weltanschauung. . . . With one step the war can bring us closer to the development of this new Weltanschauung. . . . The question is, Is the shock great enough to bring into existence a new Weltanschauung that transcends all that vulgar 'idealism,' 'positivism,' and materialism that mocks philosophy? Because on this hinges the fate of the arts—indeed of the entire culture."[21]

If Fülep retained his independence vis à vis Lukács, Emma Ritoók was openly hostile to him. Her lectures, "The Problems of Aesthetic Effect," were never published, but one can learn something about her position from an essay entitled "The Ugly in Art" that she published in 1916.[22] There is nothing of Lukács in that work. What is more, Ritoók specifically rejected Lukács's ethics, witness her letter to him of March 1917: "We are counting on you in May . . . ; in particular we have in mind four lectures on ethics. Please don't let us down. I especially should like for you to speak on ethics because I have given much thought to what you said on Sundays last year and I perceive that I must adopt a position in opposition to your views. I cannot do this on the basis of principle until I hear from you a systematic exposition."[23]

We do not possess a record of Lukács's lectures, but they certainly centered on the distinction between the first and the second ethic. Of the two seminars—Frederick Antal's "Cézanne and Post-Cézannean Painting" and Zoltán Kodály's "On the Hungarian Folk-Song"—even less is known. Despite the sophistication of the topics, however, the Free School's success exceeded all expectations; lectures attracted as many as seventy students, among whom were the most gifted young men and women in Hungary—as they were to demonstrate later, in western Europe and the United States.[24] Obviously pleased, Balázs recorded his evaluation of the first semester's work in his diary: "Fogarasi's lectures on the theory of philosophic thought were firstrate. Hauser's on aesthetics after Kant less able, but he had done an impressive amount of work. Antal's lectures were a bit weak, but Mannheim's on the logic of epistemology were excellent, exciting, and rich; the first appearance of an important philosopher of the future. Gyuri also arrived, and although he improvised the ethical lectures, they were still paramount in importance. . . . What a splendid lecturer Gyuri is! An ideal professor. Everyone who heard him could sense that a new heroic age was dawning for philosophy."[25]

The Free School's second semester began in February 1918. Preparatory to its opening, Mannheim delivered a programmatic lecture entitled "Soul and Culture," in which he elucidated the school's central preoccupation: the problem of alienation. "We are many and we live apart," he told his audience, "divorced from one another, longing for one another, but unable to draw near to one another. But it is not only the other who is out of our reach, but we ourselves as well."[26]

By way of introduction to the Free School's general orientation,

Mannheim spoke of the cultural tradition with which the faculty wished
to be identified: "In Weltanschauung and attitude toward life, Dostoevski; in our ethical convictions, Kierkegaard; in our philosophic point of
view, the German *Logos*, the Hungarian *A Szellem*, Lask, and Zalai; in
our aesthetic conviction, Paul Ernst and Riegl; in our artistic culture,
Cézanne, the new French lyric poetry, and particularly the trend represented by the *Nouvelle Revue Française*. Among our own, those
whose names can serve as rallying cries are Bartók, Ady, . . . and the
Thália Theater movement."[27] With this inventory as a background, he
turned to his topic—the relationship between the soul and culture.

Although the mystics believed that they could achieve knowledge of
the soul by withdrawing from life, Mannheim insisted that such a path
was not open to modern men, if indeed it had been open to the mystics
themselves. Modern man should not attempt to take up a position outside of events because only through the manifestations of his life could
he trace his soul's path. Hence what had to be inquired into was the relation of the soul to one's work. A privileged modality of the soul that was
prior to culture, each work necessarily became a "cultural object" as it
entered the flow of time, and, for that reason, the mystics "wanted to
cast off the *Werk*; they felt that it could not bring forth fulfillment, because it stands out against the soul, draws toward itself, becomes an end
in itself, falsifies. Nevertheless, they later acknowledged its inevitability. Meister Eckhart, in his sermon on *Mary and Martha*, proclaimed
the necessity of the *Werk*."[28]

In the sermon to which Mannheim referred, Eckhart stood the biblical
account in St. Luke 10:38–42 on its head. According to the gospel version, Jesus defended Mary, who sat at his feet, against the censure of
her sister Martha, who was busy preparing the evening meal. Eckhart,
however, praises Martha because she sacrificed pure, spiritual pleasure
in order to draw near to God through work. "Martha, and with her all
the friends of God, are careful or troubled, . . . a state in which temporal work is as good as any communing with God, for it joins us as
straitly to God as the best that can happen to us barring the vision of
God in his naked nature."[29]

According to Mannheim, then, it was through works (culture) that
men were able to confront their souls. But work had yet another mission: to serve as a temporary bridge between men. Insofar as it carried
out this mission, it was a cultural object or form. The possibilities of
human existence were thus shared by men and that was all to the good,
but inevitably cultural forms began to take on a life of their own, increasingly alienated from the soul content that inspired their creation.
Culture became a "Golem," more and more divorced from the soul,

and when alienation became complete, there arose what Mannheim, following Lukács, called "aesthetic cultures."

Having described the tragedy of culture, Mannheim suggested a schema for the soul's journey through time. There were, he argued, religious, artistic, and critical (or aesthetic) cultures. In religious cultures, creative men had a privileged relationship to the soul; they approached a mystical, formless understanding of human existence. In artistic cultures, the contents of the soul were given more or less adequate form by means of pure creative instinct. Because no alienation was as yet perceived—the soul and form being in harmony—theory and criticism were unnecessary. Critical (aesthetic) cultures emerged as the alienation of the soul from the cultural form became transparent.

It was because he and his friends were confronted with an aesthetic culture, Mannheim explained, that they had undertaken the task of cultural criticism, the analysis of the structure of each cultural form.[30] "For us, it was precisely in terms of this structural analysis that the return to Kant became timely."[31] Kant was the first to see clearly the structures peculiar to the three most important cultural formations: theory, ethics, and aesthetics. Because in Hungary it was Béla Zalai who pursued Kant's insight most consistently, "we united with him directly. Last [semester] we assayed to analyze the fundamentals and structures peculiar to ethics, aesthetics, epistemology, philosophy, and art."[32] The faculty hoped, Mannheim continued, to further this effort during the semester to come, and as a result of such analysis, he held out the prospect of a new culture, the forms of which would express more authentically the soul's new experiences. Such a culture alone could minimize human alienation.

We know relatively little about the Free School's second semester, although Lukács's "Aesthetics" lectures were undoubtedly distilled from the *Heidelberg Aesthetics*. Béla Fogarasi's "The Methods of *Geistesgeschichte*" examined the work of Dilthey, Husserl, Windelband, and Rickert, and Arnold Hauser's "Artistic Dilettantism" was directed to a phenomenon characteristic of "aesthetic cultures." Mannheim's lectures, "Structural Analysis of Epistemological Systems," constituted a continuation of his first semester's investigations. Frederick Antal's lectures, "The Evolution of Composition and Content in Modern Painting," have not survived in any form, but we know that the young art historian, inspired in part by Lukács's *Modern Drama*, laid considerable stress on sociological factors. Indeed, of all the members of the Sunday Circle, he was the most intrigued by the Marxist approach to art history.[33] Balázs offered a seminar entitled "Hungarian Lyrical Poets" and a series of lectures, "The Evolution of Lyrical Sensibility," in which he examined modern lyrics of loneliness and traced the origins of alienation to the collapse of medieval religion and of Renaissance culture: "With Rousseau begins the soul's revolt against culture, in which it no longer feels itself to be at home."[34]

Mannheim identified four other lecturers: Sándor Varjas, Zoltán Kodály, Béla Bartók, and Ervin Szabó. Varjas, a member of the "BEMBE" (Bolzano) Circle and a philosopher with an interest in psychoanalysis, chose as his theme "Phenomenological Investigations." Although these lectures may well have been delivered, there is no reliable evidence to suggest that either Kodály or Bartók presented theirs. Whether or not Szabó, the father of Hungarian Marxism, delivered his lectures is also uncertain, but he "followed with interested sympathy the *Geisteswissenschaft* lectures organized by those around György Lukács."[35]

Postwar events in Hungary were soon to overtake the Free School of the Humanistic Sciences, but despite its brief existence, the school's importance to *European* intellectual history can scarcely be exaggerated. Lukács, Balázs, Mannheim, Hauser, Antal, Fogarasi, Charles de Tolnay, Michael Polanyi; even this partial list of names suffices to indicate the significance of its work. Perhaps Tolnay summed up the school's ideals and achievements as well as anyone: "In opposition to the scholarship for scholarship's sake characteristic of Hungarian and Western universities, the Free School set a new objective for scholarly work. Knowledge would no longer be an end in itself, but rather a road to the soul's self-fulfillment. . . . Within this circle of young people of learning, a spiritual *community* took form. For the first time in modern Hungarian spiritual life, there was realized . . . the most fervent desire of every contemporary scholar and human being: the rediscovery of community."[36]

Philosophic Idealism and Politics

The Free School of the Humanistic Sciences set itself in opposition not only to official Hungarian culture but also to the circles around the journals *Nyugat* and *Huszadik Század*. At the same time that it was offering classes, Lukács propagated its, and his, ideas in print. In his most ambitious effort of the final two years of the war, he collected several of his essays on Balázs and published them under the title *Béla Balázs and His Detractors*. In the important introduction,[37] he defended his decision to publish essays written in praise of a friend, insisting, truthfully, that he and Balázs became friends because of a prior community of convictions, not vice versa. Dismissing most of Balázs's

Hungarian critics, he deemed it worthwhile to make specific reply only to Mihály Babits. Echoing what he had said in his earlier debate with the fine writer/critic, Lukács argued that Babits's charge that Balázs was a "German" writer masked his uneasiness in the presence of a profundity all too rare in Hungarian literary history.

Finally, and most important, Lukács went so far as to compare Balázs with Dostoevski. Because Babits had rightly regarded such a comparison as "shocking," Lukács called the critic's knowledge of Russian literature into question. Babits, he reminded his readers, had once compared *Oblomov* to the Hungarian penchant for inaction, when in fact the comparison would not stand the test. Hungarians knew exactly what they must do to get along in the reality attainable in *this* world. The Russian Oblomov, on the other hand, had his sight set on utopia. "He sees the absolute and if with one leap, one single 'impetuous act of heroism'—as Staretz Zossima formulated the central question of the Russian soul—it could be realized, Oblomov too would act. But he sees that this is impossible and, unable to endure living on a relative plane, he remains in bed. His inaction, therefore, belongs to the problematic of the 'impetuous act of heroism'; it takes its place in that curious sequence that leads from *Picque Dame*'s Hermann through Raskolnikov to, if you will, Ropshin's terrorists" (*IM*, 707–8).

Not only does this passage reflect Lukács's Russian spirit, it also testifies to his longing to reach utopia at a stroke. Ready as he was for his own "impetuous act of heroism," he identified himself consciously with Dostoevski's characterization of Alyosha Karamazov: "He was to a certain extent a young man of our own times, that is, honest by nature, demanding truth, seeking it, believing in it, and, believing in it, demanding to serve it with all the strength of his soul, yearning for an immediate act of heroism and wishing to sacrifice everything, even life itself, for that act of heroism."[38] All that was missing was some tangible evidence that utopia might be realizable.

Lukács did not defend in detail his identification of Balázs with Dostoevski because he had done so at some length in the most important of the essays included in the collection: *"On Tristan's Boat"* (the title of a volume of Balázs's verses) and *"Mortal Youth"* (the title of a Balázs drama).[39] In the first, he argued that the true poet was he who uncovered the soul's essence, he who recalled that unity of souls that men knew prior to the time that Jehovah built the Tower of Babel, thus making their souls, as well as their words, mutually incomprehensible. With "naked words" he revealed "naked souls." In the world of the great poets, there was but one reality—that of the soul—and in modern times it was Dostoevski who first brought men back to the soul's cosmos.

Lukács concluded that "if we wish to situate Béla Balázs's oeuvre in literary history, we may mention only Dostoevski as his predecessor" (*IM*, 649).

Similarly, Lukács characterized Balázs's *Mortal Youth* as "the new drama of the soul, the dramatic equivalent of Dostoevski's epic" (*IM*, 694). In this play, the characters lived their soul's essence free of that social determination that compelled men to live inauthentic existences in empirical (or even metaphysical) reality, and because their relationships with others were unmediated by forms, they were able to become fully human. The "soul's tireless essence" could exist only "as the trans-temporal union of two souls." Lukács cited in this regard the symbiotic relationship that existed between Myshkin and Rogozhin and between Raskolnikov and Svidrigalov. Balázs's play was "the first conscious attempt to create a drama on this plane" (*IM*, 686–87).

Not surprisingly, Balázs thought the essay collection "brilliant," but he was convinced that it would occasion a "pogrom" against the Sunday Circle. In this case, his fears were exaggerated because, although the *Nyugat* circle remained hostile, some members of the *Huszadik Század* circle, including Oszkár Jászi, had themselves begun to take a new interest in philosophic idealism. In a review of the published version of Mannheim's *Soul and Culture*, for example, Jászi praised the author and his colleagues for opposing positivism and historical materialism. "This remonstrance of idealism, pluralism, and absolute standards of value can evoke only sympathy and endorsement."[40] And in the summer of 1918, the Sociological Society proposed the creation of a "counter-university" that would initially boast two faculties, one for sociology and political economy, the other for the humanistic sciences. "The latter," Balázs wrote in his diary, "is to be staffed by members of our school. Our faculty is to have complete autonomy. This is very significant for we will no longer be so isolated. It is true that our distinguished purity is also endangered, but it is not necessary to lose it. Fülep is afraid. 'Until now,' he said, 'we were the twelve fishermen; soon we will be made into a church.' "[41]

The idea for this cooperative venture was generated by a lecture Béla Fogarasi delivered on 5 March 1918 before a joint meeting of the Sociological Society and the Sunday Circle. Entitled "Conservative and Progressive Idealism,"[42] the address and the discussion it engendered signaled a major turning point in Hungarian intellectual history, because they symbolized a new reciprocity between radical politics and philosophic idealism. For both sides, this came as something of a revelation. Many political radicals in the Sociological Society recognized that they had always been idealists without knowing it, and as for the members of the Sunday Circle, Balázs later recalled that "in the course of that great and celebrated discussion, it became evident that we did not and never had lived in an ivory tower, but that every one of our ideas implied an exacting life."[43]

Fogarasi was the ideal lecturer for so auspicious an occasion, for although he was closely identified with Lukács and the Sunday Circle, he continued to be active in the Sociological Society, to which he spoke often on the history of philosophy. No one was in a better position to refute the view according to which there existed a necessary correlation between positivism and progressive politics. Because they assumed a preestablished harmony between progressive desiderata and evolutionary transmutations, positivists put their trust in the law of development, but to embrace developmental tendencies was, as Fogarasi pointed out, to espouse *Realpolitik*. Ought collapsed into is and end goals were soon abandoned for present realities.

Progressive politics, Fogarasi insisted, could not build upon the shifting sands of natural science, but only upon the rock of an idealism that, by recognizing the absolute validity of logical truths, ethical imperatives, and aesthetic values, upheld the independence of norms vis-à-vis Being and historical fortune. To be sure, not every idealism was conducive to progressive politics; both metaphysical and aesthetic idealism —the idealism of the Romantics, the later Schelling, and Hegel—gravitated toward conservatism. But the ethical idealism associated with Kant and Fichte *was* progressive: democratic and socialist. The Königsberg philosopher first formulated this ethical idealism when he stressed the dualism of *Sein* and *Sollen*, what is and what ought to be.

But here a problem arose, because the categorical imperative recognized no norms of content. On the basis of what ethical postulate of content, Fogarasi asked rhetorically, could he and his friends demand democracy and equality? The answer, he replied, could be deduced from the Kantian-Fichtean concept of dignity (*Würdigkeit*). Man's dignity derived from his responsibility, and only democracy and socialism were capable of creating a world in which man was in a position to accept full responsibility for his actions and decisions. Fogarasi cautioned, finally, that *political ends* must never be confused with *ethical ends*. Neither democracy nor socialism could summon into being the true end of ethics—love and brotherhood beyond Kant's ethic of responsibility. The ethical transformation of human beings could transform completely the political situation, but the reverse could never be true.

Subsequent to Fogarasi's lecture, the Sociological Society convened on three occasions in order to discuss and debate his theses, and Lukács's contribution was of particular importance.[44] He insisted even more forcefully than Fogarasi that what was crucial to progressive action was the particular morality, not the metaphysical theory, on which that action was based. As an example, he cited the unprogressive character of Indian culture. That culture, he argued, was deeply connected with Indian ethics, with the teaching that holds that everyone in this life has unalterable tasks. Compliance with caste responsibilities was the highest virtue; movement out of the caste was the greatest sin. This ethic had been correlated with the most distinct epistemologies and metaphysics in the course of development, but because the ethic had remained the same, the changes in Weltanschauung from the *Rigveda* to the Buddha and beyond had not changed in the least the socially stagnant and un-progressive character of the culture. For the same reason, Lukács de-nied that there was any necessary correlation between positivism and progress, on the one hand, and a transcendent Weltanschauung and conservatism, on the other. The positing of transcendence need not have a paralyzing effect on action; it could "have as its result that imperative according to which the transcendent reality stands before us as a task. Now, immediately, this very moment, we must realize it, we must bring heaven to earth. (The Anabaptist movements following the Reformation constitute very instructive examples of this possibility.)" (*IM*, 840)

In concert with Fogarasi, Lukács made a sharp distinction between ethics and politics. Ethical action, he argued, was directed toward the inner transformation of man such that the inner intention of his actions conformed to ethical norms. Political action, on the other hand, aimed at the creation, preservation, or transformation of institutions:

> Ethical idealism, insofar as it is directed toward politics, cannot want anything other than the creation of institutions that best meet the requirements of the ethical ideal and the removal of those that stand in the way of this ideal's realization, and every politics based on ethical idealism is conscious at every moment that that which it can attain is *only* political in nature; that is, it can accomplish only the creation of institutions which contribute positively or negatively to this development. No kind of politics can produce the ethically essential—the inner perfection of man, the true realization of ethics. It can only push aside the barriers from the path of development. [*IM*, 841]

From the ethical point of view, according to Lukács, ethical *action directe* was preferable, because such action sought the transformation of the souls of men without the mediation of politics or institutions. If recourse was had to the latter, they must serve the ethical goal, for the moment that they became ends in themselves, they fell from the sphere of value to that of the merely existent. Indeed, every theory that proclaimed the autonomy of politics was obliged, according to Lukács, to abandon ethics and to adopt a metaphysics that recognized the state or the nation as the ultimate existent, the most genuine reality. The state as a complex of institutions was the very symbol and embodiment of conservatism. The most important demand of ethics must be that all institutions be opposed that stand in the way of Kantian-Fichtean *Würdigkeit*, the autonomous dignity of men. "The permanent revolution of ethical idealism opposes existence [institutions] as existence, as that which is of no value to the ethical ideal, and because it is a permanent revolution, because it is an absolute revolution, it is capable of determining the direction of the never-coming-to-rest, never-stagnating development and of regulating its movement" (*IM*, 843–44).

In conclusion, Lukács rejected the principal objection raised against Kantian-Fichtean ethics—its supposed abstract, formal character, the impossibility of drawing from it unequivocal conclusions concerning political action. Progressive criticism of every action and every institution could not better be summed up than in the categorical imperative never to treat a man as a means, but always as an end in himself. There was, Lukács maintained, no concrete demand of progressive politics that could not be shown to be the application of that principle to a special case.

In the light of some of his own criticisms, Lukács's defense of Kant's ethics appears to be contradictory, but as Ágnes Heller has pointed out, Kant wrote "several ethics."[45] In his earlier ethical works—*The Critique of Practical Reason* and the *Groundwork for the Metaphysics of Morals*—he emphasized the motivation for our actions, and this was reflected in the "formal" formulation of the categorical imperative: to act so that one's maxim of action could become a universal law. Here the categorical imperative was indeed formal, abstracting as it did from all ends.

But, Heller argues, Kant wanted to be the Solon, not the Draco of his time, and his subsequent formulation was concrete and material precisely because it was directed toward ends: always act in such a way that oneself and others are treated as ends in themselves, never as means to some other end. This was, as we have seen, the formulation the young Lukács praised. In the spirit of this new formulation, according to Heller, Kant wrote *The Metaphysics of Morals* in an effort to apply the moral law concretely to actions. When actions became the center of interest, the category of responsibility was introduced into ethics, and as Fogarasi had maintained, it was man's responsibility to the self-legislated moral law that constituted his dignity. Heller concludes that

the society based on Kant's new formulation of the categorical imperative was "utopian."

Although this latter claim will not withstand criticism, it was the view
of the young Lukács, who based his defense of Kant's ethics on part 2
of *The Metaphysics of Morals*—"Metaphysical Elements of Virtue."
When, for example, he defined the ethically essential as "the inner perfection of man," he was echoing what Kant wrote.[46] Moreover, Kant's
distinction between juridical or "external" legislation (duties that can
be enforced by the law and that concern *means*) and ethical or "internal" legislation (self-enforced duties that are also *ends*)[47] was fundamental to Lukács's utopian dreams. Utopia was a world in which *all*
legislation would be ethical.

Lukács hoped, indeed, to eliminate all institutional (political) compulsion and, at the same time, to avoid, insofar as possible, the use of
political means to bring heaven to earth. Rather than politics, which
required institutions that might take on lives of their own, he favored
ethical "direct action." As we shall see, he was at this time under the
spell of anarcho-syndicalism, having been introduced to the work of
Georges Sorel by Ervin Szabó,[48] for whom the war had been a catalyst
for rethinking. Like all those who took part in the discussion of Fogarasi's lecture, Szabó sought to end the mutual indifference of philosophy
and politics.

Politics and Apocalypse

During the last years of the war, Lukács vacillated between two alternative responses to the age of absolute sinfulness: withdrawal to a small
agricultural commune (utopia in microcosm) and direct action to change
the world (utopia in macrocosm). Withdrawal from the world had always held for him a certain fascination. In his youth, he had wanted to
enter a monastery.[49] The original plan of *The Theory of the Novel* was to
cast the work in the form of a series of conversations between young
people who had withdrawn from the world, and the members of the
Sunday Circle *did* withdraw from the world of quotidian reality, at least
for one day each week. Throughout 1917–18, Lukács and Balázs discussed frequently the possibility of living a secluded, communal life
near Heidelberg, where they were to be joined by Edith Hajós and Anna
Schlamadinger. In his diary, Balázs described this *"Mistbeet"* ("Hot-
bed") plan. "Gyuri was very enthusiastic about the idea. . . . Edith
and Anna would work, take charge of the economy, and provide for us.
Edith is fond of saying that 'one cannot even consider that the men

should work.' The men should write, make music, philosophize, be scholars—meanwhile, the women should win the bread. We talked of many beautiful things with regard to this settlement, which we see as the final solution for each of our lives."[50]

From Fourier and Owen by way of the romantics who idealized the Russian *mir* to the American young people of the 1960s and 1970s, the dream of an agricultural commune separated from and hence uncontaminated by a wicked world has been the principal utopian alternative to apocalyptic revolution. Because of his distaste for and suspicion of "politics," Lukács was very much attracted by this dream, but in the end events in Hungary and in Russia induced him to choose action in the world, his participation in the antiwar movement being the initial step in that direction.

The organization of an antiwar *movement* began in Hungary, as it did almost everywhere in Europe, only in 1916, for as the war entered its third year, even those who had welcomed it began to entertain second thoughts. Men such as Ady, Lukács, and Szabó had never succumbed to the general enthusiasm, but by 1916 they no longer constituted an isolated minority. It was Szabó, director of Budapest's Municipal Library (that today bears his name), who took the lead; during the winter of 1916, he summoned Lukács, Balázs, Babits, and several others to a meeting to discuss what they might do to shorten the war. Lukács heeded the summons because Szabó was "the spiritual/intellectual father of us all. It was he who truly stood in opposition to the whole of social democratic ideology."[51]

During 1917, the antiwar movement won increasing numbers of adherents from among the Hungarian intelligentsia, and although Szabó's health was failing, he continued to be the leader of the oppositional forces; closest to him in this effort stood Babits and Jászi. Out of the many meetings and discussions led or inspired by Szabó there eventually emerged a plan for a pacifist organization—"The Knights of Europe." According to Balázs, "Mihály Babits's suggestion persuaded Jászi to organize a spiritual and ethical order of Knighthood opposed to every militarism and every nationalism. Of course, Gyuri and I joined with enthusiasm. . . . I believe that similar associations stand ready to be organized all over Europe, and it would be a great thing if we were able to set this in motion."[52]

Jászi and Babits each drafted a manifesto for the Knights of Europe; according to the former's, the goal of the organization was the creation of "the United States of Europe."[53] Members of the association would support every effort to weaken chauvinism and nationalism; to aid in the formation of viable states and to guarantee to national minorities linguistic, cultural, and economic freedom; and to advance democracy, free trade, and social progress.

Babits's draft was longer and more literary.[54] The Knights of Europe, he wrote, would wage spiritual/intellectual war to prepare Europeans for the creation of a united Europe. Representing no political party, nation, or class, they dedicated themselves to the cause and propagation of truth. Setting aside all counsel of despair and hopelessness, they expressed their faith in a better future and intended to live on the basis of that faith, thus providing a moral/intellectual example for all Europeans.

Together with Balázs, Lukács became a Knight of Europe, but he was not as enthusiastic as his friend suggested. He was never on good terms with either Jászi or Babits, and, more important, the manifestoes lacked the immediate millennial promise he believed to be the only *realistic* hope for a world sunk in sin. Yet if Lukács was disappointed by the fate of Szabó's antiwar initiative, he was excited by the writer to whose work Szabó had introduced him—Georges Sorel. "Precisely he [Sorel]," Lukács later recalled, "exercised the greatest influence on my intellectual evolution. Positively insofar as he increased my antipathy to every revisionist or opportunistic interpretation of Marxist theory; negatively [from the standpoint of his later evolution] insofar as the mythological conception of the party as nothing but direct and immediate class struggle dominated my theoretical outlook."[55]

Although of subsequent embarrassment to him, Lukács's infatuation with Sorel should occasion no surprise, for the Frenchman had all of the right enemies. In *The Illusions of Progress*, he characterized the dominant idea of the nineteenth century as "a bourgeois doctrine";[56] the world was becoming more, not less, sinful. Scientific rationalism and individualism were in his judgment symptoms of decline rather than tokens of advance. Sorel was also an outspoken opponent of the state, and in the notes for the Dostoevski book, Lukács wrote: *"State*: Sorel: 'No correction is possible until this power is reduced to play no more than a secondary role in social relations.'"[57] The great error of the Second International, Sorel believed, was its determination to *capture* rather than to destroy the state. In this ambition, it signaled its inability, or refusal, to learn from history. Following Tocqueville, Sorel argued that the French Revolution and "all the revolutionary disturbances of the nineteenth century had ended in reinforcing the power of the State."[58] Because it was oppressive by nature, the state's continued existence would make possible only the substitution of one group of oppressors for another. Finally, Sorel detested "politics," for to engage in politics was to give tacit recognition to the world as it was; to maintain political "institutions" (i.e., the state) was to betray the revolution.

As a consequence of the "decomposition of Marxism," Sorel proposed a marriage of Marxism and syndicalism in which the moral and apocalyptic inspiration of the former was straightforwardly affirmed and the "scientific" and "political" understanding was rejected. No student of Sorel's work has failed to perceive the moral passion that informs it; Sorel himself described his pessimism as "a metaphysics of morals rather than a theory of the world."[59] He meant that his pessimism, like that of Lukács, was provisional, and did not signify an abandonment of hope. Man could make a new world, but he would have to do so through an exercise of the moral will, for to rely on a theory of inevitable development was to invite defeat. If men would *act* heroically, the state could be brought to its knees. Marxian socialism was thus defined not by its peculiar dogmas but by its clarion call for those "impetuous acts of heroism" that so fascinated Lukács.

Not only was Sorel's "new school" of Marxism explicitly moral, it was undisguisedly apocalyptic. "Apocalypse," he wrote, "which represented a scandalous ancestry to socialists who wished to make Marxism compatible with the practice of politicians in a democracy—in reality corresponds perfectly to the general strike which, for revolutionary syndicalists, represents the advent of the new world to come."[60] To be sure, the general strike was a "myth," but Sorel recognized that myths provided meaning and direction for human action. Faith in myth had done more to change the world than the ascertainment of fact because myths were "not descriptions of things, but expressions of a determination to act."[61] It was this determination to act that Sorel so admired in Lenin, whom he described in 1919 as "the greatest theoretician that socialism has had since Marx."[62] Indeed, despite Lenin's famous disparagement of Sorel, he had far more in common with the French engineer than he was ever willing to concede. Certainly Lukács perceived the essential kinship, for he believed the Russian Revolution to be the acting out of Sorel's ideas.

For men such as Sorel and Lukács who dreamed apocalyptic dreams, the Bolshevik revolution was not simply or even essentially a political event. It represented the advent of the millennium. Dostoevski's homeland had fallen to men who claimed that they possessed the keys to a new kingdom and everyone who knew him has testified to Lukács's sympathy for that claim. In her roman à clef *The Adventurers of the Spirit*, Emma Ritoók put these words in the mouth of Ervin Donáth (Lukács): "I have often suspected that it is necessary to orient oneself eastward, but until now the sure connection [with Jewish mysticism] was missing. Could it be possible that Slavic mysticism could have set the stage for the new messianic mission of the Jewish spirit?"[63] Ernst Bloch remembered that Lukács was "impassioned" by the revolution. "If the revolution had broken out in France, it wouldn't have had the same impact on him. It would have been a simple affair of the brain. But Russia was an affair of the heart."[64] According to Paul Ernst, Lukács "alluded to the Russian Revolution and to the great ideas that it has transformed into reality. The Russian Revolution is an event whose meaning for our Europe cannot yet even vaguely be surmised; it takes the initial steps leading mankind out of the bourgeois social order, mechanization and bureaucratization, militarism and imperialism, into a free world in which the spirit can again rule and the soul at least live."[65] And if the Russian Revolution was the first step in the realization of utopia, its leader was a "gnostic of the deed," the quintessential man of action.[66] After all the endless chatter of orthodox social democracy, Lukács thought, Lenin had *made* a revolution and placed utopia on the immediate agenda.

Entranced by Sorel's theories and Lenin's practice, Lukács began to take a greater interest in Hungarian politics. As a Knight of Europe he had identified himself with a political attitude that owed more to Woodrow Wilson than to Lenin, but this is not surprising when one remembers that Hungary did not then have a communist party. More important, Lukács retained two major reservations concerning Lenin and the Bolshevik revolution—the use of violence and the continued existence of the dictatorial state. He hoped, therefore, that a nonviolent transformation of Hungary might still be possible, and those hopes soared when in late October 1918, Mihály Károlyi led a successful and virtually bloodless revolution against the helpless and defeated old régime. "The triumph without apparent effort [of Károlyi's revolution], the collapse without an outpouring of blood of the Habsburg Monarchy in Hungary, had created in me the illusion that in the future, too, a nonviolent path could lead to the complete triumph of democracy and even to the victory of socialism."[67]

Lukács never, however, regarded Károlyi's republic as the final goal, and in an essay, "Republican Propaganda," published eleven days after Károlyi assumed power, he issued a warning to his countrymen:

> But let us never forget that in the achievement of the republic, the revolution has only begun, it has not been completed. The republic is today the beautiful symbol of the new order, the new Hungary that all of us are awaiting, but it is only a means and a

symbol and everything will be lost if we permit it to become an end in itself. . . . The history of every revolution exhibits this evolution. Those political institutions, the creation of which was necessary for the sake of an economic and social transformation, become ends in themselves, eclipsing that for which we first looked to them; indeed, they turn against it. This transformation of political aims into ends in themselves always signifies the end of revolutions and the victory of reaction.[68]

The Károlyi government sought to remake Hungary in the image of the Western democracies, an effort for which Lukács had little sympathy, but even such a limited change represented a considerable challenge. The victorious Allies refused to differentiate between Károlyi and István Tisza, in large part because they were bent on dismembering the crown lands and dividing the spoils among the new nation-states. At the same time, forces on the political right and left were gathering within the country, where many had cast Károlyi in the role of a Hungarian Kerensky. More than any other oppositional force, the Hungarian Communist party, organized on 24 November 1918, stood ready in the wings, waiting to move to center stage the moment the Károlyi government faltered. The party's confidence is not surprising; four great empires had fallen and the possibilities of creating a radically different world suddenly seemed very real.

Because, therefore, a soviet republic was the most likely alternative to Károlyi's democratic republic, the radical (but noncommunist) journal *Szabadgondolat* (*Free Thought*) devoted its December 1918 number to the question of bolshevism. That special number is of extraordinary importance not only because it presents, in microcosm, the debate over communism in which the Hungarian intelligentsia was then feverishly engaged, but also because it contains political statements, forged in the crucible of a mounting national crisis, of two men whose views were of fundamental importance to Hungary's future: Jászi and Lukács.

Szabadgondolat's special issue on bolshevism began with an editorial note to its readers that reflected the extravagant hopes and expectations generated by a catastrophic war. Only a radically transformed world, it seemed, could possibly redeem four years of sacrifice and destruction. "We stand on the threshold of a new world order. In opposition to the world order of armed men, *Szabadgondolat* proclaims the world order of pacifism. In place of sovereign states: universal League of Nations! In place of general armament: general disarmament! In place of wars: a compulsory court of arbitration! In place of class rule and racial oppression: democratic people's state and equal rights for all nationalities! In place of the rule of force: the rule of law! The world expects all this from the pacifistic peace."[69]

If Bolshevik practice during the first tempestuous year of Lenin's rule brought the achievement of these goals no closer, Bolshevik evangelism continued to call upon repentant Hungarians to become soldiers of the hammer and sickle. Hungarian party leader Béla Kun, a prisoner of war in Russia before his political conversion, echoed the Soviet charge that it was the self-serving opposition of defenders of the old world that was slowing the inexorable coming of the new. Uncompromising in their agitation and convinced of their vocation, Kun and his followers insisted that they be given power; no journal committed to the creation of a new world and to the free and open exchange of ideas could easily ignore such a demand.

It was only natural that the editors should ask for a contribution from Jászi, who was then serving as minister of nationalities in the Károlyi government, a government that took its ideological bearings from his extensive writings. He began his essay, "Proletarian Dictatorship,"[70] by registering his opposition to all dictatorships as antithetical to democracy and morality. For the sake of argument, however, he was prepared to set aside moral scruple and to consider proletarian dictatorship as a practical question. Even from this point of view, Jászi maintained, the Bolsheviks' promises had proved empty, for in Lenin's Russia, the dictatorship had not signaled the end of class rule but only its reversal; the oppressed had become the oppressors. He concluded with a warning against any attempt on the part of the Hungarian Communists to disrupt the Károlyi government, arguing that such action would play into the hands of counterrevolutionaries.

Lukács's "Bolshevism as a Moral Problem" was at once more critical of and more sympathetic to bolshevism. The moral problem to which he referred hinged on the issue of democracy. Was democracy an integral part of socialism or merely a tactic, useful until the proletariat assumed power? In order to clarify this question, Lukács pointed to the contradiction between Marx's sociological method and his utopian vision of the classless society. On the one hand, he had claimed that the motive force of historical development was class struggle; on the other hand, he was confident that the proletariat's victory over its class enemy, the bourgeoisie, would bring class oppression to an end. Yet viewed as sociological necessity, the victory of the proletariat signified nothing more than the ascendancy of new oppressors. If Marx had indeed discovered the propelling force of history, one would be forced to accept evil as evil, oppression as oppression.

If bolshevism's confidence in the messianic mission of the proletariat could not be justified by reference to its understanding of historical process, it could only rest on faith. Bolsheviks had to *believe* that the proletarian dictatorship would eradicate rather than perpetuate oppression. They had to believe that good (the classless society) could issue from evil (dictatorship and terror), and this, Lukács insisted, was truly an instance of *credo quia absurdum est*. Clearly, he feared that the Bolsheviks would grow too fond of the power of the state.

Lukács recognized that an eschewal of immoral means and a reliance on moral (democratic) means of achieving the goal of the classless society presented many difficulties. It might well be that most men did not share his enthusiasm for *Gemeinschaft*, and the day of the new world would therefore have to be postponed until the slow process of education convinced them of its desirability. Indeed, adherents of the democratic way themselves required considerable faith, but in summation Lukács wrote:

> I repeat: Bolshevism rests on the metaphysical assumption that good can issue from evil, that it is possible, as Razumikhin says in *Crime and Punishment*, to lie our way through to the truth.[71] The present writer is not able to share this faith and therefore he sees at the root of the bolshevik position an irresolvable moral dilemma. Democracy in his view requires only superhuman self-abnegation and self-sacrifice from those who consciously and honestly wish to persevere to the end, but this, if perhaps it necessitates superhuman strength, is not in essence an insoluble question as is bolshevism's moral problem.[72]

In the same month that this article appeared, Lukács joined the Hungarian Communist party, accompanied by Béla Balázs, Béla Fogarasi, and Ljena Grabenko Lukács. Those members of the Sunday Circle who remained uncommitted to communism received the news of his party allegiance with stunned disbelief. Anna Lesznai remembered that his "conversion took place in the interval between two Sundays: Saul became Paul."[73] Enemies as well as friends were at a loss to understand; in his autobiography, the proletarian/avant-garde writer and artist Lajos Kassák described a meeting of the *Vörös Újság* (*Red Gazette*) editorial staff late in 1918, at the time of Lukács's co-optation. "I was a little surprised that Lukács had undertaken this work, he who a few days earlier had published an article in *Szabadgondolat* in which he wrote with philosophic emphasis that the communist movement had no ethical base and was therefore inadequate for the creation of a new world. The day before yesterday he wrote this, but today he sits at the table of the *Vörös Újság* editorial staff."[74]

But Lukács's conversion was not as sudden or dramatic as it appeared. A close reading of "Bolshevism as a Moral Problem" discloses that the only stumbling blocks in the way of his entry into the party were the resort to violence and the fear that the proletarian dictatorship (the *state*) would not liquidate itself. He did not otherwise mask his sympathy for the Bolsheviks; in fact, he associated their decisiveness with those "impetuous acts of heroism" that he himself was so eager to perform.

Lukács had, we know, been fascinated by the problem of violence and terror for years. In his *Modern Drama* he had written of Hebbel: "His prayer could also have been that which Judith[75] offered before making her decision: 'If thou [God] place a sin between me and my deed: who am I that I should quarrel about it and shun thee.' "[76] For the German dramatist, life's greatest tragedy was precisely "that it imposes evils on morally pure human beings, that it is not possible to remain pure and still live."[77] Later Lukács affirmed the necessary sin in "On Poverty of Spirit" and celebrated the Russian terrorists in the notes for the Dostoevski book. In the first essay he published after joining the party—"Tactics and Ethics"[78]—he attempted to set forth the resolution of the problem of terror at which he had arrived before committing himself to the communist movement.

Lukács did not deny the terrible moral responsibility of those who employed terror, but neither did he think that they alone were morally culpable. He admitted that every man who identified himself with the communist movement was responsible for every life sacrificed in the revolutionary struggle, but, by the same token, he contended that every man who took sides with communism's opponents had to shoulder the moral responsibility for lives lost because of imperialistic wars and class oppression. It was Lukács's conviction that there was no escape for men who wished to preserve their moral purity in the age of absolute sinfulness that enabled him to overcome his eleventh-hour scruples concerning the resort to terror. All men, he persuaded himself, were caught in the tragic dilemma of having to choose between the purposeful and ephemeral violence of the revolution and the meaningless and never-ceasing violence of the old, corrupt world.

The choice was not an arbitrary one, for there existed a standard for judging the lesser evil that Lukács called "sacrifice." To explain what he meant by this word, he turned again to Savinkov[79] and to Hebbel:

> Murder is not permitted; murder is an unconditional and unforgivable sin, but it is inescapably necessary. It is not permitted, but it must be done. And in a different place in his fiction,

Savinkov sees not the justification of his act (that is impossible), but its deepest moral root in that he sacrifices not only his life, but also his purity, morality, even his soul for his brothers. In other words, only that man's murderous act can be—tragically—moral, who knows that murder is not permitted under any circumstances. Or let us express this idea that belongs to the ultimate human tragedy in the unsurpassably beautiful words of Hebbel's Judith: "And if God has placed sin between me and the deed required of me—who am I that I should be able to evade it?"[80]

It would be misleading, of course, to suggest that Lukács's decision matured in a historical vacuum. A polarization seemed to him to be developing between revolutionary and "reactionary" camps. Communist Russia was fighting for its life against "White" Russians and the Allies. Germany's Majority Social Democrats, led by Friedrich Ebert, Philipp Scheidemann, and Gustav Noske, were trying to curb the revolutionary forces in the former Reich. Hungary's new democratic government feared and hated revolutionary violence. The Armageddon that Lukács discussed with Marianne Weber in Heidelberg seemed to be at hand; like so many millenarians before him, he believed that the destiny of the world would soon be decided, and he was convinced that as a morally sensitive man, he must choose the party that offered the hope of a new world—the party of the revolution.

In his novelistic history *Optimisták* (*Optimists*), Ervin Sinkó,[81] one of the participants in the struggle for the Hungarian Soviet Republic, recreated the turbulent days of 1918–19. Lukács appeared as one of the principal characters, the revolutionary intellectual "Vértes." On being asked why, in view of his initial moral censure of bolshevism, he had joined the revolution, Vértes answered that he had become aware that he could not avoid sin. Once having recognized that inevitability, he had to decide whether he should take responsibility for every drop of blood spilled in the interest of the revolution or reject solidarity with a vision that could only be realized by means of terror. *Either* he had to support by inaction the world of Scheidemann, Noske, the German officer corps, and the White Russian officers, *or* he had to join in the revolutionary struggle for a new world. To support the old world, Vértes contended, was unthinkable; to refuse to join the revolution out of moral scruple was in effect to say to Karl Liebknecht and Rosa Luxemburg: "I want to be better than you. I want to be innocent of every sin of violence." This was also unthinkable for anyone who knew anything of the character of the Sparticist leaders. Vértes therefore committed himself to the Communist party and its revolutionary objectives.[82]

The second problem that bolshevism posed for Lukács was its inability to demonstrate conclusively that the state—the proletarian dictatorship—would liquidate itself, but during the first weeks of the Károlyi
government, he read (in German translation) Lenin's *State and Revolution.*[83] In this atypical work, the Russian leader defined the state as the
product of the irreconcilability of class antagonisms. As an organ of
class rule, it demonstrated by its very existence that society was torn by
class struggle. In order to end class oppression, therefore, Lenin concluded that the revolution would have to smash the entire apparatus
of state power. To be sure, he referred to the "bourgeois" state, but
even the proletarian state was not to last forever, for it was destined to
"wither away." It was required only so long as the dethroned bourgeoisie continued its resistance. In fact, Lenin proclaimed, the proletarian
state would begin *immediately* to wither away because the functions of
state power would devolve increasingly upon the people. In due course,
people would *"become accustomed* to observing the elementary rules
of social intercourse" and there would no longer be any need for state
compulsion. Lukács was aware that this dream might never be realized,
but Lenin was at the Russian helm, and there was at least *hope* that
the scenario of *State and Revolution* would be played out on the stage
of history.

In late November or early December 1918, Lukács met Béla Kun.
Here was a man, he told the Sunday Circle, "who *possesses the truth.*
. . . [His] thinking and conviction do not, like ours, become lost in a
vacuum, but become active reality. We freeze our principles in bourgeois formulas. For the first time, I have met someone in whom Hegel's
dialectic has become flesh and blood, someone who truly *lives out* that
about which we only prattle. He made it plain to me that I had never
drawn the consequences of my ideas, but I will now do so."[84] This important meeting was arranged by Ernő Seidler, a party member close
to Kun and, more significant, Irma Seidler's brother.[85] To Lukács, it
seemed as though Irma had entrusted her brother with a holy mission.

Encouraged by Lenin and inspired by Kun, Lukács decided on his
own "impetuous act of heroism," although he did not deceive himself
concerning the scientific predictability of communism's realization. No
amount of knowledge could ever have silenced his doubt; to join the
revolution he had to make a leap of faith. Even if, in the end, communism was unable to redeem its promises, Lukács believed that his
commitment would be justified ethically because he had exercised his
moral will to a new world. In this regard, Sinkó's valuable memoir is
again instructive, for in one of his many debates with his comrades,
Vértes maintained that Marxist theory could not in itself provide the

necessary impulse for heroic revolutionary action; action could never result from knowledge alone. No degree of erudition could impart perfect knowledge of a given situation or of the many possible consequences of an act, because the more extensive one's knowledge, the more one recognized the impossibility of perfect knowledge. This ironic truth, Vértes argued, led to skepticism and to a paralysis of the will. "Hamlet cannot act because he only knows and does not believe." To act, to place oneself in the service of a revolution, required the power of faith. "In order to think well, a correct theory is sufficient, but in order for a man who knows good and evil to be able to live and fight, faith is necessary."[86]

There is much of Weber (the *Gesinnungsethik*), Sorel, and Lenin here, and something more; how, a young comrade asks, did one acquire this faith? Vértes's answer provides the solution to the final riddle of Lukács's conversion to communism. "If the question interests you and you find some time, read Kierkegaard. I have a strong suspicion that he himself was without faith, but I know of no one who perceived more clearly than he the cardinal importance—and inaccessibility—of faith."[87] During his years in Heidelberg, Lukács had begun a study (never completed) of Kierkegaard's critique of Hegel, and he knew, therefore, that Kierkegaard had rejected the mediative nature of Hegel's philosophy and his claim that philosophy could comprehend reality through reason. Kierkegaard denied that contradictory ideas could be preserved and reconciled at a higher level of understanding and insisted that there was no escaping the necessity of choice; the moral man had to decide "either/or." Once, after Irma's suicide, Lukács condemned himself for having been neither "hot" nor "cold," and he did not intend to commit the same sin again—he chose bolshevism and the revolution.

But, in a very real sense, Lukács had made his choice as early as 1911, at the time of Irma's death. From then on, he aligned himself with the heretical tradition that stretched back to Jewish apocalyptic writings and the New Testament Apocalypse. Like all those who had come to hate this world *as it is*—from the Gnostics, Joachim of Floris, and Thomas Müntzer, through the Hasidim, Fichte, the Russian terrorists, Sorel, and Lenin, to Karl Marx—Lukács embraced the perennial heresy, the belief that heaven, understood as the reign of perfect justice, could be established on earth. Nowhere was that seductive heresy more alive during the nineteenth century than in Russia. With the coming of World War I, history had reached the age of absolute sinfulness; hence redemption could not be far off. With the Russian Revolution, the epic battle that would usher in the millennium had begun.

"I cannot tolerate this age," a fictional apocalyptic revolutionary insists, "and I will not."[88] Russia's apocalyptic revolutionaries, from Chernyshevsky to Lenin, agreed. Christian heretics that they were, they would not be satisfied with a better world, much less with the world as it was; only a completely new world peopled by new creatures would satisfy their inordinate craving for justice. Lukács now proposed to work for the realization of a utopian world without regard for the crimes he might be called upon to commit.

Gertrúd Bortstieber: Dialectics

Gertrúd Bortstieber about 1917
Courtesy Magyar Tudományos Akadémia Filozófiai Intézet
Lukács Archívum és Könyvtár
(Lukács Archives and Library, Institute of Philosophy,
Hungarian Academy of Sciences), Budapest

6

The Hungarian Soviet Republic

Gertrúd and Hegel

Lukács's conversion to communism marked the culmination of his utopian years and of his life with Ljena Grabenko, for although his wife had also joined the party, his dream of becoming one with her had ended. "When Ljena visited me after her separation from the musician [Bruno Steinbach], there existed between us a sympathetic friendship which, however, did not touch upon the central problems of life. Respect and sympathy, without that solidarity that extends to the center of life."[1] After some time in Austria, Ljena returned to Russia, and, although nothing is known concerning her subsequent fate, she, like Savinkov, may well have fallen victim to Soviet "justice."[2]

In the spring of 1917, Lukács met Gertrúd Bortstieber, one of those who attended his Free School lectures on ethics. This was not, however, their first encounter, for they had been introduced many years earlier by Mici Lukács. Even at that time, Gertrúd had been attracted to Lukács, witness a letter of 7 September 1906, in which she praised his Ibsen essay. "At first I was surprised that you describe Ibsen as a Romantic, but only because, as I see, I had a very superficial conception of Romanticism, to whose essence you introduced me. . . . I accepted the other ideas without any opposition. I do not want to criticize, nor do I consider myself competent enough to do so; indeed, you do not want this. You want only that I read with a receptive mind, and I accept this role gladly at all times. Whenever you should require a reader, I am happily at your disposal."[3]

When they renewed their acquaintance in 1917, Gertrúd was the wife of Imre Jánossy, a mathematician, and the mother of two boys. An economist by training, she united "in her person the qualities of great practical wisdom and sense of realism with an irrepressibly serene outlook on life and a radiating warmth of character."[4] In the last year of his life, Lukács remembered this woman, who was to become his second wife, with love and gratitude:

> The beginning of the new relationship: obscure, but the feeling that, finally, for the first time in my life, love, completion, solid basis for life (examination of thought), not opposition. . . . I don't know whether the inner metamorphosis of my thought (1917–19) would have occurred without the help of this examination. . . . The importance of Gertrúd in this transition. For the first time in my life: unlike the others (Irma, Ljena), my course was always constant. Relationship, also love, within a given course of development. Now with respect to every decision, Gertrúd played a major role, precisely in the most human-personal determinations. . . . And long before a spiritual *Gemeinschaft* had been formed between us, this overpowering need for harmony, this becoming-affirmative through her, was for our relationship a central question. After I met Gertrúd, the becoming-affirmative that I derived from her became the central problem of my personal life.[5]

The identification with another that Lukács had been unable to effect with his mother, Irma, or Ljena, he achieved at last with Gertrúd; for more than forty years, the two of them formed a *"Gemeinschaft* in life and thought, in work and struggle."[6] And because the alienation between man and woman had finally been overcome, that between work and life, ought and is, was soon to be transcended as well. Lukács was about to make the final turn of his early years: from utopia to dialectics. Though it appeared to be sudden and dramatic, this turn had been intellectually prepared for by his years-long study of those mystics in whose writings the origins of the dialectic may be found—Plotinus, Eckhart, Nicholas of Cusa, and Jacob Böhme.[7] Marxists, it was now clear, could learn far more from Hegel than from Fichte.

To be sure, Fichte possessed a more revolutionary disposition than Hegel did, but that disposition was purely utopian. For him, the present constituted the third of five world-historical ages—the age of absolute sinfulness; as such, it was negative through and through. The final two ages, described by Fichte in *Characteristics of the Present Age*, constituted the utopian future and were to witness the realization of that formal "ought" that had for so long stood over against reality, the "is." But *how* was history to pass from one age to the next? How was utopia to be achieved? Here, Lukács now believed, Fichte's philosophy of history revealed its Achilles heel.

If, Lukács reasoned, Hegel's "reconciliation with reality" was reactionary in politics and contemplative in philosophy, it yet made possible an understanding of the connection between logical categories and the structural forms of bourgeois society. By rejecting the utopian ought and focusing philosophy on the understanding of the present—grasped dialectically—Hegel had pointed to the only way of knowing that which was alone knowable about the future—the tendencies *in the present* that impel history forward. Hegel's "splendid realism" was expressed in "his rejection of every utopia, his attempt to comprehend philosophy as the intellectual expression of history itself and not as a philosophy about history."[8] Inspired by Hegel, Lukács had achieved his own philosophic and revolutionary reconciliation with reality that, as so often with the Romantics, was "signalized by a loving union with the feminine other."[9] For "it was Gertrúd Bortstieber's unique personality, a combination of traits of a *grande dame* of the Enlightenment and a plebeian heroine in a Gottfried Keller novella, that taught him to appreciate the 'ordinary life' he had formerly despised."[10]

The Károlyi Government

When Lukács joined the Hungarian Communist party, he was greeted by suspicion and no little open hostility, and had it not been for the support of Kun and Seidler, he might well have been turned away. Perhaps no one put the case against Lukács and his friends as strongly as József Lengyel, a no-nonsense materialist who never reconciled himself to the presence of the "ethical ones." Though antimilitarists, they had not, Lengyel charged, struggled actively against the war, and as for *The Brothers Karamazov*, *Judith*, and *Either/Or*, Lengyel could not begin to understand why revolutionaries should waste their time reading them; if he had had his way, those who passed their time discussing such works would have been shot without further ado.[11]

It was against a background of antagonism that Lukács wrote "Tactics and Ethics" sometime in late December 1918 or early January 1919. There, as we have seen, he announced the reasons for his personal decision to cast his lot with the Communists. But he did something more: he outlined for the first time his Hegelian Marxism. Revolutionary tactics, Lukács maintained, did not recognize legal perimeters because revolutionaries denied the moral raison d'être of every existing political order.

Nor were tactics determined by short-term goals, but by the ultimate objective. This objective was utopia, but *not* understood as a world wholly other than the world of experience. Utopia, Lukács now argued, was *reality* in the process of being achieved. To be sure, the old world was not simply to be reformed; it had to be transcended. But the forces of total change were already at work within the sinful world and insofar as these forces contributed to the complete realization of utopia, they *were* utopian. The Homeric world, Lukács had written in *The Theory of the Novel*, constituted a concrete totality, it did not recognize any distinction between is and ought or between immanent and transcendent. Once he had believed that in his time such a world existed only in visionary works of art; now he claimed that the Homeric world was in the process of being re-created—it had only to be made *conscious* of itself.

Marx's theory of the class struggle, informed by Hegel's philosophy, provided an account of the collapse of transcendence into immanence; "the class struggle of the proletariat is at once the objective itself and its realization" (*UM*, 1:189). Class struggle was not a means to some transcendent end. It *was* utopia in its step-by-step achievement of self-consciousness. Because the final step to utopia in its fullness could never be known beforehand, every correct tactic was important—its success might signal the achievement of the ultimate objective.

This being the case, revolutionary tactics could be selected only on the basis of the Hegelian-Marxist philosophy of history. Any tactic that advanced the self-realization of utopia was justified *historically* and hence morally, because the goal of history was utopia, a faith that Lukács never questioned. Yet he believed that he had solved the ethical problem of ends/means by abolishing it; ethics were identical with history, rightly read. To serve history, the temporal unfolding of utopia, was ethical by definition. Correct tactics was simply another way of saying ethical acts. To be sure, Lukács recognized that *as an individual* he was still liable for his crimes, and his only defense here was to appeal to Savinkov, Judith, and the concept of "sacrifice." As an individual, he had to sacrifice his moral purity, but as a co-opted member of the proletariat (alienated man writ large), the class that represented the great community of mankind, his acts were justified if history validated their objective correctness. Despite, however, the undeniable sophistication of this argument, Lukács failed to recognize that it must lead either to moral paralysis or to an immorality that is unbounded precisely because it is rooted in a fanatical moral passion.

Armed with his new revolutionary theory, Lukács was eager to engage Hungarian communism's opponents: the liberal democrats and the Social Democrats who, together with the members of Károlyi's own party, formed the beleaguered aristocrat's government. In "The Question of Intellectual Leadership and the 'Intellectual Workers,'"[12] he attacked the liberal democrats, especially Jászi and his old friend Karl Polanyi. One of the most common charges leveled against socialism, he began, was that it took insufficient account of intellectual/spiritual factors in history, concentrating instead on material being. This was a criticism that Jászi had often directed at socialism, most recently in his *Szabadgondolat* article "Proletarian Dictatorship." Following Jászi, Polanyi had made the same charge in a public lecture he gave in December 1918: "Marxism views the world *from without*. For it, social development is a pure automatism, propelled by the machinery of the class struggle. Radicalism, on the other hand, views the world *from within* and recognizes in human progress its own work. Intellectual/spiritual labor must become conscious of itself in order to take over the direction of society in accordance with the prerogatives of the intellect and the spirit, which at all times have been society's hidden guides."[13]

Lukács conceded that for Marxists the motive forces of society were independent of consciousness—of *individual* consciousness. They were not, however, independent of *class* consciousness, and at the present stage of history, only the class consciousness of the proletariat could determine the future. To be sure, that class consciousness would have to become *conscious* of the world-historical mission of the proletariat (as opposed to its awareness of its more immediate interests and struggles) in order to transform the laws of social development from blind, fatal powers into self-aware, free powers and to put an end to the age-old distinction between freedom and necessity. But class consciousness alone could be spoken of as the "intellectual leader of society." Far from denying the "intellectual/spiritual" factor, therefore, Lukács argued that true Marxists insisted upon its decisive significance.

Having entered his brief against the liberal democrats, Lukács turned in "What Is Orthodox Marxism?"[14] to the Social Democrats. Because the question of orthodoxy stood at the center of intrasocialist debates, he hoped to settle the issue by identifying Marxist orthodoxy with Marx's method: "the revolutionary dialectic." He reminded readers that Marx's method derived from Hegel, a fact that revisionists such as Bernstein and "vulgar Marxists" such as Kautsky had either forgotten or purposely suppressed. Eager to appear scientific, they looked upon Marx's Hegelian roots as an unfortunate metaphysical hangover and claimed to be students of "facts" and of "reality." Such ideas, according to Lukács, effectively removed from Marxism the revolutionary dynamic by paralyzing the will to act. By focusing on discrete facts, one simply could not perceive the total process of which they were merely moments or parts, and Marxism was thereby reduced to reformist trade unionism. Rather than the promise of a new world, it became part and parcel of the old; having won a stake in the old order, the proletariat lost the ability to perceive each "moment" as a revolutionary deed within the dialectical totality of history. "The absolute dominion of the totality, the unity, the whole over abstract isolation of the parts: this is the essence of Marx's social view, the dialectical method. Its adoption . . . constitutes orthodox Marxism" (*UM*, 1:214).

Lukács's hatred of the Social Democratic party was not only ideological. He recognized that it was the predominant partner in Károlyi's coalition, the only party that possessed any organized public support, and as such, it was the key to Károlyi's survival. Its willingness to support an essentially bourgeois regime derived from the fact that, like the German and Austrian parties that it resembled in many ways, it was deceived by its own revolutionary rhetoric. Such rhetoric came easy as long as there was no real possibility that words would have to be transformed into action, but when revolution became a real possibility and when the Bolsheviks and the Hungarian Communists called upon them to act, things were quite different. The fact of the matter was that, as party ideologist Zsigmond Kunfi (a member of Károlyi's government) put it, "as a socialist I appreciate the aims of bolshevism, but I disapprove of its terroristic, antidemocratic methods."[15] At the same time, the Social Democrats could, and did, argue that the Allies would never tolerate a Bolshevik regime, an argument that carried weight as long as there remained hope of a "Wilsonian" peace, one that would treat Hungary justly.

On 11 January 1919, Károlyi assumed the office of president of the republic, and Dénes Berinkey, an expert on international law whom Károlyi hoped would unite the heterogeneous elements of the coalition, formed a government dominated by the Social Democrats. This shift to the left did not, of course, satisfy the Communists, and their inflammatory speeches and demonstrations only increased in number; though exceedingly dangerous to him, Károlyi refused to silence his opponents lest he appear to be denying the freedom of speech for which he had long campaigned.

On 20 February, the Association of the Unemployed organized a Communist-sponsored demonstration in front of the editorial offices of *Népszava*, the Socialist paper. Fearing violence, the Socialists had asked for police protection, and as is usual in such cases, someone fired a shot. By the time the shooting had ended, four policemen lay dead, and the following day, the police began to round up Communists, including Béla Kun. After these arrests, overzealous police officers beat Kun, on one occasion in the presence of a newspaper reporter, who reported the attack the following day (22 February). A wave of sympathy for the Bolsheviks swept over the capital.

With Kun and the members of the Party Central Committee in jail, a new Central Committee was organized (or activated); chaired by Tibor Szamuely,[16] it numbered Lukács among its members. From this new position of authority, he attacked the Socialists for their part in the police crackdown.[17] There could no longer be any doubt, he wrote, that the Socialists feared the proletarian revolution as much as any bourgeois leader. Having denounced Bolshevik violence in the name of law and order, they did not scruple to lend moral support to police brutality.

Meanwhile, things were going from bad to worse for Károlyi and his government. Embarrassed by the mistreatment of Kun, he received from Lenin a telegram advising him of the arrest of the Hungarian Red Cross Mission in Moscow and reminding him that many Hungarian officers remained in Russian prisoner-of-war camps. Lenin warned him, therefore, to protect the Hungarian Communists. Károlyi quickly called a meeting of the cabinet, subsequent to which he ordered the release of twenty-nine Communists, dropped charges of incitement to murder against the others, and required that prisoners be treated in a civilized manner.[18]

As a result of this affair, increased fear of counterrevolution, and impatience with Allied unfriendliness, left-wing Socialists began to explore the possibility of a reconciliation with the Communists. In fact, men such as Jenő Varga, Jenő Landler, and József Pogány had become convinced that bolshevism represented authentic socialism. Negotiations with Kun began while he was still incarcerated and they continued into March. On the 20th, Lieutenant Colonel Vyx, the head of the French military mission to Budapest, presented the famous "ultimatum" to Károlyi that administered the coup de grace to the democratic republic and led directly to the formation of the Soviet Republic.

The ultimatum was one of the results of the insensitivity and miscalculation that characterized much of postwar diplomacy. On 13 November 1918, Károlyi had agreed to a French-sponsored military convention (the Belgrade Convention), according to which the former Kingdom of Hungary was to remain under Hungarian jurisdiction until the Peace Conference provided otherwise. As fighting between Hungarian and Rumanian forces in Transylvania continued, however, the Allied Supreme Council recommended to the Peace Conference that an armistice line more favorable to the Rumanians be established. On 26 February, the Peace Conference responded by drafting a note that moved the armistice line forty-five miles closer to Budapest.[19] Debrecen and Szeged, unambiguously Hungarian cities, were to be included in the neutral zone. Further, when Vyx handed the note to Károlyi, he informed him that Hungarian troop withdrawal would have to begin by 23 March and be completed within ten days. Most disheartening for the Hungarians was the Frenchman's suggestion that the new line was to be regarded as a definite political frontier.[20]

Cognizant of the fact that no government that agreed to such demands could possibly survive, Károlyi rejected the ultimatum and charged the Social Democrats, in conjunction with the Communists, with the formation of a new government. Pursuant to that end, Sándor Juhász-Nagy, the minister of justice, ordered the release of Kun and the remaining Communist prisoners. Meanwhile, however, the Socialists, recognizing the increasing popularity of the Communists and hoping for assistance from Soviet Russia, had concluded an agreement with their former enemies to amalgamate their two parties and to form a Soviet rather than a Social Democratic government. On 21 March, the Socialist members of the existing government proclaimed the Dictatorship of the Proletariat and asked Károlyi to resign power to the "Hungarian workers." Although he refused, *Népszava* published a letter of resignation over his forged signature.[21] As one Socialist leader put it: "The imperialists of the Entente took democracy and national self-determination as their slogans, but since victory they have acted differently. Our hope for peace was destroyed by the ukase from Colonel Vyx. There is no longer any doubt that those gentlemen in Paris wish to give us an imperialist peace. . . . From now on we must look to the east for justice, as it has been denied to us in the west."[22]

The New Culture

Károlyi's western (Wilsonian) policy had failed to protect Hungary's territorial integrity. Desperate and believing themselves to have been betrayed, Hungarians, even many who were anti-communists, now fastened their hopes on Béla Kun's eastern (Leninist) policy. Like Károlyi, Kun was obliged to form a coalition government, and again the dominant partner was the Social Democratic party. This time, however, the party's left replaced its right/center and its partner was the Communist rather than the Radical party. In an effort to present a united front, the Communists and the Social Democrats merged as the Hungarian Party of Socialist-Communist Workers. According to the "documents of unity" signed in the Budapest City Prison on 21 March, the two parties would "jointly participate in the leadership of the new party and the government." Moreover, "in order to ensure the complete authority of the proletariat and to [make a stand against] Entente imperialism, the fullest and closest military and spiritual alliance must be concluded with the Russian Soviet government."[23]

Although the merger was a desperate and tactical marriage of convenience, Lukács believed it constituted evidence of the dialectical advance of history. To a little pamphlet entitled *The Documents of Unity* (published in April 1919), he contributed an exercise in sophistry that purported to reveal "The Theoretical Significance of the Restoration of Proletarian Unity." As "Party and Class," the essay was republished in his essay collection *Tactics and Ethics* (May 1919).[24] Here he returned to a favorite theme—the dangers of institutions, in this case political parties. Because it was a natural association independent of institutions, class was diametrically opposed to the political party. What was new here was Lukács's claim that one was not confronted historically with a simple either/or situation: *either* party *or* class. That was the "error" of his earlier thinking; he had been unable to understand *how* the world of the parties could be destroyed and the world of one universal class created. He was left, therefore, with utopian dreams.

Having discovered dialectical thinking, he could set aside the absolute antitheses that he believed bourgeois thinkers could never surmount. The truth was, he argued, that party and class stood in a *dialectical* rather than an absolute relation of antagonism to each other. Both were equally necessary historically, because at a certain stage in historical development the proletariat was obliged to create its own party as a temporary means of defending its interests. In time, however, party organization stood in the way of the proletariat's ultimate conquest of power. This crisis could be resolved only when both class and party ended their independent, isolated existence and were reconciled in a higher unity, namely *"the unified proletariat, as the ruling class in society."*

Just as the creation of a proletarian party had been necessary historically, so was its supercession, because to remain a "party" would have been to accept "the forms of capitalist society." Hence, the merger of the Social Democratic and the Communist parties was not simply the result of discussions and deliberations between certain leaders; it was necessitated by the will of the proletariat become conscious. To be sure, the merger meant the creation of a new "party," but the word had been completely redefined. The Hungarian Party of Socialist-Communist Workers was only the channel through which the unified will of the unified proletariat expressed itself. "Parties," in the bourgeois sense, had ceased to exist. No longer constrained by "party" institutions, the proletariat—the universal class and hence no "class" at all in the bourgeois sense—could proceed to carry out its historic mission unencumbered by historically anachronistic encrustations.

This sort of dialectical legerdemain was lost on most Socialists and Communists, who continued to harbor mutual suspicions. The composition of the new Revolutionary Governing Council was the first major problem. Kun was the only Communist among twelve people's commissars, but as commissar of foreign affairs, he was the real leader of the Soviet Republic, nothing being more important than the effort to enlist Soviet Russia in the struggle for Hungarian national interests. Seven of the twenty-one deputy people's commissars were Communists, and Lukács was to serve under Zsigmond Kunfi as deputy people's commissar of public education. In less than one month, however, the distinction between full and deputy commissar was abolished and in many commissariats the Communists were in effective control. From the first, for example, Lukács was the republic's cultural dictator.

Even more than Weimar culture, Hungarian culture during the Soviet Republic "was the creation of outsiders, propelled by history into the inside, for a short, dizzying, fragile moment."[25] Years later, Lukács still recalled with pride how thoroughly the Commissariat of Public Education cleaned house, replacing old regime officials with countercultural leaders.[26] In a directive dated 26 March 1919, he prohibited numerous professors from teaching at the University of Budapest.[27] Among the proscribed in the liberal arts faculty were Zsolt Beöthy and Gedeon Petz, who, it will be recalled, had orchestrated the rejection of Lukács's application for habilitation.

Higher education was only the beginning. In a tersely worded directive dated 30 March 1919, Lukács ordered that meetings of the Kisfaludy Literary Society be suspended; it was this society that had honored his history of the modern drama and made possible its publication. On 14 April, he informed Albert Berzeviczy, the president of the Hungarian Academy of Sciences, that the academy was to be reorganized; until then, it was forbidden to take any action or hold any meeting. Lukács also recommended the suspension of all "bourgeois" papers and journals and transformed the Radical daily *Világ* (*World*) into *Fáklya* (*Torch*), the official daily of the Commissariat of Public Education. He proposed that religious education be discontinued, emphasizing, however, the necessity of protecting the churches.[28]

At the same time that he was clearing the decks, Lukács made a series of important assignments and appointments. Early in April, he announced several new lecture series at the university: Sándor Varjas

— "Formal Logic"; József Révai— "Cicero"; Béla Fogarasi— "The Philosophic Foundations of the Humanistic Sciences"; Karl Mannheim — "Philosophy of Culture"; Mihály Babits— "Ady-Seminar"; Marcell Benedek— "The French Naturalistic Novel"; Lajos Fülep— "Dante: Vita Nuova"; Béla Fogarasi— "Historical Materialism"; Sándor Varjas — "History of the Second Half of the Nineteenth Century"; and Frederick Antal— "Modern Painting: Folk Art."[29]

On 2 May, Lukács announced several university appointments: Mihály Babits—Modern Hungarian Literature and World Literature; Sándor Varjas—Logic and Epistemology; Lajos Fülep—Italian Language and Literature; and Gyula Szekfű—Historical Auxiliary Sciences.[30] On 11 May, he named to the faculty of Budapest's Secondary-School Teacher-Training College Karl Mannheim (Philosophy), Arnold Hauser (Theory of Literature), Marcell Benedek (French Language and Literature), and György Pólya (Mathematics).[31] To the Writers Directory he appointed himself (president), Balázs, Fülep, Béla Révész, Lajos Kassák, and Aladár Komját.[32] To the Committee for the Communization of the Theaters he named Béla Reinitz, Balázs, Kassák, and Andor Gábor; to the Musical Arts Directory he appointed Bartók, Kodály, and Ernő Dohnányi.[33]

These impressive appointments included many noncommunists who considered their work to be a national contribution, and who were attracted by Lukács's program. Even Jászi, who emigrated to Vienna on 1 May, could write that "under the direction of George Lukács, the policy of the dictators in regard to education and art was certainly distinguished by many great ideals."[34] To be more precise, Lukács's policy was guided by his determination to end alienation; the "new culture" was to be the "connecting link between human beings."[35]

In the effort to translate this goal into reality, Lukács focused his attention on those cultural realms with which he had always been fascinated. His initial step was to nationalize all of Budapest's theaters, and in an interview granted to *Színházi Élet* (*Theater Life*),[36] he discussed his decision and his plans for the future. "When we communized the theaters, we did so chiefly to open the places of culture to the proletariat, the workers: our theaters will *no* longer be the monopoly of the wealthy." The trade unions would soon dispose of all tickets at minimal prices. Balázs enlarged on the theater program in interviews he gave to *Színház* (*Theater*) and *Vörös Lobogó* (*Red Banner*).[37] The repertoire of plays would be revised to include only the greatest works of world literature, and new theaters would be built, including one devoted to experimental works. Talented actors would be given opportunities immediately, and leading companies would perform in provincial cities. All of this was reminiscent of Thália, which, according to one enthusiast, was "Hungary's first experiment in proletarian culture."[38]

In an essay entitled "The People's Theater," Balázs reflected upon the relationship between the theater and the union of human souls.[39] By giving the theaters to the people, he observed, the republic was only returning to them that which was rightfully theirs, for drama was not the creation of lonely, individual artists but a manifestation of the people's collective soul. At the source of Greek tragedy, one discovered not an individual writer but the chorus, "which is identical with the public, the people." In the past, too many modern productions had attempted to isolate each member of the audience, to create the illusion that one was alone. The communist theater regarded it as its responsibility not only to provide inexpensive tickets, but to make of the drama once again a celebration of the meeting of souls.

If the drama was the most important educational art in the struggle to forge a world free of alienation, the fairy tale was a close second. "As a result of the provisions of the Commissariat of Public Education," *Vörös Újság* reported on 17 April, "120,000 proletarian children today heard fairy tales in every school and children's hospital in Budapest."[40] According to Lukács's and Balázs's plan, "fairy tale afternoons" were to continue throughout the summer, in parks and theaters. In the 11 May number of *Fáklya*, Balázs published a defense of this policy entitled "Don't Take Fairy Tales Away from the Children!" The new economic order that the republic had created was only a means, he argued, the ultimate goal was "the new man, whose name today is still child." Many Communists, however, failed to understand how fairy tales contributed to the achievement of this goal; they insisted, he wrote, that children be taught "reality," rather than fantasy. They demanded that the Grimms and Hans Christian Andersen be taken from the children.

Such a policy would be shortsighted, because children could only understand the world within the framework of fairy tales. Moreover, the great fairy tales—Snow White, Cinderella, Aladdin's Lamp—enriched children's souls. A child who knew no fairy tales was like an adult who was ignorant of Shakespeare. For too long, proletarian children had been denied sufficient access to the treasures of fantasy, and to continue to deny them would be an act of cruelty. As for the charge that fairy tales reflected capitalist ideology, nothing, according to Balázs, was further from the truth. In them children encountered a world "in which everything is possible for everyone in accord with inner worth, where the characters change not only their class, but also their form and their life. Such a world is more communist than our communism. We abolished only the differences between human classes; with the possibility provided by enchantment, the fairy tale erased the border between animal/vegetable and human being, between every existing and nonexisting being. The communist Weltanschauung of fairy tales is far more profound, even in its most naive forms, than that of consciously socialist poetry."[41]

Together with Balázs, Lukács was involved most directly with plans for the theater and for the reading of fairy tales to children, but he initiated many other projects, including a massive plan to translate great works of world literature into Hungarian. For this purpose, he created an Office of Translators. According to the 2 July number of Vörös Újság, "it is almost natural that the first project will be the translation of Dostoevski's complete works. Zoltán Trócsányi will direct the translation work, and Comrade György Lukács will probably write the introductions. Indeed, it is necessary that those who know only Hungarian should be able to read The Brothers Karamazov, A Raw Youth, and Dostoevski's other writings."[42] The office also projected the translation of the works of Tolstoi, Ibsen, Gogol, Goethe, and Shakespeare. A distinct Marx-Translation Committee was created to oversee the task of rendering the master intelligible to Hungarian readers.

Lukács was inclined to grant to the Music Directory a free hand, because by his own admission he lacked a musical ear. Although he regarded Dohnányi as a political opportunist and was cool toward Kodály, he had a great respect for Bartók. "For our generation," he recalled later, "it was not only the Waldbauer Quartet's first concerts that constituted a great experience, but also—above all—The Wooden Prince, in which, really for the first time in Hungary, serious art took up seriously the problem of alienation."[43] Despite many plans, however, the Music Directory was unable to effect much change because, according to Bartók, "the political atmosphere is too troubled. It is impossible to work well and soundly."[44]

Whatever difficulties Bartók may have encountered, they were as nothing compared with those Lukács and Balázs confronted as those responsible for literary policies. Although both insisted that they recognized no official literature, not everyone was convinced, and on 15 April, Pál Kéri attacked the Commissariat's literary policies in the social democratic weekly Az Ember (Man).[45] According to Kéri, Lukács and Balázs had cast their lot with Lajos Kassák, János Mácza, and the circle around the avant-garde journal Ma (Today). Kéri portrayed the Ma Circle as a hopelessly muddled group of incompetents and philistines, Balázs as a journalist at best, and Lukács as a wealthy eccentric.

The following day, Vörös Újság published a rejoinder defending

Lukács and charging Kéri with "cultural counterrevolution."[46] Ferenc Göndör, editor of *Az Ember* joined in the fray by coming to Kéri's defense and renewing the attack on Mácza, Kassák, and Balázs, but he was careful not to attack Lukács.[47] It was in fact the *Ma* Circle that he feared and wished to discredit. In an attack on both Kéri and Göndör, József Révai, who had begun his literary career as a *Ma* contributor, pointed out that "the *official* cultural program of the Commissariat of Public Education has not to this day been announced."[48] Finally, in a carefully worded essay he published in *Vörös Újság* on 18 April,[49] Lukács assayed to set the record straight. *Ma* was not and never would be the official organ of the Commissariat of Public Education. The writers and artists around the journal were regarded officially as no better and no worse than any other honest and well-meaning group. What was more, he did not intend to promote officially *any* literary trend, because a communist cultural program distinguished only between good and bad literature and was unwilling to dismiss Shakespeare and Goethe because they were not socialist writers.

It was to Lukács's credit that he did not join the attack on Kassák and the *Ma* Circle,[50] for the truth is that his lifelong rejection of the avant-garde, a rejection that led to his subsequent debates with Ernst Bloch and Bertolt Brecht, had its roots in his distaste for the Hungarian avant-garde. To be sure, Kassák and his friends welcomed the coming of the Soviet Republic, but "avant-garde communism is the fruit of an eschatological state of mind, simultaneously messianic and apocalyptic."[51] Lukács recognized in the avant-garde that form of utopianism that he had only recently overcome. By insisting on a complete and radical break with past culture, it was unable, as Lukács himself had been, to transcend a rigid dualism. No doubt he had the *Ma* writers and artists in mind when he suggested that "fashion" in culture was determined by market considerations, and because fashion required complete deviation from what had gone before, organic development gave place to "directionless confusion" and "self-important and pretentious dilettantism."[52]

Although Lukács never nominated any official literary school, he was already a "realist." True reality comprised those moments that advanced history's dialectic. Thus his enthusiasm for Dostoevski began to wane (though it never disappeared)[53] at the same time that his enthusiasm for Tolstoi began to wax. He turned to the latter not simply because Lenin admired him, but because he believed that he had discovered in the author of *War and Peace* a far greater ability to detect what in his view were the principal moments in the utopian dialectic of history. Whereas Dostoevski's utopia was beyond this world, Tolstoi's was within it. The task of literature was not, as Lukács once believed, to provide a vision of a new utopian reality, but rather to bring to consciousness (and to affirm) the utopian reality moving inexorably to full consciousness (complete fulfillment).

The Fall of the Soviet Republic

Lukács was aware that he could implement his cultural program only if the Soviet Republic survived, and he worked tirelessly to rally the Hungarian proletariat to meet what he regarded as its historic responsibilities. From his point of view, even economic production represented a historical/moral problem. In an effort to increase production, Jenő Varga, the republic's principal economic adviser, had guaranteed every worker a job. Moreover, he saw to it that the government abolished piecework, instituted a forty-eight-hour week, increased salaries, and provided insurance.[54] The results of these measures were disastrous, and at a meeting of the Workers' Council on 16 June, Varga conceded that under his authority labor production had fallen precipitously. He attributed this melancholy circumstance to three factors: the absence of any labor discipline; the ruinous effect of time wages; and the regrettable fact that "men have not yet attained the higher type of Socialist mentality which will be the starting point of the coming generation."[55]

In the 20 July number of *Szociális Termelés* (*Social Production*), Lukács turned his attention to economic problems in an article entitled "The Role of Morality in Communist Production."[56] Anticipating his subsequent critique of bureaucratic socialism, he warned the proletariat that failure to achieve self-discipline would force the government to create institutions to compel it to act in its own interest, a threat reminiscent of Rousseau's insistence that the recalcitrant be forced to be free. Lukács urged the proletariat to create its own labor discipline, thus exercising its moral will. If the government were obliged to subject the workers to institutionalized coercion, a legal order would be created that would have to be destroyed before the realm of necessity could give way to the realm of freedom. Thus the question of production was not simply economic, it was also moral in nature. The realization of the realm of freedom depended on the consciousness and moral quality of the proletariat, the only class that could end morality's subordination to law, institutions, and compulsion. The ultimate goal of communism was the building of a society in which actions were regulated not by the constraint of law but by the exercise of man's moral freedom. These rather arcane entreaties fell, however, on deaf ears, and in a provocative and futile effort to increase production, Varga reinstated forced labor discipline, piecework, and incentive wages.[57]

But as difficult as the republic's economic problems were, its military difficulties were even greater. Subsequent to Károlyi's rejection of the Vyx ultimatum and Kun's assumption of power, all Entente missions withdrew from Budapest, and on 27 March, Marshal Foch presented a plan of military intervention to Wilson, Lloyd George, and Clemenceau. Because, however, of the advanced state of Allied demobilization and concern with regard to world opinion, the Big Three were reluctant to act decisively—a reluctance that was to continue throughout the 133 days of the Soviet Republic's life.[58] On 31 March, the Allies dispatched to Budapest a delegation headed by General Smuts, who assured Kun that the line of demarcation between Hungary and Rumania set by the Vyx note was not regarded in Paris as a permanent political frontier. He requested, therefore, that Hungarian troops withdraw behind it.

Because to issue such an order would have meant political suicide, Kun refused, and Smuts then proposed a new line, more favorable to Hungary. Debrecen would remain Hungarian; Arad, Nagyvárad, and Szatmár would be in the neutral, not the Rumanian, zone. Kun rejected that proposal because it would have entailed abandoning Transylvania, and he countered with a demand that the Rumanians withdraw to the line Károlyi had accepted in Belgrade the preceding November. Smuts would not accede. By the end of the first week in April, then, the Smuts mission had failed. On 16 April, Rumania launched an offensive against Hungary and, although there is no evidence to suggest that it was ordered by the Big Three, the Hungarians may be forgiven for having been suspicious.

Despite the cloud of danger hovering over the young republic, Lukács perceived a silver lining. As a consequence of the Rumanian attack, he announced to his skeptical comrades, the proletariat had forged a unity greater than it had ever known. Proletarian class consciousness, the sine qua non of world revolution, could only be attained at the cost of struggle, sacrifice, and resolution in the face of death, but until then the proletarian revolution in Hungary had never been challenged. Hence, according to Lukács, the proletariat should welcome this counterrevolutionary danger as that historical event that would *advance* the cause of world revolution by awakening the world proletariat's consciousness of its unity. Outfitted with his dialectical understanding of history, he perceived the attack not as an isolated event (and hence reactionary), but as a negative moment within a totality that could only be progressive. *His-*

torically, the attack would serve the purposes of the world-redeeming proletariat.[59]

In the event, the Rumanians advanced to the Tisza River and even crossed it at some points. They then readied themselves for a march on Budapest, but at this point the Allies intervened; in a meeting with Ionel Bratianu in Paris, Clemenceau ordered that the Rumanian advance be halted. But Rumania was not Hungary's only enemy; on 26 April, Czechoslovak troops had crossed the military demarcation line in the north. Knowing that the republic's fate hung in the balance, the Hungarian leaders ordered a counter-offensive in the second half of May, and they appointed Lukács political commissar of the Fifth Division. In his novel, *Ferenc Prenn's Storm-Tossed Life*, József Lengyel painted an unflattering picture of Lukács ("Nándor Benzy") at the front. He appeared, Lengyel recalled, in knee pants and walking shoes, looking for all the world like a German taking his Sunday stroll. He was unarmed and seemed to be unaware of the shooting. When advised by a platoon leader that the Czechs were preparing for an assault, he replied that his presence would guarantee victory. The startled commander told him that any Hungarian victory would be Pyrrhic. "Tactically," Benzy replied, "I will not argue the point. Ethically, every day and at every moment it is necessary. . . ."[60] But before he could complete his sentence, the commander turned on his heel and walked away.

That evening, Benzy invited several people to a "friendly conversation," in the course of which he spoke of accepting responsibility for the shedding of blood, of shedding one's own blood, and of the identity of theory and practice. More concretely, he spoke of the war against the Czechs and proletarian internationalism, insisting that the Red Army was not fighting for Hungary, but against the very idea of the "nation." Strangely enough, in this commitment to universality, it was akin to the Catholic church. One of the soldiers (speaking for Lengyel) was unimpressed: "Whatever international and unification goals stand before us, now we are fighting as Hungarians against the Czechs, because the Czechs invaded Hungary."[61]

Lukács's own recollections of his service with the Fifth Division were somewhat different.[62] A political commissar, he maintained, had to attend to two matters above all: mail delivery and food at the front. Often he would park his car two or three kilometers from the front and proceed on foot in order to catch the cooks unawares. Such unannounced inspections were crucial because only an army that was well fed was battle-ready. On one occasion, according to Lukács, he joined a battalion near the city of Eger, where the Czechs were preparing an assault.

When he arrived, he found the soldiers in the worst possible mood, not having received any provisions for twenty-four hours. He tried to rally them with talk of the international revolution and Hungary's mission—without success. When, however, he was able to secure food for them, they listened to him with real interest and subsequently acquitted themselves well in battle. This story was designed to illustrate Lukács's claim that a political commissar's duties transcended the making of propaganda.

Impressed by the Hungarian Red Army, Lukács conceded that many peasant-soldiers disliked the Kun government because it had not, as Lenin's government had, divided the land. In what was a major tactical blunder, Kun had refused to partition the *latifundia*, turning them instead into state concerns, in most cases with the former owner as manager. The peasant-soldiers had remained loyal to the Soviet Republic only because of national feeling. "This army," Lukács admitted, "was essentially a Hungarian army. It defended [Hungary] against foreign attacks."[63] Class consciousness had not replaced national consciousness.

It was in large measure because of the peasant-soldiers' national feeling that the Red Army was able not only to halt the Czechoslovak advance but also to occupy more than one-third of Slovakia. Desperate, Eduard Beneš appealed to Paris for assistance, and, on 8 and 13 June, Clemenceau forwarded ultimata to Kun. In the latter note, the French leader demanded that the Red Army withdraw from Slovakia. "If the Allies and Associated Governments are not informed by their representatives on the spot within four days from midday on June 14, 1919, that this operation is being effectively carried out, they will hold themselves free to advance on Budapest and to take such other steps as may seem desirable to secure a just and speedy peace."[64]

Faced with such a threat and with problems of "internal disorganization," Kun acquiesced; he and his associates were pleased to think of their capitulation as akin to Russia's acceptance of Brest-Litovsk.[65] Before the end of June, the Hungarian troops had abandoned Slovakia. That was Kun's greatest mistake. As long as his government satisfied the national feeling of the Hungarians, he could rely on widespread support, but the moment it became clear that he was unable or unwilling to defend Hungary's vital interests, his dictatorship lost all raison d'être. Shortly before Kun's acceptance of the ultimatum, Lukács returned to Budapest.

In Clemenceau's note of 13 June, he had promised Kun that "the Rumanian troops will be withdrawn from Hungarian territory as soon as the Hungarian troops have evacuated Czechoslovakia."[66] The Rumanians, however, refused to honor this pledge; their troops remained at the Tisza River. Although the Allies upbraided the Rumanian government, they took no steps to enforce compliance, and on 10 July, Hungary's Revolutionary Governing Council considered a military recommendation that an offensive be launched against the Rumanian army. Despite the risks that such an attack entailed, the council voted to accept the recommendation, and hostilities were initiated on 21 July.[67] Kun had few alternatives. Having withdrawn from Czechoslovakia, he had alienated Hungarian national sensibilities, and without nationalist support, he knew that his days were numbered. The Rumanian campaign was thus a desperate gamble not merely to win territory but, more important, to win support at home. In the event, the gamble was lost, for the attack failed to dislodge the Rumanians. Worse, the enemy soon took the offensive.

When news of the Red Army's failure and disorganization reached Budapest, Lukács was sent to rejoin the Fifth Division, then fighting in the area between the Danube and Tisza rivers.[68] His assignment was to restore the division's battle-readiness, a mission that he later conceded had "ended in complete failure." On his arrival, he discovered that "there was complete panic" among the soldiers; no one any longer believed that victory was possible. Everyone was convinced that the Rumanians would take Budapest and that the Soviet Republic was doomed. So critical was the situation that when Lukács returned to Budapest for two days, he and some members of the Sunday Circle discussed whether or not they would be justified in murdering a friend whom they knew to be plotting some action injurious to the republic.[69]

On 1 August 1919, the Hungarian Soviet Republic collapsed. Having resigned in favor of a caretaker trade-union government, Kun and many of the republic's leaders left for Austria aboard a train that was protected by the Italian military mission. Some former leaders, however, remained in Budapest in order to organize an underground movement aimed at reestablishing Communist rule; Lukács was among them. "The assignment was," he testified later, "that I should carry out the ideological part of the work, Korvin the organizational part."[70] The union of purpose that he forged with Korvin was to leave an indelible mark on his life.

Ottó Korvin (Klein) was born on 24 March 1894 in Nagybocskón,[71] and because he had curvature of the spine, he was unable to take part in normal child's play. Always an outsider, he came of age without establishing any of those friendships that make for a happy childhood. In 1906, his family moved to Budapest where, having failed a gymnasium examination, he enrolled at a school of commerce, though, like so many of his generation, he was under Ady's influence and aspired to be a poet. At one editor's suggestion, he took the magyarized nom de plume "Korvin" and began to publish his verses. At about the same time (just prior to the war), he became a socialist, though he did not join the Social Democratic party.

Early in 1918, Korvin joined the "Revolutionary Socialists," radical members of the Galileo Circle, and when most of his friends were arrested for distributing antiwar propaganda, he became the group's leader. In May, there were more arrests, but he again escaped capture. Through his friend Ernő Seidler, he met Béla Kun and became a member of the Hungarian Communist party's first Central Committee. When Kun came to power, Korvin became chief of the Political Investigation Department of the People's Commissariat of Internal Affairs (the secret police). Although he may have accepted the charge reluctantly, he worked tirelessly to prevent a "counterrevolution." His agents frequented coffee houses, playing fields, and churches—everywhere large groups of people congregated. Young terrorists who styled themselves "Lenin Boys" also worked closely with the department. Those whom Korvin imprisoned included military officers, former members of parliament, lawyers, counts, and barons.[72] One judicious student of the Soviet Republic has written that "it is difficult to determine whether Korvin was a homicidal maniac, as the contemporary anticommunist literature suggests, or an idealistic zealot of moral integrity with a messianic belief in the purity of the revolution."[73] In practice, as we have seen, it often comes to the same thing. In any event, some of the more responsible Socialist members of the government registered officially their disapproval of Korvin and his methods.

On 1 August, the day the republic collapsed, Korvin resigned and Lukács returned from the front. "I reported in uniform to the comrades, who were preparing to travel," Lukács recalled. "With regard to myself, I said that my suggestion would be that I make my way to Germany and continue to work in the German party. No, Béla Kun replied, you remain with Korvin in Budapest and organize together the illegal movement. I took note of the order and went to Korvin's room to discuss the work to be done."[74] As it turned out, the assignment was short-lived, because on 7 August, Korvin was arrested and Lukács prepared to cross the Austrian frontier.

During the brief time that he remained in the capital, Lukács stayed with Olga Máté, Béla Zalai's widow. He slept in her photography studio and hid in the attic during the day. On one occasion, an anonymous informant directed the police to Mrs. Zalai's apartment, but with Lukács in the attic, she convinced the police that the clothes and toilet articles in the wardrobe were all that remained of her late husband's possessions. In October, Lukács's friends, Karl Mannheim and the sculptor Márk Vedres among them, arranged for him to pose as the chauffeur for a German officer who was on his way to Vienna. Because, however, Lukács did not know how to drive, his friends bound up his arm so that he could claim to have had an accident en route; this would account for the fact that the officer himself was driving.[75]

Lukács had not been in Vienna for long, when, on 29 December, Korvin was hanged in Budapest. Jászi, no friend of the Communist leaders, reported on "credible authority" that Korvin, who had been brutally tortured, told his brother József Kelen, himself a prisoner, that "if you come back to power, forget what was done to me."[76] The execution precipitated among the Hungarian revolutionaries in exile a discussion concerning suicide. According to Victor Serge, Lukács considered taking his own life "in the hours when I was expecting to be arrested and hanged with him. I came to the conclusion that I had no right to it: a member of the Central Committee must set the example."[77]

In the 19 August 1920 number of *Proletár* (*Proletarian*; published in Vienna),[78] Lukács characterized Korvin as a "heroically self-sacrificing comrade" who had protected the Soviet Republic against the nefarious plottings of counterrevolutionaries. He denied that his friend had ever committed atrocities, labeling all such charges libelous legends. The "poet's" ill-repute was every bit as undeserved, according to Lukács, as was that of Thomas Müntzer, Jean-Paul Marat, and M. S. Uritskii. He should have mentioned the man with whom he clearly identified Korvin—Ivan Kaliayev.

C·H·A·P·T·E·R

Vienna

The Lure of Politics

When Lukács arrived in Vienna in October 1919, the city was no longer a proud and prosperous imperial capital. Thousands of Viennese were out of work, and even those who were able to put food on their tables looked forward to a particularly uncertain future. Under such circumstances, Karl Renner's government was not enthusiastic about the presence of the Hungarian Soviet Republic's fallen leaders, and although the Social Democrats were permitted to settle in Austria, most of the Communists were arrested.[1] Because of his scholarly reputation, Lukács was only briefly detained, but he was kept under surveillance. On 6 September, the Hungarian government had demanded the extradition of nine of the republic's leaders, including Béla Kun. Lukács's name did not appear on this list, but only because the government had learned that he was still in Hungary.[2] Once in Vienna, his life depended upon Austrian willingness to grant him political asylum.

In an effort to prevent Lukács's extradition, Franz Baumgarten and Bruno Steinbach drafted a formal appeal to which they appended the signatures of leading German intellectuals. On 12 November 1919, the *Berliner Tageblatt* published the document:

> Not Georg v. Lukács the politician, but the man and thinker ought to be vindicated. Once he gave up the allurements of the pampered life that were his by birth for the office of responsible, solitary thought. When he applied himself to politics, he sacrificed what

was most dear to him—his freedom as a thinker—for the re-
former's work he intended to accomplish. The Hungarian government demands his extradition from Austria. . . . He is said to have
instigated the murder of political opponents, but only blind hate
can believe the accusation. Lukács's salvation is no party matter.
All who have come to know personally his human purity and who
admire the high spirituality of his philosophic-aesthetic books
are duty-bound to protest the extradition.

The statement was signed by Franz Ferdinand Baumgarten, Richard
Beer-Hofmann, Richard Dehmel, Paul Ernst, Bruno Frank, Maximilian
Harden, Alfred Kerr, Heinrich Mann, Thomas Mann, Emil Praetorius,
and Karl Scheffler. Max Weber, Alfred Weber, and Ernst Troeltsch
refused to add their signatures.[3]

Aware that the extradition of Lukács and the other Hungarian Communists would be tantamount to a death sentence and concerned about
Austrian citizens still in Russia, the Austrian government refused to
comply with the Hungarian demand. Still, Lukács's initial Austrian
permit was valid for only six months,[4] and it is not surprising that he
presented "the most heart-rending spectacle; deathly pale, haggard,
nervous, and disconsolate. He . . . walks about with a revolver in his
pocket, because he has reason to fear that they will abduct him."[5]

Balázs was even more nervous, and he confessed to his diary that he
was avoiding Lukács because he did not want to compromise himself in
the eyes of the authorities. Nor did he want to have anything to do with
emigré politics: "The truth is that I do not wish to take part any longer
in politics, just as I did not take part in them before, because they are
not my concern. Communism is my religion, not my politics, and from
now on I want only to be an artist and nothing more!"[6]

For his part, Lukács chose to engage in political work—theoretical
and organizational. As a result, the alliance that he and Balázs had
forged around 1908 came to an end. In his diary, Balázs provided a
fitting epitaph:

It seems that one must choose whether one writes or lives one's
ethic, just as the philosopher of religion reckons with but does not
live God. If this is true, then it seems that György Lukács, out of
integrity and moral imperative, is going to live his life to the very
end in untruth, because Lukács the conspiratorial, active politician
and revolutionary is assuming a *mask*, [is living in] untruth; it is
not his metaphysically rooted mission. He was born a quiet
scholar, a lonely sage, a seer of things eternal; not, however, to
search for stolen party funds in spacious coffee houses, to keep an

eye on the daily stream of ephemeral politics, or to strive to influence the masses—he who *is not speaking* his own *language* if more than ten people understand. His is a terrible banishment; he is truly homeless because he has lost his home. Of course the question is: What is more important, purity or the truth? He lives an inauthentic life out of purity (he does not live his own life). He commits a metaphysical sin, but it is not given to us either to intervene in the decision of a man of such profound ethical worth or to judge him. Who knows what kind of reasons he has.[7]

Lukács's father also hoped that his son's political involvement would prove to be a passing aberration. In a letter of 20 January 1920, he appealed to Paul Ernst to do what he could "to rescue him from accursed politics" and to guide him back to his life's calling—pure scholarship. He must, the elder Lukács wrote, leave Vienna and return to Heidelberg.[8] There was little, however, that Ernst could do, for if Lukács would not listen to Balázs, he was wholly deaf to entreaties from Ernst or his father. He turned instead to the one person who seemed truly to understand him—Gertrúd Bortstieber. "Spring 1920—Gertrúd in Vienna. She and her children lived with her sister in Hütteldorf. I, for the time being, in Vienna. At first, together only on free days, but later, I too in Hütteldorf. Thus, her way of life (family, three children) became dominant for me as well."[9] Lukács and Gertrúd were married in 1920.[10]

Utopia and Bureaucracy

Before turning to a consideration of Lukács's political writings, something must be said of the Hungarian emigration in Vienna, a subject that deserves a study of its own. Although the emigrés were united in their opposition to Admiral Miklós Horthy's government, they agreed on little else. One may identify four distinct groups within the emigration: the Radicals who wrote for the *Bécsi Magyar Újság* (*Hungarian News of Vienna*), edited by Oszkár Jászi; the Social Democrats, led by Zsigmond Kunfi and Pál Szende,[11] around the journal *Világosság* (*Clarity*); the *Ma* Circle led by Kassák; and the Communists.

Life in exile was not easy for the Hungarians, who had little money and few prospects. Viewed with suspicion by the Austrian authorities, they were as homesick as their legendary countryman—Háry János. "An emigré," József Lengyel later wrote, "is that person who, living in a foreign country, neither can nor wishes to think of anything but his homeland."[12] For Balázs, homesickness came as a surprise: "It is true

that I proclaimed the synthesis of the nations, the European man. . . . It
is true that I always felt my deepest metaphysical roots to be beyond
every race and nation and I knew myself to be a wanderer, solitary. . . .
It is true that according to my biological lineage, I am a Jew; thus, there
is no more Turanian blood in me than there was in Sándor Petőfi." He
had encountered in Vienna people who listened to him with more sympathy than most Hungarians ever had. "And yet, what hurts? Why *do I
feel* myself to be an exile?"[13]

These restless wanderers passed much of their time in coffee houses,
where they critically dissected the Horthy regime and rival emigré
groups. The Radicals, Social Democrats, and *Ma*-ists did agree, however, that it had been the Communists whose failures had made their
exile necessary. Because Kun and Lukács disliked the *Ma* writers,
Kassák held them "responsible for the fact that the revolution came to
the bourgeois dead end."[14] In a devastating attack on the Communists,
Szende wrote that "the soviet system had already collapsed internally
when Rumanian bayonets brought it to an end in July 1919." Communism, he declared, was "a mixture of the messianism and simplicity of
primitive Christianity and the intolerance and orthodoxy of Catholicism."[15] And Jászi alleged that it was "the economic and moral bank-
ruptcy of the Soviet Republic" that necessitated the fatal offensive
against Rumania.[16]

As if these attacks were not enough, the Hungarian Communists had
fallen out among themselves. "The Hungarian emigration was deeply
split," Victor Serge remembered. "To the opposition within his Party,
Béla Kun was a remarkably odious figure. He was the incarnation of
intellectual inadequacy, uncertainty of will, and authoritarian corruption."[17] On his arrival in Vienna, Kun had been taken into custody and
placed under house arrest at Karlstein near the Czech border, because
his safety could not be guaranteed in Vienna. Due to the fact that the
building in which he was detained could not be heated adequately, Kun
threatened a hunger strike if he were not moved elsewhere,[18] and thus,
on 7 February 1920, he was taken to Stockerau near Vienna, where he
and his comrades occupied the local hospital's empty psychiatric ward.
Eager to be rid of Kun, the Austrians agreed to a Soviet proposal that he
be sent to Russia, and, on 11 August, he arrived in Petrograd. Physically
removed from the Viennese emigration, he was no longer in a position
to exercise leadership, and Jenő Landler, a former Social Democrat
whom Lukács had come to know well during the final days of the Soviet
Republic, organized an anti-Kun faction. Landler was, according to
Lukács, a man of great practical intelligence, who protested against
Kun's bureaucratic and utopian projects and who "endeavored to derive

the political and organizational tasks of the Hungarian communist movement from the concrete problems of Hungary's concrete situation."[19]
From the first, Lukács allied himself with the Landler group.

Against a background of factional struggles, Lukács began to work
out in print his conception of Marxism and his proposals for political
action. Between 1920 and 1922, he published numerous essays in *Proletár* and in *Kommunismus*, a journal of "left-wing" communism. Taken
together, these essays constituted a defense of the Communist party
as that organization that was capable of steering a course between the
Scylla of utopia and the Charybdis of bureaucracy.

By 1920, utopia was anathema to Lukács. "Genuine revolutionaries,"
he wrote in *Kommunismus*, "above all Lenin, distinguish themselves
from petit-bourgeois utopianism by their want of illusion."[20] The greatest illusion of all, he believed, was that to which he himself had succumbed earlier: that the new world could be brought into being at one
stroke. "This transition from 'necessity' to 'freedom,' " he had become
convinced, "cannot under any circumstances be a once-for-all, sudden,
and unmediated act, but only a *process*, the revolutionary, crisis-prone
character of which Engels very appropriately designated with the word
'leap.' "[21] To be sure, Lukács had not removed utopia from the historical
agenda, but he had abandoned the notion of an apocalyptic transformation that would bring heaven to earth in a single moment. He considered
himself to be a "realist"—a historical rather than an abstract thinker.

Filled with self-confidence and contempt for his ideological opponents, Lukács was prepared to accept criticism from only one man—
Vladimir Ilyich Lenin, the consummate revolutionary "realist." Early
in 1920, Lukács published in *Kommunismus* an essay entitled "On the
Question of Parliamentarianism."[22] Inspired by the contemporary debate
in Communist circles throughout Europe, he aligned himself with the
"left Communists" and attacked those who advocated parliamentary
participation. As bourgeois institutions, he argued, parliaments could
serve only to undermine true revolutionary action, as represented by
genuine "workers' councils" (soviets). To his dismay, Lenin was sorely
displeased: "G. L.'s article is very Left-wing and very poor. Its Marxism is purely verbal; . . . it gives no concrete analysis of precise and
definite historical situations; it takes no account of what is most essential
(the need to take over and to learn to take over, all fields of work and
all institutions in which the bourgeoisie exerts its influence over the
masses, etc.)."[23]

"Left-wing" communism had become one of Lenin's central concerns, and in April 1920, he wrote his most famous exercise in political
cynicism—*Left-Wing Communism—an Infantile Disorder*. Praising left

Communists such as Anton Pannekoek, Henriette Roland-Holst, and Amadeo Bordiga for their enthusiasm and commitment, Lenin took them severely to task for their inability or unwillingness to consider concrete historical circumstances. The *goal* of communism did not change, but the path to that goal was never the same; the true revolutionary had to make tactical compromises in the service of the revolution. The refusal, "on principle," to participate in bourgeois parliaments reflected an abstract, undialectical, and unhistorical understanding. Although Communists recognized that parliamentarianism would give place to soviets, only the rash and impatient concluded that parliaments were no longer a political reality with which to reckon. Communists had to destroy parliamentarianism from *within* parliaments; they had to co-operate with parliamentary parties in order to be in a position to *subvert* parliamentary government. Did not, Lenin asked rhetorically, the Bolsheviks participate in the elections to the Constituent Assembly in 1917? Did they not turn these elections to revolutionary account? Always depending upon circumstances, participation in a bourgeois-democratic parliament might help to render parliamentarianism "politically obsolete."[24]

In Lenin's view, the refusal to participate in parliaments reflected a more general refusal to make compromises of any sort. He conceded that many compromises *were* treacherous and intolerable, but he insisted that to generalize from this that all compromise was inadmissible bespoke an undialectical, dogmatic mentality. "Our theory is not a dogma, but a *guide to action*," said Marx and Engels. Whether or not a compromise was justified depended upon its contribution to the goal of revolution. "Only one thing is lacking," Lenin concluded, "to enable us to march forward more confidently and firmly to victory, namely, the universal and thorough awareness of all Communists in all countries, of the necessity to display the utmost *flexibility* in their tactics."[25]

Lukács was impressed by Lenin's cunning, accepting immediately *Left-Wing Communism*'s arguments;[26] he was embarrassed to discover that he had not completely overcome his utopianism. At the same time that he embraced Lenin's opportunism, however, Lukács continued to affirm his faith in the proletariat's utopian mission, for to lose sight of utopia, he believed, was to encourage the growth of bureaucracy and of a bureaucratic mentality. Remembering Max Weber's work and his old fears of institutional forms alienated from life, Lukács attacked bureaucratization within the Communist movement with all the means at his command.

The old parties, he wrote in 1920, were compromise collectivities of heterogeneous individuals. Consequently, they very rapidly became bureaucratized, generating an aristocracy of party officials who were cut off from the masses. It was precisely because of the bureaucratic character of the old parties that many revolutionaries had looked to syndicalism. But the parties were not alone guilty. The Second International itself possessed only a paper reality, a bureaucratic unity.[27] There was no greater danger to the Communist party and to the Third International than bureaucratization, and in Lukács's judgment, the Central Committee of the Hungarian Communist party headed by Béla Kun had already (by 1922) degenerated into an "empty bureaucracy."[28]

Blinded by unquestioning faith, Lukács argued that the Russian Communist party had succumbed neither to petit-bourgeois utopianism nor to bureaucratization; it constituted a *tertium datur*.[29] It was, to be sure, an "organization," but one wholly unlike bureaucratic organizations. For the Communist party, "organization is not the prerequisite of action, but rather a constant interplay of prerequisite and result *during* action. Indeed, if one of these two aspects predominates, organization ought to be understood as result rather than as prerequisite."[30] The Communist party was not simply a means to an end—the revolution; it was an end in itself. The seizure of power was an important step in the building of communism, but it was only *one* step. The party and the revolution were dialectically related; without the party there could be no revolution, and without the revolution the party would remain the home of a minority of men.

The party was an end in itself. This remarkable claim derived from Lukács's insistence that the party "must be the first incarnation of the realm of freedom. In it, the spirit of brotherhood, of true solidarity, of willingness and ability to sacrifice ought first to prevail."[31] Lukács had persuaded himself that the party was the *Gemeinschaft* for which he had searched so long. Prophetically, he warned that if the party should fail to constitute itself a true *Gemeinschaft*, the seizure of power would simply substitute one oppressor for another; bureaucracy and corruption would not disappear. But if, as Lukács believed, the party became a *Gemeinschaft*, it could act as "the educator of humanity to freedom and self-discipline."[32]

To be "educated," in Lukács's new terminology, was to be class conscious, and proletarian class consciousness was the realization of human solidarity because the proletariat was the universal class, the class that could not free itself without at the same time freeing all men. But education was not simply or even primarily the result of propaganda; it was the product of action. A "unity of the deed" could be forged even if a particular action failed to achieve its aim. "The proletariat," Lukács wrote in 1920, "can constitute itself a class only in actual class struggle."[33] When the proletariat was fully conscious and in control of political power, Lukács believed that *Gemeinschaft* would become a reality for all men.

Toward a Marxist Theory of Literature

As we have seen, Lukács was preoccupied with politics during the years 1920–22, yet he did not set literary-cultural questions completely aside. It is true that Balázs complained to his diary on 26 October 1920 that Lukács alone could reunite the members of the Sunday Circle, but "he does not now have time because he is fashioning world revolution."[34] But only three months later (16 January 1921), he reported that the Sunday Circle had reorganized—even if it met on Mondays. In addition to Balázs and Lukács, the members included József Révai, Ljena Grabenko, Béla Fogarasi, Tibor Gergely, Edith Hajós, Anna Schlamadinger, and Anna Lesznai. "Ah, once again we are together," Balázs wrote, and "not even the world revolution will break up this sect."[35]

Soon other Hungarian emigrés joined the circle—Charles de Tolnay, László Radványi, Andor Gábor, Ervin Sinkó, and György Káldor. In the fall of 1921, Karl Mannheim and Arnold Hauser contacted Balázs and Lukács, but they were not well received. "This return of theirs is probably related to the fact that the world revolution is being deferred to an ever more remote future. As a result, the Circle's commitment to serious action cannot for the time being be a topic of discussion. Consequently, it is now less dangerous to be around us."[36]

Much had changed since the happier, more hopeful days in Budapest. The subjects of discussion were not very different, but they were now approached from a communist perspective. The major problem was that of the individualistic ethic that "led us to give ourselves to a movement that excludes this individualistic ethic. For humanity, two lines of development are relevant: the evolution of classes and of individual souls. They may travel on completely distinct paths and intersect with each other in us, but they remain two in number. Under these circumstances, to renounce our ethic will be the 'most ethical' of our acts."[37]

The members of the reconstituted Sunday Circle also discussed communist art and literature. At the time, artistic and literary questions had not yet been answered in Soviet Russia, where Lunacharski directed the Commissariat of Enlightenment in a relatively liberal spirit. True, Lenin had no taste for the avant-garde. "Aren't you ashamed to vote for publication of Mayakovsky's *150 Millions* in five thousand copies?," he wrote to Lunacharski on 6 May 1921. "Rubbish, stupidity, double-dyed stupidity and pretentiousness."[38] Still, in the early 1920s, it was not yet clear that "realism" would become the official artistic mode, and among the Hungarian emigrés in Vienna, there was much discussion of expressionism and activism, of Kassák and *Ma*, of the "proletarian art" to come. But Balázs, Lukács, and their friends denied that the avant-garde represented the wave of the communist future, for to them, Kassák and his followers were nihilists who wished to sever all connection with the past. To reject the progressive traditions of literature was, they believed, to destroy the roots of a profound, traditionally grounded, communist literature.[39]

In a series of essays that he published in *Die Rote Fahne*, Lukács began to formulate his new ideas about literature. Taken together, these explorations constitute a revised version of his first book: *History of the Evolution of the Modern Drama*, a work in which he tried to account for the rise and decline of tragic ages. A tragic age, he had concluded, was "the heroic age of a class's decline."[40] The decline of the bourgeoisie made possible a rebirth of the tragic spirit and hence of the tragic drama. In the *Rote Fahne* essays, he employed the same historical/sociological theory, but by then he was more interested in the literature inspired by a class on the rise, a class that conceived of the causes of its difficulties as temporary and hence subject to change.[41] This class was the proletariat. But here a problem arose, because an authentic "proletarian" literature had not yet emerged. Lukács focused his attention, therefore, on those writers whose work reflected the optimistic, self-confident strivings of the bourgeoisie during the late eighteenth and early nineteenth centuries.

Balzac was one of the greatest of these writers. During the second half of the nineteenth century, his fame, Lukács noted,[42] had been eclipsed by that of Flaubert, Zola, Daudet, and Maupassant, and this change in fortune was not accidental; behind it were social changes and hence changes in the ideology of the nineteenth-century's ruling class—the bourgeoisie. Balzac was the literary expression of the rising bourgeoisie. Thus, unlike the disillusioned, resigned writers of the declining bourgeoisie (late nineteenth century), he not only portrayed human passions and analyzed them psychologically, but he also understood them in their essence, in their relationship to the whole of social life. After 1848, when the decline of the bourgeoisie began, Balzac's work no longer coincided with the class-dictated spirit of the age.

By 1922, Lukács perceived signs of a Balzac revival, but he denied that this rekindled interest reflected a renewal of bourgeois self-confidence. If Balzac were again to be popular with that class, it would only be because of nostalgia. The appeal of his work would be much the same as that of "One Thousand and One Nights," Chinese fairy tales, or medieval stories. For the decaying bourgeois culture, rejection was the only possible response. By the same token, because the proletariat was then the rising class, it was likely to discover in Balzac a kindred spirit. "For the proletariat," Lukács wrote in "Marxism and Literary History," for "a rising class (just as for the rising and revolutionary bourgeois class of the eighteenth century), art is avowedly class art, partisan art, a proclamation of particular aims of class struggle."[43]

To be sure, Lukács still valued the work of some fin de siècle writers, but for different reasons than he once had. In this regard, it is instructive to compare his 1903 essay, "The New Hauptmann," with his 1922 reflections, "On Hauptmann's Evolution." In the former, as we have seen, he praised Hauptmann's abandonment of naturalism and celebrated his resigned tragic vision; in the latter, it was precisely Hauptmann's *"complete resignation,"* his conviction that men could not successfully defy their fate, that Lukács deplored. According to Hauptmann, he wrote, men must suffer their "hopeless foreignness" to one another. Yet despite his inability to grasp the essence of historical processes, the German writer evidenced a "great and beautiful honesty. He never disguised his inner uncertainty."[44] Thus he held up a mirror to his age and to the decline of his class.

For the same reason, Lukács awarded Strindberg even higher marks.[45] The Swedish dramatist, he argued, had depicted with relentless honesty the nature of marriage in capitalist society. He uncovered the truth that in those marriages in which the cash-nexus was not the sum and substance of union, *mere* sexual relationship degraded them even more. Brought together by "a meaningless sexual passion" from which they were unable to free themselves, married couples in a capitalist world lived in a "frightful hell"—the very words Lukács had used to describe his own marriage to Ljena Grabenko. Yet despite his great understanding of bourgeois marriage, Strindberg, like all bourgeois intellectuals, regarded bourgeois society as an unalterable "fact of nature." He conceived of his rebellion against fate as a futile act of heroism.

In this sense, according to Lukács, Strindberg was the father of expressionism, in which his "inferno appears as a colder and more naked reflection of a final dissolution." Among the expressionists, the *bourgeois* revolt against bourgeois society had become completely trivial; no longer capable of searching self-criticism, this revolt took the form of an inarticulate death scream. The expressionists were, in sum, Strindberg's epigones, lacking the master's profound insight and ability to depict concretely the decline of the capitalist world.

But what of Dostoevski? Lukács's abandonment of utopia and quest for reality had, we know, affected his judgment of the great Russian writer. In his most important literary essay of the early 1920s—"Stavrogin's Confession"—he praised Dostoevski's ability to reduce every character and every human relationship to pure spiritual essence, but he charged that his former idol had consciously ignored the social roots of human problems, viewing them as *individual* failures. This attempt to translate social being into pure spirituality could not but run aground.

And yet, Lukács concluded, Dostoevski's very failure was transformed into artistic success, for despite his intention to ignore social reality, the Russian had succeeded in disclosing the social roots of even the purest expressions of the soul. In his "confession," Stavrogin appeared as the greatest representative of that famous Russian type—the "superfluous man." Better than any character in Turgenev, Goncharov, or Tolstoi, Stavrogin demonstrated that when a superfluous man honestly searched for an aim, he had but three choices: suicide, depravity, or revolution. Thus Dostoevski's "political damnation of revolution transformed itself unintentionally into the artistic glorification of its absolute spiritual necessity."[46]

That in the course of development the class function of a literary work was often transformed, Lukács was certain.[47] Shakespeare's dramas had, for example, originated as feudal-reactionary, courtly works of literature, but in the age of Lessing, Goethe, and Schiller, the same dramas gave expression to the bourgeoisie's struggle for spiritual emancipation—*against* French courtly literature. Even armed with this recognition, however, the Marxist critic could not rest content, because he had to attempt to discover why a *particular* work had been found useful by subsequent ages. Why did the great German writers of the late eighteenth century embrace Shakespeare rather than one of his distinguished contemporaries? Here, Lukács argued, Marxists could not avoid an *aesthetic* analysis of literature. He maintained that those writers whose work continued to live were those who understood the most profound human emotions and ideas and rendered them meaningful even to men who were unaware of the concrete life situation out of which they emerged. The conclusion was inescapable: the most profound human emotions were transformed far more slowly than were social forms.

Lukács was struggling with the same problem with which Marx himself had had to wrestle—why ancient Greek drama continued to speak to modern man so directly. His attempt to answer it amounted to a recognition of a timeless element in great works of art. Moreover, despite his insistence that historical knowledge was necessary for criticism, Lukács's conclusion here refuted the claim. Well might he argue for the necessity of historical *consciousness*—that "sense of the timeless as well as of the temporal and of the timeless and of the temporal together"

(T. S. Eliot); he could scarcely maintain, on his own showing, that historical *knowledge* was invariably crucial, and in a remarkable concession to traditional criticism, he characterized as "idle" any speculation about the supposed irrelevance of classical literature in a classless society.

Dialectical Dogmatics

Despite these initial investigations, Lukács did not work out a Marxist theory of literature in detail because he was devoting most of his efforts to a theory of practice. In 1923, he published a volume of essays that constituted "in a definite sense the summing up and conclusion of that personal period of development that had begun in 1918–19."[48] Entitled *History and Class Consciousness: Studies in Marxist Dialectics*, the book was dedicated to Gertrúd Bortstieber. In this brilliant and perverse volume, the single most influential Marxist work of the twentieth century, the young Lukács offered a solution to the problem of alienation with which he had struggled personally and publicly from his earliest years. "For the first time since Marx," he wrote with pride in 1967, "alienation is treated as the central question of the revolutionary critique of capitalism."[49] Lukács argued that the answer to that central question could be found only with the aid of the Marxist, or dialectical, method, and as he put it in the original preface: "If these essays offer the beginning or merely the occasion for a genuinely fruitful discussion of the dialectical method, a discussion that brings to general consciousness again the essence of the method, they will have fulfilled their function completely."[50]

At the same time, Lukács hoped to settle accounts with his former, utopian, self; a profoundly antiutopian thread weaves its way through the fabric of this book. Rejecting utopia (fantasy), he embraced dialectics (reality). Critical of Marxist revisionists and "opportunists," he considered utopian thinkers to be even more dangerous to a correct Marxist theory and practice. Neither the "fatalism" of the former nor the ethical dreams of the latter could serve the revolution; both had to be preserved and negated within the dialectical process that was history. To Ernst Bloch, Ljena Grabenko, and himself (ca. 1911–19), Lukács here bid a not very fond farewell.

Of the eight essays that comprise *History and Class Consciousness*, two originated in 1919: "What Is Orthodox Marxism?" and "The Changing Function of Historical Materialism." We have already discussed the former, which first appeared shortly before the proclamation of the Hungarian Soviet Republic. Although Lukács revised and expanded it, the essay was not altered in essence.[51] Here too he identified orthodox Marxism with the dialectical method, rejecting any attempt to reduce Marx's teachings to a rigid dogma. Such an attempt had, in his view, been made by the so-called orthodox Marxists of the Second International. Although all Marxists gave at least lip service to a historical point of view, Lukács was convinced that few of them had been able fully to appreciate what a truly historical theory entailed. Too often, theoretical categories had hardened into timeless verities, seduced as it were by bourgeois theorists' efforts to pass off the historical condition under capitalism as an immutable *condition humaine*. True knowledge of reality required, in Lukács's judgment, a thoroughgoing recognition of its historical character.

In "The Changing Function of Historical Materialism,"[52] the text of a lecture Lukács delivered at the time (June 1919) of the inauguration of the Budapest Institute for Research into Historical Materialism, he boldly applied the historical/dialectical method to historical materialism itself. As an ideology, historical materialism was not, he argued, relative; it was absolutely valid within a capitalist social order. It was, indeed, capitalist society's self-knowledge. The attempt made by "vulgar" Marxists to apply its categories to precapitalist societies could not, however, be successful. Such an attempt betrayed an understanding insufficiently historical, a mistaking of historically valid for eternally valid categories.

By clinging to the deterministic form of historical materialism at a time when capitalism had entered a period of mortal crisis, vulgar Marxists conspired to prolong the capitalist era. To deny the necessity of *acts* of violence in favor of a patient waiting on the immanent laws of economics was, Lukács insisted, to render an invaluable service to an overripe society. The function of historical materialism had to be altered in accordance with the demands of a changing historical reality. The necessity of the objective economic process was being transformed into the freedom of the subjective human will; historical evolution was becoming *conscious*. Viewed dialectically, necessity and freedom were identical; the passage from the realm of necessity to the realm of freedom corresponded to the increasing consciousness of that class that was alone capable of perceiving history's subject-object identity—the proletariat. This capability derived from the circumstance that the proletariat *was* the subject as well as the object of history. Proletarian class consciousness (subject) and history (proletarian action) were simply two aspects of one and the same reality.

In "Class Consciousness,"[53] an essay he wrote in March 1920, Lukács reiterated his claim that the advance of history toward the realm of freedom was "automatic" only until capitalism reached an inescapable crisis. At that point, the fate of the revolution would depend upon the class consciousness of the proletariat; only the proletariat's *conscious deeds* could lead mankind along the final path to freedom. Once again, Lukács's argument depended upon a dialectical conception of history, a *process* becoming increasingly conscious of itself through the agency of the proletariat *as a class*. Indeed, he was at pains to insist that the consciousness of individuals, no matter how great the individuals might be, could not affect the course of history decisively. Classes, not individuals, were the makers of history. This being the case, proletarian class consciousness could not be equated with the sum of the empirical consciousnesses of individual proletarians. The class consciousness of the proletariat was that which it would be if it were fully *conscious* of its (and hence humanity's) true interests and historic mission. Until consciousness became conscious, therefore, it could only be *imputed* to the proletariat.

This is an important point, for with the positing of an ideal consciousness known only to the initiated, Lukács was laying the ideological ground for a gnostic tyranny. Indeed, in "Rosa Luxemburg as Marxist,"[54] he identified the Communist party as the contemporary form taken by proletarian class consciousness. It was the party alone, therefore, that was capable of imputing class consciousness to the proletariat. As the *bearer* of proletarian class consciousness, the party was not merely a means to an end (the revolution), but an end in itself (an ever greater realm of freedom). Revolutionary process and proletarian class consciousness (in the form of the party) were dialectically related aspects of the same process. When all men were members (in the deepest sense) of the party, the realm of freedom—the goal of the revolutionary process—would be fully realized.

The ability to recognize the essential identity of party (organized class consciousness) and revolutionary process depended, Lukács pointed out, upon the category of totality that had been employed by Hegel and by Marx. Only by grasping historical development in its entirety could the bourgeois elevation of individual parts over the whole be overcome. Precisely because "bourgeois consciousness" failed to understand history as a totality, it was incapable of resolving the antinomies of capitalist life; it viewed these antinomies as immutable givens. Kant was, therefore, the quintessential bourgeois thinker not because he was a conscious apologist, but because his thinking reflected the antinomies of the capitalist world while at the same time it regarded them as absolute. Dialectical thinking, the transcendence of opposites, was the privilege of those for whom history and thought, practice and theory were one.

The failure of even the greatest bourgeois thinkers to achieve the point of view of the totality derived from the consistency with which they adopted an *individual* rather than a *class* perspective. This, as Lukács now believed, accounted for his own previous failure to achieve anything higher than a utopian hope and an ethical (individualistic) opposition to the capitalist world. As he wrote that "the new 'ethical' grounding of socialism is the subjective side of the missing category of totality that is alone capable of a unified comprehension" (*GK*, 110), he had his utopian self in mind. Although he pointed the accusing finger at men such as Bernstein, Tugan-Baranovsky, and Otto Bauer, he was in fact exorcising the ghosts of his own utopian years. As so often in the past (and future), he was conducting a debate with himself.

This was not to say, however, that Lukács had abandoned his ethical concerns. Rather, he posited a distinction between individual (bour-geois) and historical (proletarian) ethics. To regard ethics from an in-dividual point of view was a form of false consciousness. "Class con-sciousness is the 'ethics' of the proletariat, the unity of its theory and its practice, the point at which the economic necessity of its struggle for liberation changes dialectically into freedom. Because the Party is un-derstood as the historical form and as the active bearer of class con-sciousness, it becomes at the same time the bearer of the ethics of the fighting proletariat" (*GK*, 115). Just as he had argued in "Tactics and Ethics," Lukács maintained that the dialectical evolution of history was ethical by definition because its goal—a community of free men—was the highest, indeed the only true ethical ideal. But this goal was not something "above" or "beyond" history, it was a process within time. That in the end this confidence rested upon a religious faith in the in-trinsic meaning and purpose of the historical process, Lukács refused to concede: "The so-called religious faith is here nothing more than the methodological certainty that, untroubled by all momentary defeats and reverses, the historical process continues its way to the end *in and through our deeds*" (*GK*, 117).

Lukács wrote two essays especially for *History and Class Conscious-ness*: "Toward a Methodology of the Organizational Question" and "Reification and the Consciousness of the Proletariat." In the former,[55] he repeated his contention that the Communist Party was an organiza-tion unlike any other. As the form of proletarian class consciousness, it was a process, the concrete and dialectical unfolding of the realm of freedom. "For just as the realm of freedom cannot be granted to us all

at once (*gratia irresistibilis* as it were), just as the 'final goal' is not
waiting for us somewhere outside the process but inheres in every single
moment of the process, so too the Communist Party, as the revolutionary
form of proletarian consciousness, is *process-like* " (*GK*, 481–82).

Lukács emphasized, however, that the freedom to which he referred
was *not* to be mistaken for bourgeois "freedom of the individual,"
because the latter was the freedom of isolated individuals from other
isolated individuals—"a freedom of egoism, of seclusion, a freedom
for which solidarity and association come into consideration at best as
ineffective 'regulative ideas' " (*GK*, 480). True freedom was "freedom
in its union with solidarity." To act freely was to exercise a *collective*,
not an individual, will.

"Reification and the Consciousness of the Proletariat"[56] was the
longest and most important essay in *History and Class Consciousness*;
it marked the end of the young Lukács's spiritual odyssey. The resolution of the problem of alienation, with which he had struggled for so
long, was here worked out in greatest and most systematic detail. He
entitled the first of the three sections of his essay "The Phenomenon of
Reification" (*Verdinglichung*), understood as a synonym for "alienation" (*Entfremdung*).[57] The central structural problem of capitalist
society was, Lukács began, that of commodities, because commodity
structure, regarded as a thing, concealed effectively the true structure of
society, i.e., the relations between men. With the advent of capitalism,
he continued, those human relations designed to guarantee a mutual
supply of human necessities became impersonally "economic" in the
modern sense—material things designed to serve an economic mechanism that had become autonomous, an end in itself. This objectification
or reification of authentic human relationships was *the* distinguishing
characteristic of capitalist society. Rather than serving human beings,
the economic order mastered them, forcing them to conduct themselves
"rationally," in keeping with the rationalization necessary for the maxi-
mization of economic efficiency and productivity. No longer fully human, men were defined by the service they performed in the economic
order, and as that service became more specialized, man's alienation
from his fellows became more complete. What is more, this economically created isolation became the paradigm of all social relations under
capitalism—the economically organized society *par excellence*. Worse,
with the passing of time, the reified world of capitalism came to be
regarded as the "natural" and eternal order of things; men forgot that
they were men. Human consciousness itself became reified. "The transformation of the commodity relation into a thing of 'ghostly objectivity'
. . . stamps its structure on the entire consciousness of man" (*GK*, 194).

In section 2, "The Antinomies of Bourgeois Thought," Lukács attempted a critique of modern philosophy, based upon his analysis of the reified world dominated by the bourgeoisie. "Modern critical philosophy," he began, "originated in the reified structure of consciousness" (*GK*, 209). He believed that the alienated consciousness of man in bourgeois society necessitated a philosophy characterized by unresolved antinomies, and as a result even the greatest philosophies of the bourgeois era—those of Kant, Fichte, and Hegel—were, in his judgment, antinomic to the core. Kant's famous distinction between phenomena and noumena, his insistence that the "thing-in-itself" could never be known, simply pointed up for Lukács the dilemma of bourgeois thought. On the one hand, Kant sought a rational system that was unified and complete; on the other hand, because of his reified consciousness, he could not discover a means by which the thing-in-itself could be subjected to the categories of the understanding. Great as he was, therefore, the Königsberg philosopher failed to erect a system capable of grasping reality as a totality. "The 'eternal, brazen' regularity of natural events and the pure inner freedom of individual, moral praxis appear at the conclusion of the *Critique of Practical Reason* as irreconcilably separated, but at the same time—in their separation—the unchangeably given foundations of human existence" (*GK*, 244). Kant's true greatness, according to Lukács, was to have articulated clearly the philosophic antinomies of bourgeois thought and to have resisted any effort to resolve them dogmatically.

In the philosophy of Hegel, bourgeois thought came closest to overcoming Kant's antinomies; indeed, Hegel succeeded in pointing the way out of the dilemma, because in place of formal rationalism, he substituted dialectics. In place of two worlds—phenomenal and noumenal —he posited one, the historical. Having thereby eliminated the thing-in-itself, Hegel was in a far better position to realize the systematic ambitions of rationalism. He was convinced that history could be grasped as a concrete totality. But despite Hegel's great philosophic advances, he had been unable to take the final step—the correct identification of the *subject* of the historical process. The antinomic structure of bourgeois existence invaded and distorted even his consciousness, and, on the edge of the final discovery, he retreated to idealistic metaphysics, positing the "World Spirit," which, as pure subject, lay beyond history. Working its way through history, the World Spirit achieved full self-consciousness at the stage of "Absolute Spirit"—art, religion, and philosophy. For Lukács, this was nothing but sophisticated mythmaking, the inescapable limit imposed on the brilliant but reified consciousness of a thinker unable ultimately to transcend the standpoint of the bourgeoisie.

In section 3, "The Standpoint of the Proletariat," Lukács argued that it was only from the standpoint of the proletariat that the veil of the reified commodity structure of the bourgeois world could be lifted to reveal the authentic human world of men and the relations between men. Because all thinking was defined by the existence of the relevant class, bourgeois thinkers had to view the world in its *immediacy*; for them, reality was immediately given, the unalterable object of contemplation. They could not regard the world and the social order as anything but the sum of eternal, isolated "facts." Were they to abandon abstract, formal rationality, they would be forced to recognize that bourgeois class dominance was a historical, not an eternal phenomenon. To be sure, the best bourgeois thinkers were not willfully and cynically obtuse, but they possessed a consciousness that distorted ultimate reality in the interest of their class.

The superior standpoint of the proletariat was also a function of class interest. Because it was not in that class's interest to view reality in its reified immediacy, it was capable of achieving a *mediated* and hence true view of reality. Such a view required a historical/dialectical approach; what for bourgeois thinkers were static, isolated "things" could then be seen as dynamic aspects of processes, immanent tendencies and possibilities. For Lukács, that is, reality *was* not, it *became*. Hence, the proper relationship to reality was not one of contemplation, but of action; "the philosophers have only *interpreted* the world, in various ways," Marx had written. "The point, however, is to *change* it" (Eleventh Thesis on Feuerbach). The standpoint of the proletariat made possible the recognition that the contemplation of immediate data of existence was the necessary philosophic method of the bourgeoisie. Only when philosophy became praxis, thus releasing latent historic realities, could the world be changed and the immanent goal of history be brought closer to realization.

In order for philosophy to become praxis, however, historical tendencies had to become conscious. This was only another way of saying that the proletariat had to become class conscious because, Lukács proclaimed, the proletariat was the identical subject-object of the historical process. The proletariat could only achieve self-awareness, and hence become a class, by means of action in the objective world, and, at the same time, the world could only be changed essentially by the class-conscious action of the proletariat. Proletarian self-awareness and changed reality were but two aspects of *one* historical/dialectical process; one could not be discussed without constant reference to the other. This being the case, the distinction between theory and practice was overcome. True theory *was* practice. To say that this and all other bourgeois antinomies would be overcome was to say that the societal (commodity) forms taken by human relationships would be destroyed and men would recognize themselves not as isolated individuals in a legally defined *Gesellschaft*, but as members of a human *Gemeinschaft* that gave meaning to their existence. Just as the reified "facts" of the bourgeois world would give place to processes whose meaning depended upon their relationship to the totality of history, so the reified (alienated) individuals of that same world would give way to naked souls whose meaning depended upon their relationship to the totality of the human community. Indeed, these liberations were dialectically interdependent.

Thus the young Lukács's Marxism. But what is one to make of this tour de force? To begin with, *History and Class Consciousness* is not a work of philosophy; it is a dogmatics invulnerable to external criticism or argument.[58] No evidence can in principle be adduced to disprove the dogma, which is internally consistent and self-certifying. Second, the book champions a dialectic that is capable of justifying *any* deed, no matter how monstrous, for as Lukács demonstrated, no one armed with a proper "dialectical" method can ever be put to rout, because any inconvenient circumstance or argument can be declared its opposite. Finally, the book constitutes a blueprint for tyranny. Once concede that there exists an *ideal* class consciousness independent of historical experience and one is led, step by step, to defend the absolute power of gnostic visionaries. In this sense, the book bears a striking resemblance to Rousseau's *Social Contract*, which also prepares the ground for totalitarianism. Having "started out with the idea of unrestricted freedom," Lukács had "arrived at unrestricted despotism."

From Tonio Kröger to Naphta

To his generation, the young Lukács was an enigmatic figure, but almost intuitively, those who followed his career sensed an intimate relationship between his ideas and his personality, and, in an effort to lay bare the existential sources of his ideological twists and turns, they often had recourse to the creative imagination. Like Ivan Kaliayev and Sergei Nechaev, Lukács represented a challenge to novelists of ideas; by uncovering his soul's secrets, they hoped to plumb the depths of human motivation and to illuminate the inner history of an epoch. Thus, whether sympathetic or antagonistic, the novels in which Lukács appears constitute invaluable historical and psychological documents. The present study owes much to Anna Lesznai's *Kezdetben volt a kert* (*In the Beginning Was the Garden*), in which Lukács is the leader of an esoteric circle of searchers; to Ervin Sinkó's *Optimisták* (*Optimists*), in which he is a Pascalian wagerer, betting his soul on the party; to József Lengyel's *Prenn Ferenc hányatott élete* (*Ferenc Prenn's Storm-Tossed Life*), which portrays him as a muddleheaded intellectual incapable of understanding the working class; and to Emma Ritoók's *A szellem kalandorai* (*Adventurers of the Spirit*), in which he is a messianic Jew.

In this reliance upon semifictional portraits, I have followed Lukács's lead, for in the years prior to Irma Seidler's suicide, he had cast himself in the role of Thomas Mann's Tonio Kröger, the sensitive young man who could understand but not live life. In fact, it was always in Mann's creative world that Lukács was most at home. Between the two men there existed a mutual respect and understanding that transcended their many differences. They met on one occasion only: in Vienna on 17 January 1922. In Mann's room in the Hotel Imperial, Lukács expounded at length his theories concerning the contemporary function of art.[1] As the German listened, he formed a physical and spiritual image of his loquacious visitor. He had seen and heard Lukács for no more than an hour, but that, according to his wife, "was the remarkable thing about him: he got a complete picture of a person immediately."[2] Less than five months later (2 June 1922), Mann informed a friend that "Leo Naphta, a half-Jewish pupil of the Jesuits with crass views, has emerged and continu-

ally engages Settembrini in pointed debate that one day will lead to
an educational duel.''[3] And although Mann categorically denied that
Lukács served as the model for that most extraordinary figure in *The
Magic Mountain*, the similarities are too great to ignore.

About Naphta's father, whose responsibility it was to slaughter animals according to Talmudic prescription, "there was something irregu-
lar, schismatic, . . . something of the familiar of God, a Baal-Shem.''[4]
More important, his mother was horrified and alienated by his ideas.
When first he is introduced to Hans Castorp, he is living at the home of
a ladies' tailor whose name is "Lukaçek.'' Physically, he resembles
Lukács[5] and, most important, he is, like Lukács, an alarmingly cunning
defender of political terror. To Settembrini's horror, Naphta pours contempt upon bourgeois humanism with its interminable chatter about
progress, science, and democracy. An atheist, he cannot abide secularism or paganism; he is a Christian heretic who longs for heaven on
earth. Having escaped from bourgeois individualism and entered the
Jesuits' militant community, he prophesies a great sacramental shedding
of blood, after which the world will be purified. The executor of History's will is to be the proletariat: "The proletariat has taken up the task
of Gregory the Great, his religious zeal burns within it, and as little as
he may it withhold its hand from the shedding of blood. Its task is to
strike terror into the world for the healing of the world, that man may
finally achieve salvation and deliverance, and win back at length to
freedom from law and from distinction of classes, to his original status
as child of God.''[6] This is precisely the conviction that inspired Lukács's
dialectical dogmatics; it is the tragic credo of a brilliant and sensitive
man whose passion for perfect justice and harmony was greater than his
love for imperfect human beings.

N·O·T·E·S

INTRODUCTION

1. Lukács, "Gelebtes Denken," p. 4, in György Lukács, Manuscripts, Correspondence, Diaries (hereafter cited as LAK).

2. Lukács Popper, "Emlékek Lukács Györgyről," p. 1564. For many details concerning Lukács's early years I have relied upon his sister's memoir and the "Biographical Data" in Mészáros, *Lukács' Concept of Dialectic*, pp. 115–52.

3. József Lukács to György Lukács, 2 July 1910, LAK.

4. Lukács, "Gelebtes Denken," p. 7, LAK.

5. In all, four children were born to József Lukács and Adél Wertheimer: János (1884–1944) died at Mauthausen; György (1885–1971); Pál (1889–92); and Mária (1887–1981).

6. Lukács, "Gelebtes Denken," pp. 6, 16, LAK.

7. József Lukács to György Lukács, 2 August 1910, LAK.

8. Lukács, "Gelebtes Denken," p. 7, LAK.

9. Ibid., p. 10, LAK.

10. Lukács, *Magyar irodalom*, p. 6.

11. Ibid.

12. Barany, " 'Magyar Jew or: Jewish Magyar'?," p. 26. In 1840, most residential and professional restrictions on the Jews had been lifted.

13. Hanák, *Magyarország története, 1890–1918*, 1:466.

14. Marcell Benedek to Lukács, 25 June 1905, LAK.

15. Ibid., 30 July 1905, LAK.

16. Though "lengyel" means "Pole," it is also a surname; presumably Benedek refers here to a family of his acquaintance.

17. Marcell Benedek to Lukács, 4 Au-

gust 1905, LAK.

18. Hanák, "Kései rehabilitácio," p. 159.

19. Szekfű, *Magyar történet*, 5:551–55.

20. Schorske, "Politics and Patricide," p. 331.

21. The political crisis of 1905–6 subsided after József Kristóffy, minister of the interior under Baron Féjerváry, proposed that every literate male over twenty-four years of age be enfranchised. Fifteen percent of Hungary's population would then have been eligible to vote. The emperor initially supported Kristóffy's proposal as part of his campaign to bring the coalition to heel. Both Andrássy and Kossuth, sensing a threat to the Magyar ruling classes, denounced the proposal and quickly came to terms with the crown.

22. Lukács, *Magyar irodalom*, pp. 6–7.

23. Czigány, "Hungarianness," p. 336.

24. Cushing, "Problems," pp. 344–45.

25. Lukács, *Magyar irodalom*, p. 6. In that year, Lukács discovered a copy of Max Nordau's *Entartung* in his father's library. Here he was introduced for the first time to "path-finding figures" such as Baudelaire, Verlaine, Swinburne, Zola, Ibsen, and Tolstoi. "Gelebtes Denken," p. 10, LAK.

26. Lukács, *A modern dráma*, 2:499.

27. On these works and the question of the antiphilosophic character of Hungarian culture in general, see Nyíri, "Kemény, Eötvös és Madách," pp. 20–35.

28. Nisbet, *Sociology as an Art Form*, p. 115.

29. Lukács, *Művészet és társadalom*, p. 7.

30. Tönnies, *Community and Society*, pp. 64–65.

31. Ibid., pp. 65, 227.

32. Abrams, *Natural Supernaturalism*, p. 313.

33. See Nisbet, *The Quest for Community*.

CHAPTER I

1. Lukács, *Ifjúkori művek*, p. 110.

2. Ibid., p. 180.

3. Lukács destroyed all of his manuscripts shortly after completing his gymnasium studies. "Gelebtes Denken," p. 12, LAK.

4. *Irodalmi Muzeum: Emlékezések*, p. 17.

5. Lukács, *Ifjúkori művek*, pp. 69, 72, 76.

6. Ibid., p. 69.

7. Benedek, *Naplómat olvasom*, p. 121.

8. Lukács, *Magyar irodalom*, p. 574.

9. Benedek, *Naplómat olvasom*, p. 126.

10. Cited in Katona and Dénes, *A Thália története*, p. 5.

11. Ibid., p. 17.

12. Sándor Hevesi to Lukács, 1904, LAK.

13. László, *Hevesi Sándor*, p. 56.

14. Cited in Katona and Dénes, *A Thália története*, p. 51.

15. Ibid., pp. 23, 12.

16. Lukács, *Magyar irodalom*, p. 576, and López Soria, "L'expérience théâtrale de Lukács," p. 127.

17. Benedek, *Naplómat olvasom*, p. 164.

18. László Bánóczi to Lukács, 7 August 1908, LAK. Hevesi had never resigned his position with the National Theater and as his responsibilities increased there he had less time for Thália.

19. Katona and Dénes, *A Thália története*, p. 155.

20. Cited in Fekete, "Lukács esszékorszaka," p. 85.

21. On Somló (who married László

Bánóczi's sister), a professor of law turned moral philosopher, see Litván, "Egy magyar tudós tragikus pályája," pp. 32–42. On Lukács's continued interest in the work of legal philosophers—especially that of Somló and Gustav Radbruch—see the articles by Varga: "Az ifjú Lukács és a jog," pp. 664–71, and "A jog helye Lukács *Ontológiá*jában," pp. 39–50.

22. Lukács, "Curriculum vitae," p. 5. Although he only worked mornings, Lukács soon reported to his father that he could not tolerate such a life. Lukács Popper, "Emlékek Lukács Györgyről," p. 1570.

23. Lukács, *Ifjúkori művek*, pp. 84–89.

24. Ibid., pp. 90–105. Lukács had traveled to Norway to meet Ibsen and Björnson in 1902.

25. This transformation of Romanticism was, in Lukács's judgment, the key to the intellectual history of the nineteenth century. In a book to be titled *The Romanticism of the Nineteenth Century*, he planned to work his idea out in detail. See Márkus, "Lukács' 'erste' Ästhetik," pp. 233–34n.

26. Lukács, *A modern dráma*, 1:434.

27. See also Lukács, *Ifjúkori művek*, pp. 476–88.

28. Hilda Bauer to Lukács, 7 March 1909, LAK.

29. Ibid., 3 April 1909, LAK.

30. Lukács, *Essays on Thomas Mann*, p. 10.

31. Mann, "Tonio Kröger," pp. 104, 99.

32. Lukács, *Esztétikai kultura*, p. 73.

33. Cited in Fekete, "Lukács esszékorszaka," p. 85.

34. Gábor, "Alexander Bernát levelei Lukács Györgyhöz," pp. 225–26.

35. Simmel, *Philosophie des Geldes*, pp. 390–96.

36. Simmel, "Der Begriff und die Tragödie der Kultur," p. 270.

37. Simmel, *Philosophie des Geldes*, p. 488.

38. Weber, "Georg Simmel as

Sociologist," p. 161.

39. Lenk, "Das Tragische Bewusstsein," p. 260.

40. Lukács, "Megjegyzések," pp. 388–421.

41. Watnick, "Georg Lukács: Or Aesthetics and Communism," p. 65.

42. Lukács, *A modern dráma*, I:iv–vi.

43. Lukács, "Mein Weg zu Marx," pp. 226–27.

44. Lukács, *A modern dráma*, I:iv.

45. Ibid., I:3–68.

46. Ibid., I:69–216.

47. Ibid., I:219–306.

48. Ibid., I:307–48.

49. Ibid., I:351–425.

50. Ibid., I:426–91.

51. Ibid., 2:3–179.

52. Ibid., 2:181–410.

53. Lukács, *Esztétikai kultura*, p. 15. Arnold Hauser later restated Lukács's views: "The primacy of the moment, of change and chance implies, in terms of aesthetics, the dominion of the passing mood over the permanent qualities of life"; "impressionism is the climax of self-centred aesthetic culture"; "this outlook has one constant, always predominant and ever more profoundly rooted characteristic: the consciousness of estrangement and loneliness." *Social History of Art*, 4:170, 207.

54. Lukács, *Esztétikai kultura*, p. 18.

55. Márkus, "The Soul and Life," p. 106.

56. See Hanák, *A filozófus Lukács*, pp. 12–21.

57. Lukács, *Magyar irodalom*, p. 57. Following Lukács, Arnold Hauser was later to write: "The Viennese represent the purest form of the impressionism which forgoes all resistance to the stream of experience." *Social History of Art*, 4:207.

58. Lukács, *A modern dráma*, 2:411–531.

59. Balázs, *Álmodó ifjúság*, p. 86.

60. Ibid., p. 293.

61. Ibid., p. 374.

62. Balázs, Diaries, MTAK:K,

MS 5024/3, section IX, pp. 1–2, 22 August 1905.

63. Nagy, *Balázs Béla világa*, p. 96.

64. Balázs, Diaries, MTAK:K, MS 5024/3, "Berlin I," p. 7, 23 January 1907.

65. Simmel, "Zur Metaphysik des Todes," pp. 29–36. The essay first appeared in *Logos* in 1910. It may well be that Simmel discussed his early ideas about the "metaphysics of death" in his seminar. In any event, the idea was "in the air."

66. Balázs cited that famous line of Claudio: "Erst da ich sterbe, spür ich, dass ich bin." Hofmannsthal, "Der Tor und der Tod," p. 134. The citation is on p. 14 of *Halálesztetika*.

67. Balázs, *Halálesztetika*, pp. 12–13.

68. Ibid., pp. 36–37.

69. The model for Margit Szélpál was Aranka Bálint, Balázs's girl friend during his university years, but the ideas and dilemmas of the heroine are clearly those of Balázs himself.

70. Balázs, "Doktor Szélpál Margit," in *Halálos fiatalság*, p. 49.

71. Ibid., p. 75.

72. Ibid., p. 100.

73. Lukács, *Ifjúkori művek*, p. 235.

74. Sándor Radnóti, "Előszó" to Balázs, *A vándor énekel*, pp. 25–26.

75. The *Holnap* poetry anthologies were published by the Holnap Literary Society in 1908–9. As the title suggests, the poets included in the collections were regarded as heralds of a new literature.

76. Lukács, *Magyar irodalom*, pp. 78–80.

77. Ferenc Fehér first used this term to describe the Lukács-Balázs alliance.

CHAPTER 2

1. So great is the contrast between the two books that some scholars have taken the view that Lukács had an almost schizophrenic personality or alternatively that the essays were written in German, a

more philosophic language, even though they appeared first in Hungarian. The latter supposition is as fallacious as the former. János Kristóf Nyíri, in "Lukács 'Die Seele und die Formen,' " has demonstrated conclusively that the essays were written in Hungarian.

2. Lukács, *Ästhetik*, 1:673ff.

3. See Lukács to Charles de Tolnay, 23 March 1969; 14 October 1969; and 10 March 1970, LAK.

4. Gy. Lukács, "Leó Popper. Ein Nachruf," first published in the German-language newspaper *Pester Lloyd* in 1911. I am following the republished article that appears on plate XV in Mészáros, *Lukács' Concept of Dialectic*.

5. Cited by Fekete, introduction to "Lukács-Popper," p. 16.

6. Tolnay, "Popper Leó," p. 249.

7. Popper, "Volkskunst und Formbeseelung," p. 39.

8. Popper, "Die Bildhauerei, Rodin und Maillol," pp. 34–35.

9. Lukács, "Megjegyzések," p. 404.

10. József Lukács to György Lukács, 23 August 1909, LAK. Lukács's father did not hold Popper in high regard. The young man's plans to wed Beatrice de Waard despite his illness and want of financial resources seemed to him to betoken poor character. Nevertheless, in a gesture typical of his generosity, the elder Lukács offered to send Beatrice de Waard a large sum of money with the understanding that the source of the assistance should be kept secret from Popper. József Lukács to György Lukács, 9 December 1910, LAK.

11. Karl became a distinguished economic historian, author of the classic *The Great Transformation* (1944). Michael was a scientist of international reputation who later turned to philosophy; his *Personal Knowledge* (1958) was a major milestone in post-World War II thought. Laura made her mark as a scholarly defender of Captain John Smith's reputation.

12. Like many Hungarian Jews, Pollacsek chose to Magyarize his children's name (but not his own) to "Polányi," in the

expectation that their social and economic opportunities would thereby be greater.

13. Cited in Fekete, "Lukács esszékorszaka," p. 86.

14. Ibid.

15. Irma Seidler to Lukács, 3 July 1908, LAK.

16. Ibid., 25 October 1908, LAK.

17. Ibid., 2 November 1908, LAK.

18. Cited in Lendvai, "Lukács György és Seidler Irma," p. 35.

19. Lukács, *Ifjúkori művek*, pp. 188–98.

20. Hilda Bauer to Lukács, 7 April 1909, LAK.

21. Lukács to Irma Seidler, March 1910, LAK.

22. György Lukács's Diary, pp. 6–7, 11 May 1910, LAK.

23. Ibid., pp. 30–31, 29 September 1910, LAK.

24. Fekete, "Lukács-Popper," p. 29.

25. Ibid., p. 32.

26. Lukács to Irma Seidler, 22 March 1911, LAK.

27. Heller, *Portrévázlatok*, p. 420.

28. Fekete, "Lukács-Popper," p. 19.

29. Ibid., p. 24.

30. Lukács, *Ifjúkori művek*, pp. 130–43.

31. "Even from the extreme individualism which some of the romantics cultivated in their youth, almost all of them found the way to community, the community of marriage, state, church, etc." Paul Kluckhohn, cited in Mitzman, *Sociology and Estrangement*, p. 21n.

32. Lukács, *Ifjúkori művek*, pp. 203–21.

33. Ibid., pp. 287–303.

34. Ibid., pp. 160–73.

35. Ibid., pp. 352–84.

36. Fekete, "Lukács-Popper," p. 22.

37. Lukács, *Ifjúkori művek*, pp. 304–21, 144–53, 322–51.

38. According to one reviewer: "Whether we accept or reject its points of view, György Lukács's book is ideally suited to bring new life to our old-fashioned, fact-assembling literary his-

tory." b., "A modern dráma," p. 124.

39. Timár, "Popper Leó elfelejtett Lukács-ismertetése," pp. 967-72; Ritoók, "Esztétikai kutatások, I," pp. 502-4.

40. Kutasi, "Esztétikai kutatások, II," pp. 504-7.

41. Arany (1817-82), one of nineteenth-century Hungary's most gifted poets, was a master of the Hungarian language.

42. Cited by István Gál in Gál, "Lukács György levelei Babitshoz," p. 600.

43. Babits, Arcképek és tanulmányok, pp. 267-71.

44. Gál, "Lukács György levelei Babitshoz," pp. 597-98.

45. Lukács, Ifjúkori művek, pp. 779-83.

46. Gál, "Lukács György levelei Babitshoz," pp. 610-12.

47. See Johnston, The Austrian Mind, pp. 165-80.

48. Lukács, Ifjúkori művek, p. 321; see also Lendvai, "Weininger és Lukács," pp. 35-37.

49. Komlós, Problémák a Nyugat körül, p. 11.

50. Irodalmi Muzeum: Emlékezések, p. 21.

51. Ibid., pp. 20, 24-27.

52. Lukács, Magyar irodalom, p. 11.

53. Irodalmi Muzeum: Emlékezések, p. 35.

54. Oszkár Jászi to Lukács, 26 August 1909, LAK.

55. "Jelentés," p. xiv.

56. See Tömöry, Új vizeken járok, photographic plate between pp. 48 and 49.

57. See Károly Polányi to Lukács, 18 August 1908, LAK.

58. Ady, Összes versei, p. 7. When the Hungarians occupied their present homeland in 896, they entered the territory by way of the Verecke Pass through the Carpathians. Dévény was Hungary's westernmost frontier township at the turn of the century.

59. Fenyő, Följegyzések, p. 65.

60. Irodalmi Muzeum: Emlékezések, p. 21.

61. Ady, Költészet és forradalom, p. 106; Vezér, "Hajós Edit," p. 8.

62. Lukács to Lajos Fülep, 24 May 1910, LAK.

63. Béla Balázs to Mihály Babits, 26 September 1910, Babits Papers, OSZK:K, Fond III/190.

64. Fekete, "Lukács-Popper," p. 29. Lukács may also have learned that Renaissance had been started with money provided by Archduke Franz Ferdinand, who hoped to promote his political purposes.

65. Vekerdi, "A fiatal Fülep," pp. 10, 15.

66. Fülep, A művészet forradalmától, 1:449.

67. Fekete, "Lukács-Popper," p. 32.

68. Lajos Fülep to Lukács, early January 1911, LAK.

69. Fülep, A művészet forradalmától, 2:601.

70. Lukács, Magyar irodalom, p. 12.

71. Fülep, "Az emlékezés," pp. 56-90.

72. The members were Róbert Berény, Béla Czóbel, Dezső Czigány, Károly Kernstok, Ödön Márffy, Dezső Orbán, Bertalan Pór, and Lajos Tihanyi.

73. Passuth, A Nyolcak festészete, pp. 141, 148.

74. Fülep, "Új Suso-kiadás," p. 254.

75. Irodalmi Muzeum: Emlékezések, p. 34.

76. Lukács to Lajos Fülep, 9 November 1910, LAK.

77. See Lajos Fülep to Lukács, 14 July and 28 August 1911, LAK.

78. See Mannheim, "Letters to Lukács," pp. 93-105.

79. Szilasi made his philosophic reputation in Germany after World War II. His work constitutes an attempt to achieve a synthesis of the philosophies of Husserl and Heidegger.

80. See Szilasi, Platon; "A kritika elmélete," pp. 638-51.

81. Vilmos Szilasi to Lukács, summer 1910, LAK.

82. Balázs, Diaries, MTAK:K, MS 5023/18, appended to p. 7, letter of 17 August 1911.

83. In Lukács's diary, too, Hungarian eventually gave place to German.

84. Baumgarten (1880–1927) was a literary scholar of independent means. His acquaintances included Beer-Hofmann, the members of the Stefan George Circle, the brothers Mann, Rilke, E. R. Curtius, and Ernst Troeltsch.

85. Lukács, *Die Seele und die Formen*, pp. 133–54. This is a new printing without changes (except for pagination) of the original edition: Georg von Lukács, *Die Seele und die Formen/Essays* (Berlin: Egon Fleischel & Co., 1911).

86. Fekete, "Lukács-Popper," p. 29.

87. Lukács, *Die Seele und die Formen*, pp. 218–50.

88. Kutzbach, *Paul Ernst und Georg Lukács*, p. xvii.

89. Ernst, *Der Weg zur Form*, pp. 7–8, 10.

90. Cited in Faesi, *Paul Ernst*, p. 96.

91. Goldmann, "Georg Lukács: L'essayiste," pp. 247–48.

92. See Rochlitz, "Lukács et Heidegger," pp. 87–94.

93. Cited in Lukács, *Die Seele und die Formen*, p. 221.

94. Ernst, *Der Weg zur Form*, p. 121.

95. Lukács, *Die Seele und die Formen*, p. 29. Lukács was well aware that *Parerga und Paralipomena* was published in 1851, after *The World as Will and Representation*. His point was that the former work was logically prior; in fact, it was Schopenhauer's essays that first brought him wide recognition.

96. Of Mandl little is known, except that he lived in Germany and seems to have been of Hungarian origin. Lórsy was a Budapest journalist. See Nyíri, "Lukács 'Die Seele und die Formen'," pp. 401–4.

97. Fekete, "Lukács-Popper," pp. 25, 27.

98. György Lukács's Diary, 9 June 1910, LAK.

99. In a letter to Lukács, Irma wrote: "I read Kassner once again and liked it very much. Ravenna is in it, you and I are in it."

Cited in Lendvai, "Lukács György és Seidler Irma," p. 34.

100. Cited in Fekete, "Lukács esszékorszaka," p. 88.

101. Lukács to Irma Seidler, 22 March 1911, LAK.

102. Irma Seidler to Lukács, undated, LAK.

103. Fekete, "Lukács-Popper," p. 29.

104. Lukács to Irma Seidler, 22 March 1911, LAK.

105. Cited in Novák, *A Vasárnap Társaság*, p. 201n.

106. Balázs, "Notes from a Diary," p. 124. I have modified the translation very slightly.

107. See Irma Seidler to Lukács, 28 April 1911, LAK.

108. Mária Lukács to György Lukács, 8 May 1911, LAK.

109. Fekete, "Lukács-Popper," p. 36.

110. Béla Balázs to Lukács, 28 October 1911, LAK.

111. György Lukács's Diary, 27 October 1911, LAK.

112. Ibid., 15 December 1911, LAK.

113. Georg von Lukács, "Brief," in Schlösser, *Für Margarete Susman*, p. 304. The letter was dated 25 September 1912. Margarete Susman (1874–1966) was a critic, philosopher, and friend of Georg Simmel.

114. Lukács, "Von der Armut am Geiste," pp. 67–92; *Ifjúkori művek*, pp. 537–51. I have followed the Hungarian version, which is a translation by Béla Balázs of the original German.

115. Cf. Heller, "'Von der Armut am Geiste,'" p. 365.

116. On the ethic "beyond duty," see Heller, "A kötelességen túl," pp. 31–41.

CHAPTER 3

1. Lukács, *Magyar irodalom*, pp. 45, 8.

2. For the details of Bloch's early years, I have relied on Ernst Bloch, "Lebenslauf," in Traub and Wieser, *Gespräche*

mit *Ernst Bloch*, pp. 300–302, and Bahr, *Ernst Bloch*.

3. Traub and Wieser, *Gespräche mit Ernst Bloch*, p. 30.

4. Löwy, "Interview with Ernst Bloch," p. 36.

5. Karádi, "Dokumentumok Lukács György heidelbergi korszakából," p. 28.

6. Kutzbach, *Paul Ernst und Georg Lukács*, p. 23.

7. Lukács, "Leopold Ziegler," p. 255.

8. Lukács, "Wilhelm Dilthey," p. 253.

9. Lukács, "Georg Simmel," p. 2.

10. Lukács, *Magyar irodalom*, p. 8.

11. Copleston, *A History of Philosophy*, vol. 7, pt. 1, p. 49.

12. Lukács, *A modern dráma*, 1:153.

13. Löwy, "Interview with Ernst Bloch," p. 37.

14. Benz, *Les sources mystiques*, p. 8.

15. Lukács, *Magyar irodalom*, pp. 45–52; Ady, *Összes versei*, p. 183.

16. Lajos Fülep to Lukács, 16 November 1910, LAK.

17. Buber, *Begegnung*, p. 6. "In Buber's case one can scarcely resist the surmise that he was permanently damaged by his mother's abandonment of him when he was a small child." Kaufmann, "Martin Buber," p. 34.

18. Scholem, "Martin Buber's Interpretation of Hasidism," in *The Messianic Idea in Judaism*, pp. 228–50.

19. Lukács to Martin Buber, November 1911, LAK.

20. Martin Buber to Lukács, 21 February 1911, LAK.

21. Lukács to Martin Buber, November 1911, LAK.

22. Buber, *Hasidism and Modern Man*, pp. 101–2, 107.

23. Ibid., pp. 113, 118, 120–21.

24. Buber, *The Tales of Rabbi Nachman*, pp. 19–20.

25. Lukács to Martin Buber, 20 December 1911, LAK.

26. Lukács, "Zsidó miszticizmus," p. 256.

27. Balázs, *Diaries*, MTAK:K,

MS 5023/18, p. 54, July/August 1912.

28. Cohen, *Religion of Reason*, p. 33.

29. Lukács, *Ifjúkori művek*, p. 786.

30. Erzsébet Vezér, "Lesznai Anna költői világa," in Gergely, *Lesznai-Képeskönyv*, p. 84.

31. Karádi and Vezér, *A Vasárnapi Kör*, pp. 102–3.

32. Lukács, *Ifjúkori művek*, pp. 712, 716–17.

33. Ibid., pp. 719–20.

34. Ferenc Fehér, "Balázs Béla meséi és misztériumai" in Balázs, *Az álmok köntöse*, p. 13.

35. I have followed here the Hungarian translation by Ágnes Erdélyi in Lukács, *Ifjúkori művek*, pp. 519–23.

36. I have followed here the Hungarian translation by Ágnes Erdélyi in ibid., pp. 784–806.

37. Kutzbach, *Paul Ernst und Georg Lukács*, p. 22.

38. Ibid., pp. 56–57.

39. Mária Lukács to György Lukács, 28 October 1912, LAK; Fekete, "Balázs Béla naplójegyzeteiből," p. 83.

40. On Ritoók and on Bloch's eroticism, see Bloch to Lukács, 22 February 1911, LAK. Of her break with Bloch, Ritoók told Lukács: "In the end, one can neither love nor befriend a philosophic system, no matter how beautiful and great it may be." Emma Ritoók to Lukács, 1913, LAK.

41. Emma Ritoók to Lukács, 23 June 1912, 17 January 1913, and 6 August 1912, LAK.

42. Ernst Bloch to Lukács, 6 September 1911, LAK.

43. Lukács, *Magyar irodalom*, p. 13. And yet by 1914, Emma Ritoók could write: "The other day a complete stranger (a gymnasium teacher) expressed enthusiasm for your writings and said that you have a great influence on young people; at the university there is a veritable Lukács Circle, the members of which are outspokenly your followers." Ritoók to Lukács, 22 April 1914, LAK.

44. Gábor, "Alexander Bernát levelei Lukács Györgyhöz," p. 234.

45. József Lukács to György Lukács, 4 May 1911, LAK.

46. Gábor, "Alexander Bernát levelei Lukács Györgyhöz," pp. 242–45.

47. Testimony of Samu Szemere, then a professor of philosophy. Cited by Gábor in ibid., pp. 242n., 251n.

48. Ibid., p. 251.

49. Zalai, "Levelei kortársaihoz," p. 9. In a letter to Ottó Beöthy (8 February 1975), Bloch denied that he had any intention of applying for a position as *Privatdozent*.

50. Conversation with Professor Samu Szemere in Budapest, 1978.

51. József Lukács to György Lukács, 24 July and 1 August 1912, LAK.

52. Franz Baumgarten to Lukács, 15 April 1912, LAK.

53. Ibid., 8 July 1912, LAK.

54. Honigsheim, *On Max Weber*, p. 28.

55. Weber, *Max Weber*, p. 466.

56. Marianne Weber to Lukács, 31 July 1912, LAK.

57. Ibid., 22 July 1912, LAK.

58. Ernst Troeltsch to Lukács, 31 July 1912; Alfred Weber to Lukács, 8 November 1912, LAK.

59. Honigsheim, *On Max Weber*, p. 19; Weber, *Max Weber*, p. 529.

60. Emil Lask to Lukács, 11 June 1912, LAK.

61. Lukács, "Emil Lask," pp. 349–50.

62. Rosshoff, *Emil Lask als Lehrer von Georg Lukács*, p. 102.

63. Gerth and Mills, *From Max Weber*, p. 155.

64. Ibid., p. 342.

65. Honigsheim, *On Max Weber*, p. 109.

66. Eduard Baumgarten, cited in Mitzman, *The Iron Cage*, p. 218.

67. Weber, *The Protestant Ethic*, p. 115.

68. Ibid., pp. 169, 172, 180.

69. Ibid., p. 180.

70. "That was what drew him [Weber] to Lukács—the common admiration for Tolstoi and Dostoevski." Löwy, "Interview with Ernst Bloch," p. 45.

71. Weber, *Max Weber*, p. 327; Honigsheim, *On Max Weber*, p. 81.

72. Gerth and Mills, *From Max Weber*, pp. 120–26.

73. Lukács, "Curriculum vitae," p. 6.

74. Löwy, "Interview with Ernst Bloch," p. 43.

75. Balázs, Diaries, MTAK:K, MS 5023/18, p. 23, 28 February 1912. For an account of some of Ljena Grabenko's better-known comrades, see Knight, "Female Terrorists in the Russian Socialist Revolutionary Party," pp. 139–59.

76. Hilda Bauer to Lukács, 4 July 1912, LAK.

77. Balázs, Diaries, MTAK:K, MS 5023/18, p. 54, July 1913.

78. Lukács Popper, "Emlékek Lukács Györgyről," p. 1565.

79. Balázs, Diaries, MTAK:K, MS 5023/18, p. 55, July 1913.

80. Ljena Grabenko to Lukács, 12–14 October 1913, LAK. These letters were written in French because Lukács did not then know Russian.

81. Ljena Grabenko to Lukács, 27 October 1913, LAK.

82. Marianne Weber to Lukács, 15 November 1913, LAK.

83. József Lukács to György Lukács, 15 December 1913, LAK; Mária Lukács to György Lukács, 17 December 1913, LAK.

84. József Lukács to György Lukács, 22 December 1913, 11 April 1914 and 7 June 1914, LAK.

85. Mária Lukács to György Lukács, summer 1914, LAK.

86. József Lukács to György Lukács, 1 June 1911, LAK.

87. Ibid., 7 June 1914, LAK.

88. Löwy, "Interview with Ernst Bloch," pp. 43–44.

89. Lukács, *Ifjúkori művek*, p. 685. In a letter of 4 May 1915, Lukács wrote to

Ernst: "The problem lies in finding the road that leads from soul to soul, and everything else is *only an instrument*, only ancillary." Kutzbach, *Paul Ernst und Georg Lukács*, p. 73.

90. Cited in György Márkus, "Nachwort," in Lukács, *Heidelberger Ästhetik*, p. 255.

91. Weber, *Max Weber*, p. 465.

92. Gerth and Mills, *From Max Weber*, p. 154.

93. For the details of their labor of love, see Márkus, "Nachwort," in Lukács, *Heidelberger Ästhetik*, pp. 255–78.

94. Lukács, *Heidelberger Philosophie der Kunst*, p. 9.

95. Ibid., p. 15.

96. Ibid., p. 31.

97. Ibid., p. 56.

98. Ibid., p. 40.

99. Ibid., p. 37.

100. Georg Lukács, "Das Formproblem der Malerei," in *Heidelberger Ästhetik*, p. 233. This lecture, previously unpublished, dates to late 1913 or early 1914; it stands in close relationship to the *Philosophy of Art*.

101. Weber, *Max Weber*, p. 466.

CHAPTER 4

1. Stromberg, "The Intellectuals and the Coming of War in 1914," pp. 109–22.

2. Lukács, "Die deutschen Intellektuellen und der Krieg," pp. 65–69.

3. Weber, *Max Weber*, pp. 518–19.

4. Balogh, "The Turning of the World," p. 190.

5. Balázs, "Paris-e vagy Weimar?," pp. 200–203.

6. Balázs, *A vándor énekel*, p. 313.

7. Balázs, Diaries, MTAK:K, MS 5023/19, pp. 6–7, 9 April 1915.

8. Balázs, *A vándor énekel*, p. 312.

9. Lukács, *Die Theorie des Romans*, p. 5.

10. Béla Fogarasi to Lukács, 17 March 1915, LAK. In a letter to Lukács dated

20 March 1915, Emma Ritoók wrote: "Perhaps you were closer to him [Zalai] than all of us thought," LAK.

11. Kutzbach, *Paul Ernst und Georg Lukács*, p. 64.

12. Lukács, "Th. G. Masaryk: Zur russischen Geschichts-und Religionsphilosophie," pp. 871–75.

13. Kutzbach, *Paul Ernst und Georg Lukács*, p. 82.

14. Lukács, *Die Theorie des Romans*, p. 6.

15. Ibid., p. 66.

16. Ibid., p. 42.

17. Ibid., p. 53.

18. Ibid., p. 108.

19. Ibid., p. 154.

20. Lukács, Dosztojevszki Könyvvázlata és Jegyzetek (hereafter cited as DKJ), n. 76, LAK. Lukács referred here to Ernst Troeltsch's work. The idea that the state was as much the "anti-Christ" as the church (autocracy and orthodoxy) is also to be found in the fantastic speculations of Dmitri Merezhkovski. See Scherrer, *Die Petersburger Religiös-Philosophischen Vereinigungen*, pp. 168–74.

21. Lukács, *Ifjúkori művek*, p. 645.

22. Fehér, "Am Scheideweg," pp. 290–91.

23. Lukács, DKJ, n. 66, LAK.

24. Ljena Grabenko to Lukács, 25 June 1914, LAK. The letter was postmarked in Odessa, where she was visiting relatives and friends.

25. Lukács, *Ifjúkori művek*, p. 685.

26. Ibid., p. 651.

27. Lukács, DKJ, n. 39, LAK. According to Lukács, the basic question of Western atheism—represented by Hebbel, Ibsen, and Paul Ernst—was *"How can one die without God?"*

28. Ibid., n. 10, LAK.

29. Ibid.

30. Ibid.

31. Azev's treachery was unmasked in 1908 by the Socialist Revolutionary leader Vladimir Burtsev; he escaped retribution, however, and after extensive travel settled

in Berlin under an assumed name. Recognized in 1915 by the German police, he was arrested as an "anarchist" and imprisoned until 1917; he died in the following year.

32. Savinkov, *Memoirs*, p. 47.

33. Ibid., p. 38.

34. Ibid., p. 99.

35. Ropshin [Boris Savinkov], *The Pale Horse*, p. 5.

36. When Vania refuses to attack the governor's house, George asks for an explanation. Vania replies: "I can't . . . because of the children." Ibid., p. 124.

37. The words are those of W. H. Auden from "Spain" (1937). Subsequently, Auden changed the line to read: "The conscious acceptance of guilt in the fact of murder." See McCabe, " 'Necessary Murder,' " pp. 51-57.

38. Ropshin, *The Pale Horse*, pp. 10-11.

39. Kutzbach, *Paul Ernst und Georg Lukács*, p. 65.

40. Ibid., p. 74.

41. Lukács, DKJ, n. 129, LAK. In n. 143, we read: "Germany and Russia . . . (1) India: Identity with Atman; negligible individuality. (2) Germany: the individual soul—in relation to God. (3) Russia: the individual soul—in community with other souls, as willed and created by God," LAK.

42. Ibid., n. 31, LAK.

43. Cited in Fehér, "Am Scheideweg," p. 324n.

44. Lukács, *Esztétikai kultura*, p. 20.

45. Lukács, *Magyar irodalom*, pp. 46-47.

46. Dostoyevsky, *The Brothers Karamazov*, 1:26-27.

47. Lukács, *Ifjúkori művek*, pp. 651, 764.

48. Dostoyevsky, *The Brothers Karamazov*, 1:32.

49. Ibid., pp. 350, 356-57.

50. Ibid., 2:596.

51. Ibid., p. 694.

52. Lukács, DKJ, n. 12, LAK.

53. Dostoyevsky, *The Idiot*, p. 87.

54. "For him [Lukács], this woman [Ljena] was a Sonia, or another character from Dostoyevsky, a personification of the 'Russian soul.' " Löwy, "Interview with Ernst Bloch," p. 44.

55. Lukács, "Stawrogins Beichte," n.p.

56. Lukács, DKJ, n. 115, LAK.

57. Cohn, *The Pursuit of the Millennium*, p. 35.

58. Hegyi, "Lukács György nézetei," p. 402.

59. Lukács, DKJ, n. 143, LAK.

60. Fichte, *Werke*, 7:12.

61. Cited in Kelly, *Idealism, Politics and History*, p. 239.

62. Sinkó, *Optimisták*, 1:303.

63. Ady, *Összes versei*, p. 7. Cf. Revelation 20:8. Gog and Magog were also the legendary forebears of the Magyars.

64. Ibid., p. 746.

65. Ibid., pp. 749-50.

66. Kutzbach, *Paul Ernst und Georg Lukács*, p. 95.

67. Bloch, *Geist der Utopie*, pp. 420-21, 426, 428-29. This is a facsimile of the first (1918) edition.

68. Ibid., p. 406.

69. Ibid., pp. 231, 407.

70. Ibid., pp. 407-8.

71. Ernst Bloch, *Geist der Utopie* (Frankfurt am Main: Suhrkamp Verlag, 1973), p. 306. This is a new printing of the second (1923) edition.

72. Bloch, *Geist der Utopie* (1918), p. 432.

73. Ibid., p. 347.

74. "You know . . . that from the very first I have regarded essential points of your Aesthetics with complete hostility." Ernst Bloch to Lukács, 24 August 1915, LAK.

75. Ibid., 6 November 1916, LAK.

76. Alfred Weber to Lukács, 20 December 1916; Ernst Troeltsch to Lukács, 10 January 1917, LAK.

77. Balázs, Diaries, MTAK:K, MS 5023/19, pp. 32-33, 27 August 1915.

78. Karádi, "Dokumentumok Lukács György heidelbergi korszakából," pp. 33-34.

79. For the details of the editorial reconstruction, see Márkus's "Nachwort" to Lukács's *Heidelberger Ästhetik*, pp. 255-78.

80. Chapter II: "Phenomenology of the Creative and Receptive Attitudes."

81. Lukács, "Curriculum vitae," p. 6.

82. Karádi and Vezér, *A Vasárnapi Kör*, pp. 73-74.

83. Lukács, "Emil Lask," p. 350.

84. Ibid., p. 358.

85. Once again, I think that the limitations imposed on Lukács by academic form constituted the principal reason for his failure to complete the work. There is, significantly enough, not a single reference to Dostoevski in the *Aesthetics*. Yet in several Hungarian-language occasional pieces from these years, the Russian writer's name is omnipresent.

86. Maerker, *Die Ästhetik der Südwestdeutschen Schule*, p. 22.

87. "From the last few years," he wrote in reply to a query in 1918, "I can report on the great influence of only one book: the decisive impact of reading afresh the *Critique of Judgment*." *Ifjúkori művek*, p. 767.

88. Lukács, "Die Subjekt-Objekt-Beziehung in der Aesthetik," p. 8n.

89. Lukács, *Heidelberger Ästhetik*, p. 12.

90. Ibid., pp. 36, 64.

91. Ibid., pp. 53, 79.

92. Ibid., pp. 71-73.

93. Ibid., pp. 71, 73, 76-77.

94. Lukács, "Die Subjekt-Objekt-Beziehung in der Aesthetik," p. 33.

95. Ibid., p. 19.

96. Ibid., pp. 23, 35, 39.

97. Márkus, "Nachwort," in Lukács, *Heidelberger Ästhetik*, pp. 271, 267.

98. Balázs, Diaries, MTAK:K, MS 5023/19, p. 104, 28 May 1917.

99. Kutzbach, *Paul Ernst und Georg Lukács*, p. 122.

100. Ljena Grabenko to Karl Jaspers, 6 May 1915, LAK.

101. Lukács to Karl Jaspers, 3 May 1916, LAK.

102. Cited in Fekete, "Lukács György az első világháború éveiben," p. 40.

103. Balázs, Diaries, MTAK:K, MS 5023/19, p. 104, 28 May 1917.

CHAPTER 5

1. Kutzbach, *Paul Ernst und Georg Lukács*, pp. 81-82.

2. Karádi and Vezér, *A Vasárnapi Kör*, p. 72.

3. Ibid., p. 8. Spitz (1887-1974) became a well-known psychoanalyst; Wilde (1891-1971) an art historian; and Révész (1878-1955) a psychologist.

4. *Irodalmi Muzeum: Emlékezések*, p. 12.

5. Interview with Arnold Hauser in London, 28 August 1971.

6. Karádi and Vezér, *A Vasárnapi Kör*, pp. 133-34.

7. Anna Schlamadinger to Lukács, 8 March 1917, LAK.

8. Karádi and Vezér, *A Vasárnapi Kör*, plate between pp. 240 and 241.

9. Anna Schlamadinger to Lukács, 8 March 1917, LAK.

10. Karádi and Vezér, *A Vasárnapi Kör*, p. 141.

11. Cited in Novák, *A Vasárnap Társaság*, pp. 110-11.

12. Éva Gábor, "Adalékok a fiatal Mannheim Károly portréjához," in Nyíri and Kiss, *A magyar filozófiai gondolkodás*, p. 448.

13. Cited in ibid., p. 450n.

14. See his "Letters to Lukács," pp. 93-105.

15. Mannheim, "Georg Simmel, mint filozófus," p. 196.

16. Mannheim, "E. Bloch: *Geist der Utopie*," pp. 207-11.

17. See Timár, "Hauser Arnold pályakezdése," pp. 191-204.

18. Anna Schlamadinger to Lukács, 8 March 1917, LAK.

19. Hauser, "Az esztétikai rendszerezés problémája," pp. 331–57.

20. See Fülep, *Művészet és világnézet*, pp. 260–309.

21. Cited in Novák, *A Vasárnap Társaság*, p. 117.

22. Ritoók, "A rút a művészetben," pp. 177–205.

23. Karádi and Vezér, *A Vasárnapi Kör*, p. 139.

24. The students included Charles de Tolnay, János Radványi (sociologist and later the husband of the German Communist writer Anna Seghers), and Tibor Gergely (later the husband of Anna Lesznai and a well-known illustrator).

25. Karádi and Vezér, *A Vasárnapi Kör*, pp. 83, 85.

26. Mannheim, *Lélek és kultura*, pp. 10–11.

27. Ibid., p. 7.

28. Ibid., p. 10.

29. Eckhart, "Mary and Martha" in *Works*, 2:94–95.

30. Here Mannheim allowed that there was some kind of relationship, still problematic, between cultural and social forms. Though he credited Marx with this discovery, he hastened to add that he and his colleagues rejected the "*Überbau*" theory. *Lélek és kultura*, p. 24.

31. Ibid., p. 19.

32. Ibid., p. 20.

33. See Wessely, "Antal and Lukács," pp. 114–25.

34. Balázs, *Válogatott cikkek*, p. 139.

35. Oszkár Jászi, "Szabó Ervin és életmunkája," in Szabó, *Társadalmi és pártharcok*, p. 23.

36. Tolnai, *Ferenczy Noémi*, p. 10.

37. Lukács, *Ifjúkori művek*, pp. 695–709.

38. Dostoyevsky, *The Brothers Karamazov*, 1:26.

39. Lukács, *Ifjúkori művek*, pp. 643–56; 678–94.

40. Jászi, "Mannheim Károly: *Lélek és kultura*," p. 192.

41. Karádi and Vezér, *A Vasárnapi Kör*, p. 91.

42. Fogarasi, "Konzervativ és progressziv idealizmus," pp. 193–206.

43. Balázs, *Válogatott cikkek*, p. 91.

44. Lukács, *Ifjúkori művek*, pp. 837–44.

45. Heller, "Kant etikái," in *Portrévázlatok*, pp. 212–88. So completely has Heller mastered the young Lukács's work that her prose *reads* as if it were his.

46. Kant, *Werke*, 6:387.

47. These duties/ends are one's own perfection and the happiness of others. Ibid., p. 385.

48. Lukács, *Magyar irodalom*, p. 9.

49. Löwy, "Interview with Ernst Bloch," p. 40.

50. Gál, "Balázs Béla naplója," *Kritika*, no. 11 (1975): 20.

51. "Ady forradalmi hatása," p. 6. Szabó was also Irma Seidler's cousin.

52. Balázs, Diaries, MTAK:K, MS 5023/20, p. 17, 15 July 1918.

53. For Jászi's text with Babits's corrections, see Gál, "Babits békeírásaiból," pp. 529–30.

54. For Babits's text, see ibid., pp. 530–32.

55. Lukács to the editor in Remete, *Szabó Ervin*, pp. 327–28.

56. Sorel, *The Illusions of Progress*, p. xlii.

57. Lukács, DKJ, n. 56, LAK.

58. Sorel, *Reflections on Violence*, p. 39.

59. Ibid., p. 33. I have altered the translation.

60. Sorel, "The Decomposition of Marxism," in Horowitz, *Radicalism and the Revolt against Reason*, p. 251.

61. Sorel, *Reflections on Violence*, p. 50.

62. Ibid., p. 279. From Sorel's "In Defense of Lenin" ("*Pour Lénine*").

63. Ritoók, *A szellem kalandorai*, 2:168. This book describes the radicalization of Lukács and Bloch. Though marred by anti-Semitism, it is not simply a tirade. Lukács always refused to recognize him-

self in Donáth, whom he described as a cross between Bloch and Zalai.

64. Löwy, "Interview with Ernst Bloch," p. 44.

65. Kutzbach, *Paul Ernst und Georg Lukács*, pp. 128-29.

66. See Lukács, "Lenin—Theoretician of Practice," p. 36.

67. Georg Lukács, "Autobiographie" (1941), cited in Löwy, *Pour une sociologie des intellectuels révolutionnaires*, pp. 163-64.

68. Lukács, "A köztársasági propaganda," p. 17.

69. "Olvasóinkhoz!," *Szabadgondolat* 8, no. 10 (1918), p. 224.

70. Jászi, "Proletárdiktatúra," pp. 225-26.

71. Dostoevski has Razumikhin say: "People who tell lies can always be forgiven. There's nothing wrong about a lie, for it leads to the truth." *Crime and Punishment*, p. 153.

72. Lukács, "A bolsevizmus mint erkölcsi problema," pp. 228-32.

73. Cited in Kettler, "Culture and Revolution," p. 69.

74. Kassák, *Egy ember élete*, 4:216.

75. Hebbel, "Judith," in *Werke*, 1:141-210. The play was inspired by the Book of Judith in the Old Testament Apocrypha. The tragedy centers around Judith's terrible deed: the murder of Holofernes, Nebuchadnezzar's commander-in-chief. In this way, she saved her people, the Israelites.

76. Lukács, *A modern dráma*, 1:360-61. Hebbel's Judith is a virgin who sacrifices her physical and moral purity by first submitting to Holofernes and then assassinating him. Her words to God made a deep and lasting impression on Lukács: "Der Weg zu meiner Tat geht durch die Sünde! Dank, Dank dir, Herr! Du machst mein Auge hell. Vor dir wird das Unreine rein; wenn du zwischen mich und meine Tat eine Sünde stellst: wer bin ich, dass ich mit dir darüber hadern, dass ich mich dir entziehen sollte!" Hebbel, *Werke*, 1:160.

77. Lukács, *A modern dráma*, 1:391.

78. Lukács, *Utam Marxhoz*, 1:187-97.

79. Savinkov on Dora Brilliant: "Terror for her, as for Kaliayev, was something which acquires the color of justification only with the sacrifice of the terrorist himself." On Yegor Sazonov: "For him, too, terror was, above all, a matter of personal sacrifice, of heroic deed." *Memoirs*, pp. 42-43.

80. One of the characters in Emma Ritoók's *The Adventurers of the Spirit* (probably modeled after Balázs) says: "The true revolutionary is confronted with sin just as is the tragic hero and he accepts sin together with every one of its consequences. This is his greatness—and our greatness—because the greatest sacrifice is not made by the hero who dies for his ideas, but by the one who is able consciously to sacrifice his soul's salvation for them, so that the future may live ethically." *A szellem kalandorai*, 2:175-76.

81. In 1919, Sinkó (1898-1967) was a member of the Central Workers' Council of Budapest. His book is made up in large part of conversations and debates between revolutionary intellectuals.

82. Sinkó, *Optimisták*, 1:313-14.

83. Georg Lukács, "Autobiographie" (1941), cited in Löwy, *Pour une sociologie des intellectuels révolutionnaires*, p. 164. I follow here the English translation of Vladimir Lenin, "State and Revolution," in Mendel, *Essential Works of Marxism*, pp. 101-98.

84. Lesznai, *Kezdetben volt a kert*, 2:472.

85. Fekete, "Lukács György az első világháború éveiben," pp. 42-43. Like Kun, Seidler had been a prisoner of war in Russia and a founding member of the Hungarian Communist party.

86. Sinkó, *Optimisták*, 2:290-91.

87. Ibid., p. 293.

88. Percy, *Lancelot*, p. 157.

CHAPTER 6

1. Lukács, "Gelebtes Denken," p. 27, LAK.

2. Savinkov served as governor-general of Petrograd under Kerensky and committed suicide or was murdered in a Soviet prison in 1925.

3. Gertrúd Bortstieber to Lukács, 7 September 1906, LAK.

4. Mészáros, *Lukács' Concept of Dialectic*, pp. 130-31.

5. Lukács, "Gelebtes Denken," pp. 28-31, LAK.

6. Lukács, *Ästhetik*, 1:5.

7. See Kolakowski, *Main Currents*, 1:9-80.

8. See Lukács, "Die neue Ausgabe von Lassalles Briefen," p. 405; "Moses Hess," pp. 113, 116-17.

9. Abrams, *Natural Supernaturalism*, p. 255.

10. Fehér et al., "Notes on Lukács' Ontology," p. 160.

11. Lengyel, *Visegrádi utca*, pp. 138-39, 245-50.

12. Lukács, *Utam Marxhoz*, 1:198-206.

13. Polányi, *A radikalizmus programmja és célja*, p. 11.

14. Lukács, *Utam Marxhoz*, 1:207-17.

15. Cited in Gábor Vermes, "The October Revolution in Hungary: From Károlyi to Kun" in Völgyes, *Hungary in Revolution*, p. 50.

16. Szamuely (1890-1919) became a Communist while a prisoner in Russia.

17. József, *Mindenki*, 4:973-76.

18. Pastor, *Hungary between Wilson and Lenin*, p. 119.

19. Pastor, "The Vix Mission in Hungary," p. 493.

20. Jászi, *Revolution and Counter-Revolution*, p. 92.

21. Károlyi, *Memoirs*, p. 155. Whether or not Károlyi signed the resignation is, however, still a matter of controversy. See for example Siklós, "Károlyi Mihály lemondása," p. 2.

22. Sándor Garbai, cited in Pastor, *Hungary between Wilson and Lenin*, p. 142.

23. For the text of "The Documents of Unity," see Tőkés, *Béla Kun*, p. 247.

24. József, *Mindenki*, 4:223-29. In addition to this essay, *Tactics and Ethics* included the title essay, "The Question of Intellectual Leadership and the 'Intellectual Workers,'" and "What Is Orthodox Marxism?"

25. Peter Gay, *Weimar Culture: The Outsider as Insider* (New York: Harper & Row, 1968), p. xiv.

26. Lukács, *Magyar irodalom*, p. 645.

27. József, *Mindenki*, 4:930-31. Kunfi *may* have issued this directive, but from the first, Lukács made all the plans and decisions.

28. Ibid., pp. 709, 726, 720, 722, 206-7, 967.

29. Ibid., pp. 930-31.

30. Ibid., pp. 750, 1094. Szekfű was one of the greatest Hungarian historians of the twentieth century.

31. Ibid., pp. 336-37. Pólya later became a mathematician of world renown.

32. Ibid., pp. 84, 771. Révész (1876-1944) was a socialist writer who had championed Ady's poetry. Komját (1891-1937) was a Communist poet.

33. Ibid., pp. 705, 761. Reinitz (1878-1943) was a composer and critic; he set some of Ady's verses to music. Gábor (1884-1953) was a satirist/journalist turned Communist. With the exception of Bartók and Kodály, Dohnányi is perhaps the best-known Hungarian composer of the twentieth century.

34. Jászi, *Revolution and Counter-Revolution*, p. 146.

35. József, *Mindenki*, 4:206.

36. Ibid., pp. 913-14.

37. Ibid., pp. 101-3, 971.

38. Ibid., p. 934.

39. Ibid., pp. 219-20.

40. Ibid., p. 187.

41. Ibid., pp. 339-41.

42. Trócsányi was a writer, translator,

and university professor. See ibid., p. 573.

43. Lukács, *Magyar irodalom*, pp. 646, 648.

44. Demény, *Bartók Béla*, pp. 90–92.

45. József, *Mindenki*, 4:955–56. Kéri (1882–1960) was a Socialist journalist.

46. Ibid., pp. 170–71.

47. Ibid., pp. 171–74.

48. Ibid., pp. 186–88. Initially hostile to Lukács's ideas, Révai was soon won over completely. On his sympathy for Lukács during the period of the Soviet Republic, see Lengyel, "A fiatal Révai 'etikus' nézeteiről," pp. 283–311.

49. József, *Mindenki*, 4:196–98.

50. Kun was not so restrained. In remarks to party leaders he characterized the literature in *Ma* as "the product of bourgeois decadence." Ibid., p. 463.

51. Renato Poggioli, *The Theory of the Avant-Garde*, trans. Gerald Fitzgerald (New York: Harper & Row, 1971), p. 100.

52. József, *Mindenki*, 4:473–74.

53. Consider the final two paragraphs of an essay that Lukács wrote in the Soviet Union in 1943. "The golden age: genuine and harmonious relations between genuine and harmonious men. Dostoevsky's characters know that this is a dream in the present age but they cannot and will not abandon the dream. They cannot abandon the dream even when most of their feelings sharply contradict it. This dream is the truly genuine core, the real gold of Dostoevsky's Utopias; a state of the world in which men may know and love each other, in which culture and civilization will not be an obstacle to the development of men. The spontaneous, wild, and blind revolt of Dostoevsky's characters occurs in the name of the golden age, whatever the contents of the mental experiment may be. This revolt is poetically great and historically progressive in Dostoevsky: here really shines a light in the darkness of Petersburg misery, a light that illuminates the road to the future of mankind." "Dostoevsky," in Wellek, *Dostoevsky: A Collection of Critical Essays*, p. 158.

54. Frank Eckelt, "The Internal Policies of the Hungarian Soviet Republic," in Völgyes, *Hungary in Revolution*, p. 75.

55. Cited in Jászi, *Revolution and Counter-Revolution*, pp. 138–39.

56. József, *Mindenki*, 4:635–39.

57. Tőkés, *Béla Kun*, p. 196; Eckelt, "The Internal Policies," p. 76.

58. Alfred D. Low, "Soviet Hungary and the Paris Peace Conference," in Völgyes, *Hungary in Revolution*, pp. 140–41. I have relied on this article for many details.

59. József, *Mindenki*, 4:217–19.

60. Lengyel, *Prenn Ferenc*, pp. 206–8.

61. Ibid., pp. 217–18, 222.

62. Borus, *A század nagy tanúi*, pp. 187–91.

63. Ibid., p. 189.

64. Cited in Low, "Soviet Hungary and the Paris Peace Conference," p. 149.

65. Zsuzsa L. Nagy, "Problems of Foreign Policy before the Revolutionary Governing Council," in Völgyes, *Hungary in Revolution*, p. 134.

66. Cited in Low, "Soviet Hungary and the Paris Peace Conference," p. 149.

67. Nagy, "Problems of Foreign Policy," p. 135.

68. Borus, *A század nagy tanúi*, pp. 191–94.

69. Karádi and Vezér, *A Vasárnapi Kör*, p. 65.

70. Borus, *A század nagy tanúi*, p. 194.

71. András Simor, "Korvin Ottó," in Simor, *Korvin Ottó*, p. 5. For the details of Korvin's life, I have relied upon Simor's biographical essay.

72. Ferenc Stein, "A nép nevében," in Hollósi, *Nagy idők tanúi emlékeznek*, pp. 135–36. Stein was Korvin's deputy.

73. Tőkés, *Béla Kun*, p. 159n.

74. Cited in Simor, "Korvin Ottó," pp. 55–56.

75. Borus, *A század nagy tanúi*, pp. 194–95.

76. Jászi, *Revolution and Counter-Revolution*, p. 121.

77. Cited in Serge, *Memoirs*,

pp. 187–88.

78. Lukács, *Történelem és osztálytudat*, pp. 64–68.

CHAPTER 7

1. Borsányi, "Az emigráció első éve," pp. 36–37.
2. Bourdet, *Figures de Lukács*, pp. 44–45.
3. Kutzbach, *Paul Ernst und Georg Lukács*, pp. 154–56.
4. Bourdet, *Figures de Lukács*, p. 47.
5. Karádi and Vezér, *A Vasárnapi Kör*, p. 93. This description is in Balázs's diary.
6. Ibid., pp. 93–94.
7. Ibid., p. 93.
8. Kutzbach, *Paul Ernst und Georg Lukács*, p. 157.
9. Lukács, "Gelebtes Denken," p. 36, LAK. The third child to whom Lukács referred was Anna, his daughter by Gertrúd.
10. Mészáros, *Lukács' Concept of Dialectic*, p. 130. Yvon Bourdet claims that they were married twice: once when Lukács was negotiating for a professorship in Germany and a second time (the papers having been lost) when they decided to emigrate to the Soviet Union. *Figures de Lukács*, p. 57n.
11. A former Radical and member of the Károlyi government, Szende pioneered what is now known as *Ideologiekritik*.
12. Lengyel, *Bécsi portyák*, p. 135.
13. Gál, "Balázs Béla naplója," *Kritika*, no. 11 (1975): 22. Perhaps the most celebrated of all Hungarian national poets, Petőfi was of Slovak descent.
14. Németh, *A szélén behajtva*, p. 598.
15. Szende, "Die Krise der mitteleuropäischen Revolution," pp. 365, 367.
16. Jászi, *Revolution and Counter-Revolution*, p. 153.
17. Serge, *Memoirs*, p. 187.
18. Borsányi, "Az emigráció első éve," p. 38.
19. Lukács, *Utam Marxhoz*, 1:20–21.

20. Lukács, *Taktik und Ethik*, p. 220.
21. Lukács, *Revolution und Gegenrevolution*, p. 243.
22. Lukács, *Taktik und Ethik*, pp. 175–87.
23. Cited in Rodney Livingstone, "Introduction," in Lukács, *Tactics and Ethics*, pp. xvi–xvii.
24. Tucker, *The Lenin Anthology*, p. 582.
25. Ibid., pp. 591, 616.
26. Kovács, "Beszélgetés Leninről," p. 11.
27. Lukács, *Taktik und Ethik*, pp. 222–23, 189.
28. Lukács, *Tactics and Ethics*, p. 120.
29. Lukács, *Taktik und Ethik*, p. 223.
30. Lukács, *Revolution und Gegenrevolution*, p. 49.
31. Lukács, *Taktik und Ethik*, p. 226.
32. Ibid., p. 225.
33. Lukács, *Revolution und Gegenrevolution*, pp. 24–25.
34. Karádi and Vezér, *A Vasárnapi Kör*, p. 96.
35. Ibid., p. 97.
36. Ibid., pp. 99–100.
37. Ibid., p. 99. Compare what Lukács told Ilona Duczynska in 1921: "Communist ethics make it the highest duty to accept the necessity of acting wickedly. This, he said, was the greatest sacrifice revolution asked from us. The conviction of the true communist is that evil transforms itself into bliss through the dialectics of historical evolution." Cited in Borkenau, *World Communism*, pp. 172–73.
38. Tucker, *The Lenin Anthology*, p. 677.
39. Nagy, *Balázs Béla világa*, p. 274.
40. Lukács, *A modern dráma*, 1:58.
41. Ibid., p. 59.
42. Lukács, *Organisation und Illusion*, pp. 114–17.
43. Ibid., pp. 167–70.
44. Ibid., pp. 144–47.
45. Ibid., pp. 148–51.
46. Ibid., pp. 152–57.
47. On what follows, see ibid., pp. 171–74.

48. Lukács, *Geschichte und Klassen-*
bewusstsein, p. 30.
49. Ibid., p. 23.
50. Ibid., p. 56.
51. Ibid., pp. 58–93.
52. Ibid., pp. 356–400.
53. Ibid., pp. 119–69.
54. Ibid., pp. 94–118.
55. Ibid., pp. 452–513.
56. Ibid., pp. 170–355.
57. Ibid., p. 27.
58. Kolakowski, *Main Currents*, 3:298.

CONCLUSION

1. Tar, "Thomas Mann und Georg
Lukács," p. 76.
2. Mann, *Unwritten Memories*, p. 73.
3. Cited in Tar, "Thomas Mann und
Georg Lukács," p. 78.
4. Mann, *The Magic Mountain*, p. 441.
5. Bourdet, *Figures de Lukács*,
pp. 108–10.
6. Mann, *The Magic Mountain*, p. 404.

...iai Közlöny [General philological bulletin] (1909): 41–55, 132–39.
...tes from a Diary, 1911–1921." New Hungarian Quarterly 13, no. 47
123–28.
...ris-e vagy Weimar?" [Paris or Weimar?]. Nyugat [West] 7 (1914): 200–203.
...ogatott cikkek és tanulmányok [Selected articles and studies]. Edited by
K. Nagy. Budapest: Kossuth Könyvkiadó, 1968.
..., Franz. "Georg von Lukács: Die Seele und die Formen." Logos 3
...13): 249.
...Marcell. Naplómat olvasom [Reading my diary]. Budapest: Szépirodalmi
...kiadó, 1965.
...st. Geist der Utopie. Frankfurt am Main: Suhrkamp Verlag, 1971.
...sa, ed. A század nagy tanúi [Great witnesses of the century]. Budapest: RTV.
...va, 1978.
...rtin. Begegnung. Stuttgart: W. Kohlhammer Verlag, 1960.
...Hasidism and Modern Man. Translated by Maurice Friedman. New York: Harper
...ow, 1966.
...Paths in Utopia. Translated by R. F. C. Hull. Boston: Beacon Press, 1958.
...The Tales of Rabbi Nachman. Translated by Maurice Friedman. New York:
...zon Press, 1956.
...Hermann. Religion of Reason out of the Sources of Judaism. Translated by Simon
...lan. New York: Frederick Ungar, 1972.
..., János, ed. Bartók Béla. Budapest: Magyar Művészeti Tanács, 1948.
...vsky, Fyodor. The Brothers Karamazov. 2 vols. Translated by David Magarshack.
...timore: Penguin Books, 1958.
... Crime and Punishment. Translated by David Magarshack. Baltimore: Penguin
...oks, 1951.
... The Idiot. Translated by Henry and Olga Carlisle. New York: New American
...ibrary, 1969.
... The Notebooks for "The Brothers Karamazov." Edited and translated by Edward
...Wasiolek. Chicago: University of Chicago Press, 1971.
... The Possessed. Translated by Andrew R. MacAndrew. New York: New Ameri-
...an Library, 1962.
...rt, Meister. Works. Vol. 2. Translated by C. de B. Evans. London: John M.
...Watkins, 1952.
..., Paul. Der Weg zur Form. Berlin: Verlag Julius Bard, 1906.
...te, Éva, ed. "Balázs Béla naplójegyzeteiből, 1911–1920" [From Béla Balázs's diary
...notes]. Valóság [Reality] 16, no. 2 (1973): 82–89.
... "Levelek Lukács Györgyhöz" [Letters to György Lukács]. Irodalomtörténet
...[Literary history] 6, no. 3 (1974): 602–17.
... "Lukács György és Popper Leó levélváltásából, 1909–1911" [From the corre-
...spondence of György Lukács and Leó Popper]. Valóság [Reality] 17, no. 9 (1974)
...16–37.
..., and Karádi, Éva, eds. Lukács György élete képekben és dokumentumokban [L
...of György Lukács in pictures and documents]. Budapest: Corvina Kiadó, 1980
...nyő, Miksa. Följegyzések a 'Nyugat' folyóiratról és környékéről [Notes on the jo
...Nyugat and its world]. N.p.: Pátria Könyvkiadó Kiadása, 1960.
...chte, Johann G. Werke. Vol. 7. Berlin: Walter de Gruyter & Co., 1971.
...garasi, Béla. "Az ítélet voluntaristikus elmélete" [The voluntaristic theory o
...judgment]. Athenaeum 22, no. 1 (1913): 58–100; 22, no. 2 (1913): 32–

MANUSCRIPT SOURCES

Babits, Mihály. Papers. Országos Széchenyi Könyvtára: Kézirattár. Budapest, Hungary.
Balázs, Béla. Diaries. Magyar Tudományos Akadémia Könyvtára: Kézirattár. Budapest, Hungary.
Hauser, Arnold. Conversation. London, 28 August 1971.
Lukács, György. Manuscripts, Correspondence, Diaries. Magyar Tudományos Akadémia Filozófiai Intézet Lukács Archívum és Könyvtár. Budapest, Hungary.
Szemere, Samu. Conversation. Budapest, Hungary, 1978.

GYÖRGY LUKÁCS'S WORKS

"A bolsevizmus mint erkölcsi problema" [Bolshevism as a moral problem]. Szabadgondolat [Free thought] 8, no. 10 (1918): 228–32.
A drámaírás főbb irányai a múlt század utolsó negyedében [The main directions of dramaturgy during the final quarter of the last century]. Edited by L. Ferenc Lendvai. Budapest: Akadémiai Kiadó, 1980.
"Ady forradalmi hatása: Filminterjú Lukács Györggyel" [The revolutionary influence of Ady: film interview with György Lukács]. Élet és Irodalom [Life and literature], 29 January 1977, p. 6.
"A konzervativ és progressziv idealizmus vitája" [The debate concerning conservative and progressive idealism]. Huszadik Század [Twentieth century] 19 (1918):378–82.
"A köztársasági propaganda" [Republican propaganda]. Világ [World], 10 November 1918, p. 17.
A modern dráma fejlődésének története [History of the evolution of the modern drama]. 2 vols. Budapest: Franklin-Társulat, 1911.
Ästhetik. Vol. 1. Neuwied: Hermann Luchterhand Verlag, 1963.
"Bartók Béla." Nagyvilág [Wide world] 15, no. 9 (1970): 1283–94.
"Beszélgetés Leninről és a forradalmiság mai tartalmáról" [Conversation on Lenin and the contemporary meaning of the revolutionary spirit]. Edited by András Kovács. Új Írás [New writing] 11, no. 8 (1971): 10–19.
"Brief." In Für Margarete Susman: Auf gespaltenem Pfad, edited by Manfred Schlösser, pp. 303–7. Darmstadt: Erato-Presse, 1964.
"Croce, Benedetto: Zur Theorie und Geschichte der Historiographie." Archiv für Sozialwissenschaft und Sozialpolitik 39 (1915): 878–85.
"Curriculum vitae." Text und Kritik 39/40 (1973): 5–7.
"Die deutschen Intellektuellen und der Krieg." Text und Kritik 39/40 (1973): 65–69.
"Die neue Ausgabe von Lassalles Briefen." Archiv für die Geschichte des Sozialismus und der Arbeiterbewegung 11 (1925): 401–23.
Die Seele und die Formen: Essays. Neuwied: Hermann Luchterhand Verlag, 1971.
"Die Subjekt-Objekt-Beziehung in der Aesthetik." Logos 7 (1917/18): 1–39.
Die Theorie des Romans: Ein geschichtsphilosophischer Versuch über die Formen der grossen Epik. Neuwied: Hermann Luchterhand Verlag, 1963.

"Dostoevsky." In *Dostoevsky: A Collection of Critical Essays*, edited by René Wellek, pp. 146–58. Englewood Cliffs, N.J.: Prentice-Hall, 1962.

"Egy ismeretlen Lukács György-levél" [An unknown letter of György Lukács's]. Edited by György Litván. *Kritika* [Criticism], no. 3 (1974): 16–17.

"Emil Lask: Ein Nachruf." *Kantstudien* 22 (1918): 349–70.

"Emlékezés Károlyi Mihályra" [Recollections of Mihály Károlyi]. *Új Írás* [New writing], 9, no. 8 (1969): 61–62.

Essays on Thomas Mann. Translated by Stanley Mitchell. New York: Grosset & Dunlap, 1965.

Esztétikai kultúra: Tanulmányok [Aesthetic culture: studies]. Budapest: Athenaeum Irodalmi és Nyomdai Részvényt Kiadása, 1913.

"Georg Simmel." *Pester Lloyd*, 2 October 1918, pp. 2–3.

Geschichte und Klassenbewusstsein: Studien über marxistische Dialektik. Neuwied: Hermann Luchterhand Verlag, 1970.

Heidelberger Ästhetik, 1916–1918. Edited by György Márkus and Frank Benseler. Neuwied: Hermann Luchterhand Verlag, 1974.

Heidelberger Philosophie der Kunst, 1912–1914. Edited by György Márkus and Frank Benseler. Neuwied: Hermann Luchterhand Verlag, 1974.

Ifjúkori művek, 1902–1918 [Youthful works]. Edited by Árpád Tímár. Budapest: Magvető Kiadó, 1977.

"Lenin—Theoretician of Practice." *New Hungarian Quarterly* 11, no. 40 (1970): 30–36.

"Leopold Ziegler." *A Szellem* [Spirit], 1, no. 2 (1911): 255.

"Levél" [Letter]. In *Szabó Ervin, 1877–1918*, edited by László Remete, pp. 327–28. Budapest: Fővárosi Szabó Ervin Könyvtár Kiadása, 1968.

"Levelei Babitshoz" [Letters to Babits]. Edited by István Gál. *Irodalomtörténet* [Literary history], 6, no. 3 (1974): 595–601.

Magyar irodalom—Magyar kultúra: Válogatott tanulmányok [Hungarian literature—Hungarian culture: selected studies]. Edited by Ferenc Fehér and Zoltán Kenyeres. Budapest: Gondolat Kiadó, 1970.

"Megjegyzések az irodalomtörténet elméletéhez" [Notes toward the theory of literary history]. In *Emlékkönyv Alexander Bernát* [Festschrift for Bernát Alexander], pp. 388–421. Budapest: Franklin-Társulat, 1910.

"Mein Weg zu Marx." In *Georg Lukács: Zum siebzigsten Geburtstag*, pp. 225–31. Berlin: Aufbau-Verlag, 1955.

"Moses Hess und die Probleme der idealistischen Dialektik." *Archiv für die Geschichte des Sozialismus und der Arbeiterbewegung* 12 (1926): 105–55.

Művészet és társadalom: Válogatott esztétikai tanulmányok [Art and society: selected aesthetic studies]. Edited by Ferenc Fehér. Budapest: Gondolat Kiadó, 1968.

Napló-Tagebuch, 1910–11 [Diary]. Edited by L. Ferenc Lendvai. Budapest: Akadémiai Kiadó, 1981.

Organisation und Illusion: Politische Aufsätze, III, 1921–1924. Edited by Jörg Kammler and Frank Benseler. Neuwied: Hermann Luchterhand Verlag, 1977.

Revolution und Gegenrevolution: Politische Aufsätze, II, 1920–1921. Edited by Jörg Kammler and Frank Benseler. Neuwied: Hermann Luchterhand Verlag, 1976.

"Solovjeff, Wladimir: Ausgewählte Werke." *Archiv für Sozialwissenschaft und Sozialpolitik* 39 (1915): 572–73.

"Solovjeff, Wladimir: Die Rechtfertigung des Guten." *Archiv für Sozialwissenschaft und Sozialpolitik* 40 (1916/1917): 978–80.

"Stawrogins Beichte." *Die Rote Fahne*, 16 July 1922, n.p.

Tactics and Ethics: Political Essays, 1919–1929. Translated by Michael McColgan, edited

by Rodney Livingstone. New York: Ha...

Taktik und Ethik: Politische Aufsätze, I, 191... Benseler. Neuwied: Hermann Luchterha...

"The Importance and Influence of Ady." *New...* 56–63.

"Th. G. Masaryk: Zur russischen Geschichts-... *Sozialwissenschaft und Sozialpolitik* 38 (1...

Történelem és osztálytudat [History and class c... Budapest: Magvető Kiadó, 1971.

Utam Marxhoz [My road to Marx]. Vol. 1. Edit... Magvető Könyvkiadó, 1971.

"Von der Armut am Geiste." *Neue Blätter* 2, nos...

"Wilhelm Dilthey." *A Szellem* [Spirit], 1, no. 2 (...

"Zsidó miszticizmus" [Jewish mysticism]. *A Szel...

"Zum Wesen und zur Methode der Kultursoziologi... *Sozialpolitik* 39 (1915): 216–22.

OTHER PRIMARY S...

Ady, Endre. *Költészet és forradalom* [Poetry and revo... Budapest: Kossuth Könyvkiadó, 1969.

———. *Összes versei* [Collected poems]. Edited by G... Szépirodalmi Könyvkiadó, 1967.

b. "A modern dráma fejlődésének története" [History o... drama]. *Huszadik Század* [Twentieth century] 14 (1...

Babits, Mihály. *Arcképek és tanulmányok* [Portraits and ... Budapest: Szépirodalmi Könyvkiadó, 1977.

Babits—Juhász—Kosztolányi levelezése [Correspondence... Kosztolányi]. Budapest: Akadémiai Kiadó, 1959.

Balázs, Béla. *Álmodó ifjúság* [Dreaming youth]. Budapest... Könyvkiadó, 1976.

———. *A színjáték elmélete* [Theory of the drama]. Wien:... Könyvtár, 1922.

———. "A tragédiának metafizikus teóriája a német romant... [Metaphysical theory of tragedy in German romanticism... *Nyugat* [West], 16 January 1908, pp. 87–90.

———. *A vándor énekel* [The wanderer sings]. Edited by Sá... Magyar Helikon, 1975.

———. *Az álmok köntöse* [Mantle of dreams]. Edited by Fere... Radnóti. Budapest: Magyar Helikon, 1973.

———. *Dialogus a dialogusról* [Dialogue on dialogue]. Budap... Kiadása, 1913.

———. "Életrajz" [Biography]. *Tiszatáj* [Region of the Tisza]... 382–84.

———. *Halálesztetika* [Death aesthetics]. Budapest: Deutsch Zs... Könyvkereskedése, n.d.

———. *Halálos fiatalság* [Mortal youth]. Edited by Ferenc Fehé... Budapest: Magyar Helikon, 1974.

———. "Hebbel Frigyes pantragizmusa" [Friedrich Hebbel's pan-...

Philológ...

———. "N... (1972):...

———. "P...

———. *Vá...*

Magda...

Baumgarten... (1912-...

Benedek,... Köny...

Bloch, Er...

Borus, Ró... Mine...

Buber, M...

———. & R...

———...

Hor...

Cohen,... Ka...

Demény...

Dostoy... Ba...

Be...

L...

V...

Eckh...

Ernst... Feke...

Fe...

Fi... Fő...

_____. *Bevezetés a marxi filozófiába* [Introduction to Marxist philosophy]. Wien: Europa Ismeretterjesztő Könyvtár, 1922.

_____. "Konzervatív és progresszív idealizmus" [Conservative and progressive idealism]. *Huszadik Század* [Twentieth century] 19 (1918): 193–206.

_____. *Visszaemlékezések a párt megalakulásának harcaira* [Recollections of the struggles to form the party]. Budapest: Magyar Tudomány, 1959.

_____. "Zalai Béla: In Memoriam." *Athenaeum* 1 (1915): 428–41.

Fülep, Lajos. *A művészet forradalmától a nagy forradalomig: Cikkek, tanulmányok* [From artistic revolution to the great revolution: articles, studies]. 2 vols. Edited by Árpád Tímár. Budapest: Magvető Könyvkiadó, 1974.

_____. "Az emlékezés a művészi alkotásban" [Remembrance in artistic creation]. *A Szellem* [Spirit] 1, no. 1 (1911): 56–90.

_____. *Művészet és világnézet* [Art and world view]. Edited by Árpád Tímár. Budapest: Magvető Könyvkiadó, 1976.

_____. "Új Suso-kiadás" [New edition of Suso]. *A Szellem* [Spirit] 1, no. 2 (1911): 254.

Gábor, Éva, ed. "Alexander Bernát levelei Lukács Györgyhöz, 1908–1913" [Bernát Alexander's letters to György Lukács]. *Irodalomtörténet* [Literary history] 10, no. 1 (1978): 224–54.

Gál, István, ed. "Babits béke-írásaiból" [From Babits's writings on peace]. *Irodalomtörténeti Közlemények* [Proceedings of literary history] 80, no. 4 (1976): 520–33.

_____, ed. "Balázs Béla naplója" [Béla Balázs's diary]. *Kritika* [Criticism] no. 9 (1975): 3–10; no. 10 (1975): 14–18; no. 11 (1975): 20–23.

_____. "Balázs és Lukács elitfolyóirat-terve 1910-ben" [Balázs and Lukács's plan for an elite journal in 1910]. *Tiszatáj* [Region of the Tisza] 30, no. 11 (1976): 46–53.

_____. "Kodály és Balázs Béla barátsága" [The Kodály-Béla Balázs friendship]. *Tiszatáj* [Region of the Tisza] 28, no. 11 (1974): 66–72.

Gassen, Kurt, and Landmann, Michael, eds. *Buch des Dankes an Georg Simmel: Briefe, Erinnerungen, Bibliographie*. Berlin: Duncker & Humblot, 1958.

Gergely, Tibor, ed. *Lesznai képeskönyv: Lesznai Anna írásai, képei és hímzései* [Lesznai picture book: Anna Lesznai's writings, paintings, and needlework]. Budapest: Corvina Kiadó, 1978.

Gerth, H. H., and Mills, C. Wright, eds. *From Max Weber: Essays in Sociology*. New York: Oxford University Press, 1958.

Hauser, Arnold. "Az esztétikai rendszerezés problémája" [The problem of aesthetic systematization]. *Athenaeum* 4 (1918): 331–57.

_____. *Im Gespräch mit Georg Lukács*. Munich: Verlag C. H. Beck, 1978.

_____. *The Social History of Art*. Vol. 4. New York: Vintage Books, 1951.

Hebbel, Friedrich. "Judith." In *Werke*. Vol. 1, pp. 141–210. Hamburg: Hoffmann und Campe Verlag, n.d.

Hegel, G. W. F. *Phenomenology of Spirit*. Translated by A. V. Miller. Oxford: Oxford University Press, 1977.

Hofmannsthal, Hugo von. "Der Tor und der Tod." In *Poems and Verse Plays*, edited by Michael Hamburger, pp. 92–137. New York: Pantheon Books, 1961.

Hollósi, Mrs. Tibor, ed. *Nagy idők tanúi emlékeznek, 1918–1919* [Witnesses of great days remember]. Budapest: Kossuth Könyvkiadó, 1958.

Honigsheim, Paul. *On Max Weber*. Translated by Joan Rytina. New York: Free Press, 1968.

Irodalmi Muzeum: Emlékezések [Literary museum: recollections]. Budapest, 1967.

212   BIBLIOGRAPHY

Jászi, Oszkár. "Mannheim Károly: *Lélek és kultura* " [Karl Mannheim: soul and culture].
    Huszadik Század [Twentieth century] 19 (1918): 192.
_____. "Proletárdiktatúra" [Proletarian dictatorship]. *Szabadgondolat* [Free thought]
    8, no. 10 (1918): 225–26.
_____. *Revolution and Counter-Revolution in Hungary.* New York: Howard Fertig,
    1969.
"Jelentés a Társadalomtudományok Szabad Iskolájának 1907–1908-ik évi működéséről"
    [Report on the Free School of the Sociological Society's 1907–8 activities]. *Hu-
    szadik Század* [Twentieth century] 9 (1908): xiv.
József, Farkas, ed. *"Mindenki újakra készül . . ."*: *Az 1918/19-es forradalmak irodalma*
    [Everyone is preparing for the new: the literature of the 1918/19 revolutions]. Vol.
    4. Budapest: Akadémiai Kiadó, 1967.
Kant, Immanuel. *Werke.* Vol. 6. Berlin: Druck und Verlag von Georg Reimer, 1907.
Karádi, Éva, ed. "Dokumentumok Lukács György heidelbergi korszakából" [Documents
    from György Lukács's Heidelberg period]. *Valóság* [Reality] 17, no. 11 (1974):
    28–44.
_____, and Vezér, Erzsébet, eds. *A Vasárnapi Kör* [The Sunday circle]. Budapest:
    Gondolat, 1980.
Károlyi, Michael. *Memoirs: Faith without Illusion.* Translated by Catherine Károlyi. New
    York: E. P. Dutton & Co., 1957.
Kassák, Lajos. *Egy ember élete* [One man's life]. Vol. 4. Budapest: Pantheon Kiadás,
    n.d.
Komlos, Aladár. *Problémák a Nyugat körül* [Problems around *Nyugat*]. Budapest: Mag-
    vető Kiadó, 1978.
Kutasi, Elemér. "Esztétikai kutatások, II" [Aesthetic investigations]. *Huszadik Század*
    [Twentieth century] 12 (1911): 504–7.
Kutzbach, Karl August, ed. *Paul Ernst und Georg Lukács: Dokumente einer
    Freundschaft.* Emsdetten: Verlag Lechte, 1974.
Lask, Emil. *Die Logik der Philosophie und die Kategorienlehre.* Tübingen: Verlag von J.
    C. B. Mohr (Paul Siebeck), 1911.
Lengyel, József. *Bécsi portyák* [Tours of Vienna]. Budapest: Magvető Kiadó, 1970.
_____. *Prenn Ferenc hányatott élete* [Ferenc Prenn's storm-tossed life]. Budapest:
    Magvető, 1969.
_____. *Visegrádi utca* [Visegrád street]. Budapest: Szépirodalmi Könyvkiadó, 1962.
Lesznai, Anna. *Kezdetben volt a kert* [In the beginning was the garden]. 2 vols. Budapest:
    Szépirodalmi Könyvkiadó, 1966.
Löwy, Michael, ed. "Interview with Ernst Bloch." *New German Critique*, no. 9 (1976):
    35–45.
Mann, Katia. *Unwritten Memories.* Translated by Hunter and Hildegarde Hannum. New
    York: Alfred A. Knopf, 1975.
Mann, Thomas. *The Magic Mountain.* Translated by H. T. Lowe-Porter. New York:
    Vintage Books, 1969.
_____. "Tonio Kröger." In *Death in Venice and Seven Other Stories.* Translated by H. T.
    Lowe-Porter, pp. 76–134. New York: Vintage Books, 1930.
Mannheim, Károly. "A háboru bölcseletéhez [Toward a philosophy of the war]. *Huszadik
    Század* [Twentieth century] 18 (1917): 416–18.
_____. "Ernst Bloch: *Geist der Utopie.*" *Athenaeum* 5 (1919): 207–11.
_____. *Essays on Sociology and Social Psychology.* Edited by Paul Kecskemeti. Lon-
    don: Routledge & Kegan Paul, 1953.

———. "Georg Simmel, mint filozófus" [Georg Simmel as philosopher]. *Huszadik Század* [Twentieth century] 19 (1918): 194–96.

———. *Lélek és kultura* [Soul and culture]. Budapest: Benkő Gyula Cs. és Kir. Udvari Könyvkereskedése, 1918.

———. "Letters to Lukács, 1910–1916." Edited by Éva Gábor. *New Hungarian Quarterly* 16, no. 57 (1975): 93–105.

Masaryk, Thomas G. *The Spirit of Russia*. Vol. 2. Translated by Eden and Cedar Paul. London: George Allen & Unwin, 1955.

Mendel, Arthur P., ed. *Essential Works of Marxism*. New York: Bantam Books, 1965.

Molnár, Antal. "Emlékezés a Vasárnapi Társaságra" [Recollections of the Sunday society]. *Irodalomtörténet* [Literary history] 10, no. 2 (1978): 489–90.

Németh, Andor. *A szélén behajtva* [On the brink]. Budapest: Magvető Könyvkiadó, 1973.

New Hungarian Quarterly 13, no. 47 (1972).

Philosophical Forum 3, nos. 3–4 (1972).

Polányi, Károly. *A radikalizmus programmja és célja* [Radicalism's program and aim]. Szeged: Polgári Radikális Párt, n.d.

Popper, Leó. "Der Kitsch." *Die Fackel*, 31 December 1910, pp. 36–43.

———. "Die Bildhauerei, Rodin und Maillol." *Die Fackel*, 29 April 1911, pp. 33–41.

———. "Volkskunst und Formbeseelung." *Die Fackel*, 2 June 1911, pp. 37–39.

Popper Lukács, Mici. "Emlékek Lukács Györgyről" [Recollections of György Lukács]. *Nagyvilág* [Wide world] 20, no. 10 (1975): 1560–71.

Révai, Josef. "Georg Lukács, Geschichte und Klassenbewusstsein." *Archiv für die Geschichte des Sozialismus und der Arbeiterbewegung* 11 (1925): 227–36.

Ritoók, Emma. "A rút a művészetben" [The ugly in art]. *Athenaeum* 2 (1916): 177–205.

———. *A szellem kalandorai* [Adventurers of the spirit]. 2 vols. Budapest: A Göncöl Kiadása, 1922.

———. "Esztétikai kutatások, I" [Aesthetic investigations]. *Huszadik Század* [Twentieth century] 12 (1911): 502–4.

Ropshin [Boris Savinkov]. *The Pale Horse*. Translated by Z. Vengerova. New York: Alfred A. Knopf, 1919.

Savinkov, Boris. *Memoirs of a Terrorist*. Translated by Joseph Shaplen. New York: Albert & Charles Boni, 1931.

Serge, Victor. *Memoirs of a Revolutionary, 1901–1941*. Translated and edited by Peter Sedgwick. London: Oxford University Press, 1963.

Simmel, Georg. "Der Begriff und die Tragödie der Kultur." In *Philosophische Kultur*, pp. 245–77. Leipzig: Verlag von Dr. Werner Klinkhardt, 1911.

———. *Philosophie des Geldes*. Leipzig: Verlag von Duncker & Humblot, 1900.

———. "Zur Metaphysik des Todes." In *Brücke und Tür*, edited by Michael Landmann and Margarete Susman, pp. 29–36. Stuttgart: K. F. Koehler Verlag, 1957.

Simor, András, ed. *Korvin Ottó: ". . . a Gondolat él . . ."* [Ottó Korvin: the idea lives]. Budapest: Magvető Könyvkiadó, 1976.

Sinkó, Ervin. *Optimisták: Történelmi regény 1918–19-ből* [Optimists: historical novel from 1918–19]. 2 vols. Újvidék: Testvériség-Egység Könyvkiadóvállalat, 1953–55.

Sorel, Georges. *The Illusions of Progress*. Translated by John and Charlotte Stanley. Berkeley: University of California Press, 1969.

———. *Reflections on Violence*. Translated by T. E. Hulme and J. Roth. New York: Collier Books, 1961.

Szabó, Ervin. *Társadalmi és pártharcok a 48–49-es magyar forradalomban* [Social and party conflicts in the 1848–49 Hungarian revolution]. Bécs: Bécsi Magyar Kiadó, 1921.

Szende, Paul. "Die Krise der mitteleuropäischen Revolution." *Archiv für Sozialwissenschaft und Sozialpolitik* 47 (1920/1921): 337–75.

Szilasi, Vilmos. "A kritika elmélete [The theory of criticism]. In *Emlékkönyv: Alexander Bernát* [Festschrift for Bernát Alexander], pp. 638–51. Budapest: Franklin-Társulat, 1910.

———. *Platon* [Plato]. Budapest: Franklin-Társulat, 1910.

Tímár, Árpád, ed. "Popper Leó elfelejtett Lukács-ismertetése" [Leó Popper's forgotten Lukács-review]. *Irodalomtörténet* [Literary history] 3, no. 4 (1971): 967–72.

———. "Újabb adalék a Babits-Lukács-vitához" [Fresh data concerning the Babits-Lukács debate]. *Irodalomtörténet* [Literary history] 6, no. 3 (1974): 618–26.

Tolnai, Károly. *Ferenczy Noémi*. Budapest: Bisztrai Farkas Ferencz Kiadása, 1934.

———. "Popper Leó és a művészettörténet: Megjegyzések egy elfelejtett művészeti kritikusról" [Leó Popper and art history: notes on a forgotten art critic]. *Magyar Filozófiai Szemle* [Hungarian philosophical review] 16, no. 2 (1972): 249–61.

Tönnies, Ferdinand. *Community and Society*. Translated and edited by Charles P. Loomis. New York: Harper & Row, 1963.

Traub, Reiner, and Wieser, Harald, eds. *Gespräche mit Ernst Bloch*. Frankfurt am Main: Suhrkamp Verlag, 1975.

Tucker, Robert C., ed. *The Lenin Anthology*. New York: W. W. Norton and Company, 1975.

Weber, Marianne. *Fichte's Sozialismus und sein Verhältnis zur Marx'schen Doktrin*. Tübingen: Verlag von J. C. B. Mohr (Paul Siebeck), 1900.

———. *Max Weber: A Biography*. Translated by Harry Zohn. New York: John Wiley, 1975.

Weber, Max. "Georg Simmel as Sociologist." Translated by Donald N. Levine. *Social Research* 39, no. 1 (1972): 155–63.

———. *The Protestant Ethic and the Spirit of Capitalism*. Translated by Talcott Parsons. New York: Charles Scribner's Sons, 1958.

Zalai, Béla. "A filozófiai rendszerezés problémája" [The problem of philosophic systematization]. *A Szellem* [Spirit] 1, no. 2 (1911): 159–86.

———. "Levelei kortársaihoz" [Letters to contemporaries]. Edited by Ottó Beöthy. *Kritika* [Criticism], no. 8 (1975): 5–10.

SECONDARY SOURCES

Abrams, M. H. *Natural Supernaturalism*. New York: W. W. Norton and Company, 1971.

Almási, Miklós. "Lukács's 'Heidelberg Aesthetics.'" *New Hungarian Quarterly* 18, no. 65 (1977): 152–55.

Apitzsch, Ursula. *Gesellschaftstheorie und Ästhetik bei Georg Lukács bis 1933*. Stuttgart: Frommann-Holzboog, 1977.

Arato, Andrew. "Georg Lukács: The Search for a Revolutionary Subject." In *The Unknown Dimension: European Marxism since Lenin*, edited by Dick Howard and Karl E. Klare, pp. 81–106. New York: Basic Books, 1972.

———. "Lukács' Path to Marxism, 1910–1923." *Telos*, no. 7 (1971): 128–36.

———, and Breines, Paul. *The Young Lukács and the Origins of Western Marxism*. New York: Seabury Press, 1979.

Bahr, Ehrhard. *Ernst Bloch*. Berlin: Colloquium Verlag, 1974.

————. *Georg Lukács*. Berlin: Colloquium Verlag, 1970.

Balogh, Eva S. "The Turning of the World: Hungarian Progressive Writers on the War." In *The Habsburg Empire in World War I*, edited by Robert A. Kann et al., pp. 185–201. Boulder: East European Quarterly, 1977.

Barany, George. " 'Magyar Jew or: Jewish Magyar'?" *Canadian-American Slavic Studies* 8, no. 1 (1974): 1–44.

Baumer, Franklin L. "Twentieth-Century Version of the Apocalypse." In *European Intellectual History since Darwin and Marx*, edited by W. Warren Wagar, pp. 110–34. New York: Harper & Row, 1967.

Bellér, Béla. "Tanácsköztársaság és erkölcs" [Soviet republic and morality]. *Világosság* [Clarity] 10, nos. 8–9 (1969): 519–26.

Benseler, Frank, ed. *Festschrift zum achtzigsten Geburtstag von Georg Lukács*. Neuwied: Hermann Luchterhand Verlag, 1965.

Benz, Ernst. *Les sources mystiques de la philosophie romantique allemande*. Paris: Librairie Philosophique J. Vrin, 1968.

Berdyaev, Nicolas. *The Origin of Russian Communism*. Ann Arbor: University of Michigan Press, 1960.

————. *The Russian Idea*. New York: Macmillan Company, 1948.

Bettelheim, Bruno. *The Uses of Enchantment: The Meaning and Importance of Fairy Tales*. New York: Alfred A. Knopf, 1976.

Boella, Laura. *Il giovane Lukács*. Bari: De Donato Editore, 1977.

Bori, Imre. "Lukács György és a magyar irodalom [György Lukács and Hungarian literature]. *Híd* [Bridge] 29, no. 4 (1965): 441–63.

Borkenau, Franz. *World Communism*. Ann Arbor: University of Michigan Press, 1962.

Borsányi, György. "Az emigráció első éve: Fejezetek Kun Béla életéből" [The first year of exile: chapters from the life of Béla Kun]. *Valóság* [Reality] 20, no. 12 (1977): 36–49.

Bosnyák, István. "Lukács György tanácsköztársasági messianizmusa" [György Lukács's messianism during the Soviet republic]. *Valóság* [Reality] 22, no. 8 (1979): 51–55.

Bourdet, Yvon. *Figures de Lukács*. Paris: Éditions Anthropos, 1972.

Breines, Paul. "Marxism, Romanticism, and the Case of Georg Lukács: Notes on Some Recent Sources and Situations." *Studies in Romanticism* 16, no. 4 (1977): 473–89.

————. "Young Lukács, Old Lukács, New Lukács." *Journal of Modern History* 51, no. 3 (1979): 533–46.

Breuer, János. "Babits és Lukács vitájához" [On the Babits-Lukács debate]. *Irodalomtörténet* [Literary history] 8, no. 3 (1976): 745–48.

Campbell, T. M. *Hebbel, Ibsen and the Analytic Exposition*. Heidelberg: Carl Winters Universitätsbuchhandlung, 1922.

Camus, Albert. *The Rebel*. Translated by Anthony Bower. New York: Vintage Books, 1956.

Charzat, Michel. *Georges Sorel et la révolution au XX siècle*. Paris: Librairie Hachette, 1977.

Cohn, Norman. *The Pursuit of the Millennium: Revolutionary Millenarians and Mystical Anarchists of the Middle Ages*. New York: Oxford University Press, 1970.

Congdon, Lee. "Lukács, Camus, and the Russian Terrorists." *Continuity*, no. 1 (1980): 17–36.

————. "The Making of a Hungarian Revolutionary: The Unpublished Diary of Béla Balázs." *Journal of Contemporary History* 8, no. 3 (1973): 57–74.

————. "The Tragic Sense of Life: Lukács's *The Soul and the Forms*." In *Austrian Philosophy*, edited by J. C. Nyíri, pp. 43–74. Munich: Philosophia Verlag, 1981.

———. "The Unexpected Revolutionary: Lukács's Road to Marx." *Survey* 20, nos. 2–3 (91/92) (1974): 176–205.

Copleston, Frederick, S. J. *A History of Philosophy.* Vol. 7, Part 1. Garden City, N. Y.: Image Books, 1965.

Csanak, Dóra F. *Balázs Béla hagyatéka az akadémiai könyvtár kézirattárában (MS 5009–MS 5024* [Béla Balázs's literary remains in the manuscripts archive of the academy library]. Budapest: Bibliotheca Academiae Scientiarum Hungaricae, 1966.

Cushing, G. F. "Problems of Hungarian Literary Criticism." *Slavonic and East European Review* 40, no. 95 (1962): 341–55.

Czigány, L. G. "Hungarianness: The Origin of a Pseudo-Linguistic Concept." *Slavonic and East European Review* 52, no. 128 (1974): 325–36.

"Der Mann mit dem Koffer." *Der Spiegel,* 27 August 1973, pp. 100–1.

Faesi, Robert. *Paul Ernst und die neuklassischen Bestrebungen im Drama.* Leipzig: Xenien-Verlag, 1913.

Fehér, Ferenc. "Am Scheideweg des romantischen Antikapitalismus. Typologie und Beitrag zur deutschen Ideologiegeschichte gelegentlich des Briefwechsels zwischen Paul Ernst und Georg Lukács." In *Die Seele und das Leben: Studien zum frühen Lukács,* edited by Ágnes Heller, pp. 241–327. Frankfurt am Main: Suhrkamp, 1977.

———. "Balázs Béla és Lukács György szövetsége a forradalomig" [The Béla Balázs–György Lukács alliance until the revolution]. *Irodalomtörténet* [Literary history] 1, no. 2 (1969): 317–46; 1, no. 3 (1969): 531–60.

———. "Die Geschichtsphilosophie des Dramas, die Metaphysik der Tragödie und die Utopie des untragischen Dramas. Scheidewege der Dramentheorie des jungen Lukács." In *Die Seele und das Leben: Studien zum frühen Lukács,* edited by Ágnes Heller, pp. 7–53. Frankfurt am Main: Suhrkamp, 1977.

———. "Lucien Goldmann, the 'Mere Recipient' of Georg Lukács." *Philosophy and Social Criticism* 6, no. 1 (1979): 1–24.

———, et al. "Notes on Lukács' Ontology." *Telos,* no. 29 (1976): 160–81.

Fekete, Éva. "Lukács esszékorszaka" [Lukács's essay period]. *Mozgó Világ* [Restless world] 2, no. 6 (1976): 85–95.

———. "Lukács György az első világháború éveiben" [György Lukács during the years of the First World War]. *Valóság* [Reality] 20, no. 2 (1977): 33–44.

Földényi, F. László. *A fiatal Lukács* [The young Lukács]. Budapest: Magvető Kiadó, 1980.

———. "Az egyértelműség igézetében: Az etika és esztétika a fiatal Lukács gondol-kodásában" [Under the spell of harmony: ethics and aesthetics in the young Lukács's thinking]. *Világosság* [Clarity] 20, no. 5 (1979): 304–10.

Fuerst, Norbert. *Ideologie und Literatur: Zum Dialog zwischen Paul Ernst und Georg Lukács.* Emsdetten: Verlag Lechte, 1976.

Gluck, Mary. "Politics versus Culture: Radicalism and the Lukács Circle in Turn-of-the-Century Hungary." *East European Quarterly* 14, no. 2 (1980): 129–54.

Goldmann, Lucien. "The Early Writings of Georg Lukács." Translated by Joy N. Humes. *Tri-Quarterly,* no. 9 (1967): 165–81.

———. "Georg Lukács: L'essayiste." In *Recherches dialectiques,* pp. 247–59. Paris: Librairie Gallimard, 1959.

———. *Lukács et Heidegger.* Paris: Éditions Denoël, 1973.

Hanák, Péter. "Kései rehabilitáció" [Belated rehabilitation]. *Világosság* [Clarity] 10, no. 3 (1969): 158–61.

———, ed. *Magyarország története, 1890–1918* [History of Hungary]. 2 vols.

B·I·B·L·I·O·G·R·A·P·H·Y

MANUSCRIPT SOURCES

Babits, Mihály. Papers. Országos Széchenyi Könyvtára: Kézirattár. Budapest, Hungary.

Balázs, Béla. Diaries. Magyar Tudományos Akadémia Könyvtára: Kézirattár. Budapest, Hungary.

Hauser, Arnold. Conversation. London, 28 August 1971.

Lukács, György. Manuscripts, Correspondence, Diaries. Magyar Tudományos Akadémia Filozófiai Intézet Lukács Archívum és Könyvtár. Budapest, Hungary.

Szemere, Samu. Conversation. Budapest, Hungary, 1978.

GYÖRGY LUKÁCS'S WORKS

"A bolsevizmus mint erkölcsi problema" [Bolshevism as a moral problem]. *Szabadgondolat* [Free thought] 8, no. 10 (1918): 228–32.

A drámaírás főbb irányai a múlt század utolsó negyedében [The main directions of dramaturgy during the final quarter of the last century]. Edited by L. Ferenc Lendvai. Budapest: Akadémiai Kiadó, 1980.

"Ady forradalmi hatása: Filminterjú Lukács Györggyel" [The revolutionary influence of Ady: film interview with György Lukács]. *Élet és Irodalom* [Life and literature], 29 January 1977, p. 6.

"A konzervativ és progressziv idealizmus vitája" [The debate concerning conservative and progressive idealism]. *Huszadik Század* [Twentieth century] 19 (1918):378–82.

"A köztársasági propaganda" [Republican propaganda]. *Világ* [World], 10 November 1918, p. 17.

A modern dráma fejlődésének története [History of the evolution of the modern drama]. 2 vols. Budapest: Franklin-Társulat, 1911.

Ästhetik. Vol. 1. Neuwied: Hermann Luchterhand Verlag, 1963.

"Bartók Béla." *Nagyvilág* [Wide world] 15, no. 9 (1970): 1283–94.

"Beszélgetés Leninről és a forradalmiság mai tartalmáról" [Conversation on Lenin and the contemporary meaning of the revolutionary spirit]. Edited by András Kovács. *Új Írás* [New writing] 11, no. 8 (1971): 10–19.

"Brief." In *Für Margarete Susman: Auf gespaltenem Pfad*, edited by Manfred Schlösser, pp. 303–7. Darmstadt: Erato-Presse, 1964.

"Croce, Benedetto: Zur Theorie und Geschichte der Historiographie." *Archiv für Sozialwissenschaft und Sozialpolitik* 39 (1915): 878–85.

"Curriculum vitae." *Text und Kritik* 39/40 (1973): 5–7.

"Die deutschen Intellektuellen und der Krieg." *Text und Kritik* 39/40 (1973): 65–69.

"Die neue Ausgabe von Lassalles Briefen." *Archiv für die Geschichte des Sozialismus und der Arbeiterbewegung* 11 (1925): 401–23.

Die Seele und die Formen: Essays. Neuwied: Hermann Luchterhand Verlag, 1971.

"Die Subjekt-Objekt-Beziehung in der Aesthetik." *Logos* 7 (1917/18): 1–39.

Die Theorie des Romans: Ein geschichtsphilosophischer Versuch über die Formen der grossen Epik. Neuwied: Hermann Luchterhand Verlag, 1963.

"Dostoevsky." In *Dostoevsky: A Collection of Critical Essays*, edited by René Wellek, pp. 146–58. Englewood Cliffs, N.J.: Prentice-Hall, 1962.

"Egy ismeretlen Lukács György-levél" [An unknown letter of György Lukács's]. Edited by György Litván. *Kritika* [Criticism], no. 3 (1974): 16–17.

"Emil Lask: Ein Nachruf." *Kantstudien* 22 (1918): 349–70.

"Emlékezés Károlyi Mihályra" [Recollections of Mihály Károlyi]. *Új Írás* [New writing], 9, no. 8 (1969): 61–62.

Essays on Thomas Mann. Translated by Stanley Mitchell. New York: Grosset & Dunlap, 1965.

Esztétikai kultura: Tanulmányok [Aesthetic culture: studies]. Budapest: Athenaeum Irodalmi és Nyomdai Részvényt Kiadása, 1913.

"Georg Simmel." *Pester Lloyd*, 2 October 1918, pp. 2–3.

Geschichte und Klassenbewusstsein: Studien über marxistische Dialektik. Neuwied: Hermann Luchterhand Verlag, 1970.

Heidelberger Ästhetik, 1916–1918. Edited by György Márkus and Frank Benseler. Neuwied: Hermann Luchterhand Verlag, 1974.

Heidelberger Philosophie der Kunst, 1912–1914. Edited by György Márkus and Frank Benseler. Neuwied: Hermann Luchterhand Verlag, 1974.

Ifjúkori művek, 1902–1918 [Youthful works]. Edited by Árpád Tímár. Budapest: Magvető Kiadó, 1977.

"Lenin—Theoretician of Practice." *New Hungarian Quarterly* 11, no. 40 (1970): 30–36.

"Leopold Ziegler." *A Szellem* [Spirit], 1, no. 2 (1911): 255.

"Levél" [Letter]. In *Szabó Ervin, 1877–1918*, edited by László Remete, pp. 327–28. Budapest: Fővárosi Szabó Ervin Könyvtár Kiadása, 1968.

"Levelei Babitshoz" [Letters to Babits]. Edited by István Gál. *Irodalomtörténet* [Literary history], 6, no. 3 (1974): 595–601.

Magyar irodalom—Magyar kultúra: Válogatott tanulmányok [Hungarian literature—Hungarian culture: selected studies]. Edited by Ferenc Fehér and Zoltán Kenyeres. Budapest: Gondolat Kiadó, 1970.

"Megjegyzések az irodalomtörténet elméletéhez" [Notes toward the theory of literary history]. In *Emlékkönyv Alexander Bernát* [Festschrift for Bernát Alexander], pp. 388–421. Budapest: Franklin-Társulat, 1910.

"Mein Weg zu Marx." In *Georg Lukács: Zum siebzigsten Geburtstag*, pp. 225–31. Berlin: Aufbau-Verlag, 1955.

"Moses Hess und die Probleme der idealistischen Dialektik." *Archiv für die Geschichte des Sozialismus und der Arbeiterbewegung* 12 (1926): 105–55.

Művészet és társadalom: Válogatott esztétikai tanulmányok [Art and society: selected aesthetic studies]. Edited by Ferenc Fehér. Budapest: Gondolat Kiadó, 1968.

Napló-Tagebuch, 1910–11 [Diary]. Edited by L. Ferenc Lendvai. Budapest: Akadémiai Kiadó, 1981.

Organisation und Illusion: Politische Aufsätze, III, 1921–1924. Edited by Jörg Kammler and Frank Benseler. Neuwied: Hermann Luchterhand Verlag, 1977.

Revolution und Gegenrevolution: Politische Aufsätze, II, 1920–1921. Edited by Jörg Kammler and Frank Benseler. Neuwied: Hermann Luchterhand Verlag, 1976.

"Solovjeff, Wladimir: Ausgewählte Werke." *Archiv für Sozialwissenschaft und Sozialpolitik* 39 (1915): 572–73.

"Solovjeff, Wladimir: Die Rechtfertigung des Guten." *Archiv für Sozialwissenschaft und Sozialpolitik* 40 (1916/1917): 978–80.

"Stawrogins Beichte." *Die Rote Fahne*, 16 July 1922, n.p.

Tactics and Ethics: Political Essays, 1919–1929. Translated by Michael McColgan, edited

BIBLIOGRAPHY

209

by Rodney Livingstone. New York: Harper & Row, 1975.
Taktik und Ethik: Politische Aufsätze, I, 1918–1920. Edited by Jörg Kammler and Frank Benseler. Neuwied: Hermann Luchterhand Verlag, 1975.
"The Importance and Influence of Ady." *New Hungarian Quarterly* 10, no. 35 (1969): 56–63.
"Th. G. Masaryk: Zur russischen Geschichts-und Religionsphilosophie." *Archiv für Sozialwissenschaft und Sozialpolitik* 38 (1914): 871–75.
Történelem és osztálytudat [History and class consciousness]. Edited by Mihály Vajda. Budapest: Magvető Kiadó, 1971.
Utam Marxhoz [My road to Marx]. Vol. 1. Edited by György Márkus. Budapest: Magvető Könyvkiadó, 1971.
"Von der Armut am Geiste." *Neue Blätter* 2, nos. 5–6 (1912): 67–92.
"Wilhelm Dilthey." *A Szellem* [Spirit], 1, no. 2 (1911): 253.
"Zsidó miszticizmus" [Jewish mysticism]. *A Szellem* [Spirit] 1, no. 2 (1911): 256.
"Zum Wesen und zur Methode der Kultursoziologie." *Archiv für Sozialwissenschaft und Sozialpolitik* 39 (1915): 216–22.

OTHER PRIMARY SOURCES

Ady, Endre. *Költészet és forradalom* [Poetry and revolution]. Edited by József Varga. Budapest: Kossuth Könyvkiadó, 1969.
———. *Összes versei* [Collected poems]. Edited by Gyula Földessy. Budapest: Szépirodalmi Könyvkiadó, 1967.
b. "A modern dráma fejlődésének története" [History of the evolution of the modern drama]. *Huszadik Század* [Twentieth century] 14 (1913): 120–24.
Babits, Mihály. *Arcképek és tanulmányok* [Portraits and studies]. Edited by István Gál. Budapest: Szépirodalmi Könyvkiadó, 1977.
Babits—Juhász—Kosztolányi levelezése [Correspondence of Babits, Juhász, and Kosztolányi]. Budapest: Akadémiai Kiadó, 1959.
Balázs, Béla. *Álmodó ifjúság* [Dreaming youth]. Budapest: Magvető és Szépirodalmi Könyvkiadó, 1976.
———. *A szinjáték elmélete* [Theory of the drama]. Wien: Europa Ismeretterjesztő Könyvtár, 1922.
———. "A tragédiának metafizíkus teóriája a német romantikában és Hebbel Frigyes" [Metaphysical theory of tragedy in German romanticism and Friedrich Hebbel]. *Nyugat* [West], 16 January 1908, pp. 87–90.
———. *A vándor énekel* [The wanderer sings]. Edited by Sándor Radnóti. Budapest: Magyar Helikon, 1975.
———. *Az álmok köntöse* [Mantle of dreams]. Edited by Ferenc Fehér and Sándor Radnóti. Budapest: Magyar Helikon, 1973.
———. *Dialogus a dialogusról* [Dialogue on dialogue]. Budapest: Az Athenaeum R. T. Kiadása, 1913.
———. "Életrajz" [Biography]. *Tiszatáj* [Region of the Tisza] 19, no. 5 (1965): 382–84.
———. *Halálesztetika* [Death aesthetics]. Budapest: Deutsch Zsigmond és Társa Könyvkereskedése, n.d.
———. *Halálos fiatalság* [Mortal youth]. Edited by Ferenc Fehér and Sándor Radnóti. Budapest: Magyar Helikon, 1974.
———. "Hebbel Frigyes pantragizmusa" [Friedrich Hebbel's pan-tragedy]. *Egyetemes*

Philológiai Közlöny [General philological bulletin] (1909): 41–55, 132–39.
————. "Notes from a Diary, 1911–1921." *New Hungarian Quarterly* 13, no. 47 (1972): 123–28.
————. "Paris-e vagy Weimar?" [Paris or Weimar?]. *Nyugat* [West] 7 (1914): 200–203.
————. *Válogatott cikkek és tanulmányok* [Selected articles and studies]. Edited by Magda K. Nagy. Budapest: Kossuth Könyvkiadó, 1968.
Baumgarten, Franz. "Georg von Lukács: Die Seele und die Formen." *Logos* 3 (1912–13): 249.
Benedek, Marcell. *Naplómat olvasom* [Reading my diary]. Budapest: Szépirodalmi Könyvkiadó, 1965.
Bloch, Ernst. *Geist der Utopie*. Frankfurt am Main: Suhrkamp Verlag, 1971.
Borus, Rózsa, ed. *A század nagy tanúi* [Great witnesses of the century]. Budapest: RTV. Minerva, 1978.
Buber, Martin. *Begegnung*. Stuttgart: W. Kohlhammer Verlag, 1960.
————. *Hasidism and Modern Man*. Translated by Maurice Friedman. New York: Harper & Row, 1966.
————. *Paths in Utopia*. Translated by R. F. C. Hull. Boston: Beacon Press, 1958.
————. *The Tales of Rabbi Nachman*. Translated by Maurice Friedman. New York: Horizon Press, 1956.
Cohen, Hermann. *Religion of Reason out of the Sources of Judaism*. Translated by Simon Kaplan. New York: Frederick Ungar, 1972.
Demény, János, ed. *Bartók Béla*. Budapest: Magyar Művészeti Tanács, 1948.
Dostoyevsky, Fyodor. *The Brothers Karamazov*. 2 vols. Translated by David Magarshack. Baltimore: Penguin Books, 1958.
————. *Crime and Punishment*. Translated by David Magarshack. Baltimore: Penguin Books, 1951.
————. *The Idiot*. Translated by Henry and Olga Carlisle. New York: New American Library, 1969.
————. *The Notebooks for "The Brothers Karamazov."* Edited and translated by Edward Wasiolek. Chicago: University of Chicago Press, 1971.
————. *The Possessed*. Translated by Andrew R. MacAndrew. New York: New American Library, 1962.
Eckhart, Meister. *Works*. Vol. 2. Translated by C. de B. Evans. London: John M. Watkins, 1952.
Ernst, Paul. *Der Weg zur Form*. Berlin: Verlag Julius Bard, 1906.
Fekete, Éva, ed. "Balázs Béla naplójegyzeteiből, 1911–1920" [From Béla Balázs's diary notes]. *Valóság* [Reality] 16, no. 2 (1973): 82–89.
————. "Levelek Lukács Györgyhöz" [Letters to György Lukács]. *Irodalomtörténet* [Literary history] 6, no. 3 (1974): 602–17.
————. "Lukács György és Popper Leó levélváltásából, 1909–1911" [From the correspondence of György Lukács and Leó Popper]. *Valóság* [Reality] 17, no. 9 (1974): 16–37.
————, and Karádi, Éva, eds. *Lukács György élete képekben és dokumentumokban* [Life of György Lukács in pictures and documents]. Budapest: Corvina Kiadó, 1980.
Fenyő, Miksa. *Följegyzések a 'Nyugat' folyóiratról és környékéről* [Notes on the journal *Nyugat* and its world]. N.p.: Pátria Könyvkiadó Kiadása, 1960.
Fichte, Johann G. *Werke*. Vol. 7. Berlin: Walter de Gruyter & Co., 1971.
Fogarasi, Béla. "Az ítélet voluntaristikus elmélete" [The voluntaristic theory of judgment]. *Athenaeum* 22, no. 1 (1913): 58–100; 22, no. 2 (1913): 32–52.

———. *Bevezetés a marxi filozófiába* [Introduction to Marxist philosophy]. Wien: Europa Ismeretterjesztő Könyvtár, 1922.

———. "Konzervativ és progressziv idealizmus" [Conservative and progressive idealism]. *Huszadik Század* [Twentieth century] 19 (1918): 193–206.

———. *Visszaemlékezések a párt megalakulásának harcaira* [Recollections of the struggles to form the party]. Budapest: Magyar Tudomány, 1959.

———. "Zalai Béla: In Memoriam." *Athenaeum* 1 (1915): 428–41.

Fülep, Lajos. *A művészet forradalmától a nagy forradalomig: Cikkek, tanulmányok* [From artistic revolution to the great revolution: articles, studies]. 2 vols. Edited by Árpád Tímár. Budapest: Magvető Könyvkiadó, 1974.

———. "Az emlékezés a művészi alkotásban" [Remembrance in artistic creation]. *A Szellem* [Spirit] 1, no. 1 (1911): 56–90.

———. *Művészet és világnézet* [Art and world view]. Edited by Árpád Tímár. Budapest: Magvető Könyvkiadó, 1976.

———. "Új Suso-kiadás" [New edition of Suso]. *A Szellem* [Spirit] 1, no. 2 (1911): 254.

Gábor, Éva, ed. "Alexander Bernát levelei Lukács Györgyhöz, 1908–1913" [Bernát Alexander's letters to György Lukács]. *Irodalomtörténet* [Literary history] 10, no. 1 (1978): 224–54.

Gál, István, ed. "Babits béke-írásaiból" [From Babits's writings on peace]. *Irodalomtörténeti Közlemények* [Proceedings of literary history] 80, no. 4 (1976): 520–33.

———, ed. "Balázs Béla naplója" [Béla Balázs's diary]. *Kritika* [Criticism] no. 9 (1975): 3–10; no. 10 (1975): 14–18; no. 11 (1975): 20–23.

———. "Balázs és Lukács elitfolyóirat-terve 1910-ben" [Balázs and Lukács's plan for an elite journal in 1910]. *Tiszatáj* [Region of the Tisza] 30, no. 11 (1976): 46–53.

———. "Kodály és Balázs Béla barátsága" [The Kodály-Béla Balázs friendship]. *Tiszatáj* [Region of the Tisza] 28, no. 11 (1974): 66–72.

Gassen, Kurt, and Landmann, Michael, eds. *Buch des Dankes an Georg Simmel: Briefe, Erinnerungen, Bibliographie.* Berlin: Duncker & Humblot, 1958.

Gergely, Tibor, ed. *Lesznai képeskönyv: Lesznai Anna írásai, képei és hímzései* [Lesznai picture book: Anna Lesznai's writings, paintings, and needlework]. Budapest: Corvina Kiadó, 1978.

Gerth, H. H., and Mills, C. Wright, eds. *From Max Weber: Essays in Sociology.* New York: Oxford University Press, 1958.

Hauser, Arnold. "Az esztétikai rendszerezés problémája" [The problem of aesthetic systematization]. *Athenaeum* 4 (1918): 331–57.

———. *Im Gespräch mit Georg Lukács.* Munich: Verlag C. H. Beck, 1978.

———. *The Social History of Art.* Vol. 4. New York: Vintage Books, 1951.

Hebbel, Friedrich. "Judith." In *Werke.* Vol. 1, pp. 141–210. Hamburg: Hoffmann und Campe Verlag, n.d.

Hegel, G. W. F. *Phenomenology of Spirit.* Translated by A. V. Miller. Oxford: Oxford University Press, 1977.

Hofmannsthal, Hugo von. "Der Tor und der Tod." In *Poems and Verse Plays*, edited by Michael Hamburger, pp. 92–137. New York: Pantheon Books, 1961.

Hollósi, Mrs. Tibor, ed. *Nagy idők tanúi emlékeznek, 1918–1919* [Witnesses of great days remember]. Budapest: Kossuth Könyvkiadó, 1958.

Honigsheim, Paul. *On Max Weber.* Translated by Joan Rytina. New York: Free Press, 1968.

Irodalmi Muzeum: Emlékezések [Literary museum: recollections]. Budapest, 1967.

Jászi, Oszkár. "Mannheim Károly: *Lélek és kultura*" [Karl Mannheim: soul and culture].
   Huszadik Század [Twentieth century] 19 (1918): 192.
_____. "Proletárdiktatúra" [Proletarian dictatorship]. *Szabadgondolat* [Free thought]
   8, no. 10 (1918): 225–26.
_____. *Revolution and Counter-Revolution in Hungary*. New York: Howard Fertig,
   1969.
"Jelentés a Társadalomtudományok Szabad Iskolájának 1907–1908-ik évi működéséről"
   [Report on the Free School of the Sociological Society's 1907–8 activities]. *Hu-
   szadik Század* [Twentieth century] 9 (1908): xiv.
József, Farkas, ed. "*Mindenki újakra készül . . .": Az 1918/19-es forradalmak irodalma*
   [Everyone is preparing for the new: the literature of the 1918/19 revolutions]. Vol.
   4. Budapest: Akadémiai Kiadó, 1967.
Kant, Immanuel. *Werke*. Vol. 6. Berlin: Druck und Verlag von Georg Reimer, 1907.
Karádi, Éva, ed. "Dokumentumok Lukács György heidelbergi korszakából" [Documents
   from György Lukács's Heidelberg period]. *Valóság* [Reality] 17, no. 11 (1974):
   28–44.
_____, and Vezér, Erzsébet, eds. *A Vasárnapi Kör* [The Sunday circle]. Budapest:
   Gondolat, 1980.
Károlyi, Michael. *Memoirs: Faith without Illusion*. Translated by Catherine Károlyi. New
   York: E. P. Dutton & Co., 1957.
Kassák, Lajos. *Egy ember élete* [One man's life]. Vol. 4. Budapest: Pantheon Kiadás,
   n.d.
Komlos, Aladár. *Problémák a Nyugat körül* [Problems around *Nyugat*]. Budapest: Mag-
   vető Kiadó, 1978.
Kutasi, Elemér. "Esztétikai kutatások, II" [Aesthetic investigations]. *Huszadik Század*
   [Twentieth century] 12 (1911): 504–7.
Kutzbach, Karl August, ed. *Paul Ernst und Georg Lukács: Dokumente einer
   Freundschaft*. Emsdetten: Verlag Lechte, 1974.
Lask, Emil. *Die Logik der Philosophie und die Kategorienlehre*. Tübingen: Verlag von J.
   C. B. Mohr (Paul Siebeck), 1911.
Lengyel, József. *Bécsi portyák* [Tours of Vienna]. Budapest: Magvető Kiadó, 1970.
_____. *Prenn Ferenc hányatott élete* [Ferenc Prenn's storm-tossed life]. Budapest:
   Magvető, 1969.
_____. *Visegrádi utca* [Visegrád street]. Budapest: Szépirodalmi Könyvkiadó, 1962.
Lesznai, Anna. *Kezdetben volt a kert* [In the beginning was the garden]. 2 vols. Budapest:
   Szépirodalmi Könyvkiadó, 1966.
Löwy, Michael, ed. "Interview with Ernst Bloch." *New German Critique*, no. 9 (1976):
   35–45.
Mann, Katia. *Unwritten Memories*. Translated by Hunter and Hildegarde Hannum. New
   York: Alfred A. Knopf, 1975.
Mann, Thomas. *The Magic Mountain*. Translated by H. T. Lowe-Porter. New York:
   Vintage Books, 1969.
_____. "Tonio Kröger." In *Death in Venice and Seven Other Stories*. Translated by H. T.
   Lowe-Porter, pp. 76–134. New York: Vintage Books, 1930.
Mannheim, Károly. "A háboru bölcseletéhez [Toward a philosophy of the war]. *Huszadik
   Század* [Twentieth century] 18 (1917): 416–18.
_____. "Ernst Bloch: *Geist der Utopie*." *Athenaeum* 5 (1919): 207–11.
_____. *Essays on Sociology and Social Psychology*. Edited by Paul Kecskemeti. Lon-
   don: Routledge & Kegan Paul, 1953.

_____. "Georg Simmel, mint filozófus" [Georg Simmel as philosopher]. *Huszadik Század* [Twentieth century] 19 (1918): 194–96.

_____. *Lélek és kultura* [Soul and culture]. Budapest: Benkő Gyula Cs. és Kir. Udvari Könyvkereskedése, 1918.

_____. "Letters to Lukács, 1910–1916." Edited by Éva Gábor. *New Hungarian Quarterly* 16, no. 57 (1975): 93–105.

Masaryk, Thomas G. *The Spirit of Russia.* Vol. 2. Translated by Eden and Cedar Paul. London: George Allen & Unwin, 1955.

Mendel, Arthur P., ed. *Essential Works of Marxism.* New York: Bantam Books, 1965.

Molnár, Antal. "Emlékezés a Vasárnapi Társaságra" [Recollections of the Sunday society]. *Irodalomtörténet* [Literary history] 10, no. 2 (1978): 489–90.

Németh, Andor. *A szélén behajtva* [On the brink]. Budapest: Magvető Könyvkiadó, 1973.

New Hungarian Quarterly 13, no. 47 (1972).

Philosophical Forum 3, nos. 3–4 (1972).

Polányi, Károly. *A radikalizmus programmja és célja* [Radicalism's program and aim]. Szeged: Polgári Radikális Párt, n.d.

Popper, Leó. "Der Kitsch." *Die Fackel,* 31 December 1910, pp. 36–43.

_____. "Die Bildhauerei, Rodin und Maillol." *Die Fackel,* 29 April 1911, pp. 33–41.

_____. "Volkskunst und Formbeseelung." *Die Fackel,* 2 June 1911, pp. 37–39.

Popper Lukács, Mici. "Emlékek Lukács Györgyről" [Recollections of György Lukács]. *Nagyvilág* [Wide world] 20, no. 10 (1975): 1560–71.

Révai, Josef. "Georg Lukács, Geschichte und Klassenbewusstsein." *Archiv für die Geschichte des Sozialismus und der Arbeiterbewegung* 11 (1925): 227–36.

Ritoók, Emma. "A rút a művészetben" [The ugly in art]. *Athenaeum* 2 (1916): 177–205.

_____. *A szellem kalandorai* [Adventurers of the spirit]. 2 vols. Budapest: A Göncöl Kiadása, 1922.

_____. "Esztétikai kutatások, I" [Aesthetic investigations]. *Huszadik Század* [Twentieth century] 12 (1911): 502–4.

Ropshin [Boris Savinkov]. *The Pale Horse.* Translated by Z. Vengerova. New York: Alfred A. Knopf, 1919.

Savinkov, Boris. *Memoirs of a Terrorist.* Translated by Joseph Shaplen. New York: Albert & Charles Boni, 1931.

Serge, Victor. *Memoirs of a Revolutionary, 1901–1941.* Translated and edited by Peter Sedgwick. London: Oxford University Press, 1963.

Simmel, Georg. "Der Begriff und die Tragödie der Kultur." In *Philosophische Kultur,* pp. 245–77. Leipzig: Verlag von Dr. Werner Klinkhardt, 1911.

_____. *Philosophie des Geldes.* Leipzig: Verlag von Duncker & Humblot, 1900.

_____. "Zur Metaphysik des Todes." In *Brücke und Tür,* edited by Michael Landmann and Margarete Susman, pp. 29–36. Stuttgart: K. F. Koehler Verlag, 1957.

Simor, András, ed. *Korvin Ottó: ". . . a Gondolat él . . ."* [Ottó Korvin: the idea lives]. Budapest: Magvető Könyvkiadó, 1976.

Sinkó, Ervin. *Optimisták: Történelmi regény 1918–19-ből* [Optimists: historical novel from 1918–19]. 2 vols. Újvidék: Testvériség-Egység Könyvkiadóvállalat, 1953–55.

Sorel, Georges. *The Illusions of Progress.* Translated by John and Charlotte Stanley. Berkeley: University of California Press, 1969.

_____. *Reflections on Violence.* Translated by T. E. Hulme and J. Roth. New York: Collier Books, 1961.

Szabó, Ervin. *Társadalmi és pártharcok a 48–49-es magyar forradalomban* [Social and party conflicts in the 1848–49 Hungarian revolution]. Bécs: Bécsi Magyar Kiadó, 1921.

Szende, Paul. "Die Krise der mitteleuropäischen Revolution." *Archiv für Sozialwissenschaft und Sozialpolitik* 47 (1920/1921): 337–75.

Szilasi, Vilmos. "A kritika elmélete [The theory of criticism]. In *Emlékkönyv: Alexander Bernát* [Festschrift for Bernát Alexander], pp. 638–51. Budapest: Franklin-Társulat, 1910.

―――. *Platon* [Plato]. Budapest: Franklin-Társulat, 1910.

Tímár, Árpád, ed. "Popper Leó elfelejtett Lukács-ismertetése" [Leó Popper's forgotten Lukács-review]. *Irodalomtörténet* [Literary history] 3, no. 4 (1971): 967–72.

―――. "Újabb adalék a Babits-Lukács-vitához" [Fresh data concerning the Babits-Lukács debate]. *Irodalomtörténet* [Literary history] 6, no. 3 (1974): 618–26.

Tolnai, Károly. *Ferenczy Noémi.* Budapest: Bisztrai Farkas Ferencz Kiadása, 1934.

―――. "Popper Leó és a művészettörténet: Megjegyzések egy elfelejtett művészeti kritikusról" [Leó Popper and art history: notes on a forgotten art critic]. *Magyar Filozófiai Szemle* [Hungarian philosophical review] 16, no. 2 (1972): 249–61.

Tönnies, Ferdinand. *Community and Society.* Translated and edited by Charles P. Loomis. New York: Harper & Row, 1963.

Traub, Reiner, and Wieser, Harald, eds. *Gespräche mit Ernst Bloch.* Frankfurt am Main: Suhrkamp Verlag, 1975.

Tucker, Robert C., ed. *The Lenin Anthology.* New York: W. W. Norton and Company, 1975.

Weber, Marianne. *Fichte's Sozialismus und sein Verhältnis zur Marx'schen Doktrin.* Tübingen: Verlag von J. C. B. Mohr (Paul Siebeck), 1900.

―――. *Max Weber: A Biography.* Translated by Harry Zohn. New York: John Wiley, 1975.

Weber, Max. "Georg Simmel as Sociologist." Translated by Donald N. Levine. *Social Research* 39, no. 1 (1972): 155–63.

―――. *The Protestant Ethic and the Spirit of Capitalism.* Translated by Talcott Parsons. New York: Charles Scribner's Sons, 1958.

Zalai, Béla. "A filozófiai rendszerezés problémája" [The problem of philosophic systematization]. *A Szellem* [Spirit] 1, no. 2 (1911): 159–86.

―――. "Levelei kortársaihoz" [Letters to contemporaries]. Edited by Ottó Beöthy. *Kritika* [Criticism], no. 8 (1975): 5–10.

SECONDARY SOURCES

Abrams, M. H. *Natural Supernaturalism.* New York: W. W. Norton and Company, 1971.

Almási, Miklós. "Lukács's 'Heidelberg Aesthetics.'" *New Hungarian Quarterly* 18, no. 65 (1977): 152–55.

Apitzsch, Ursula. *Gesellschaftstheorie und Ästhetik bei Georg Lukács bis 1933.* Stuttgart: Frommann-Holzboog, 1977.

Arato, Andrew. "Georg Lukács: The Search for a Revolutionary Subject." In *The Unknown Dimension: European Marxism since Lenin,* edited by Dick Howard and Karl E. Klare, pp. 81–106. New York: Basic Books, 1972.

―――. "Lukács' Path to Marxism, 1910–1923." *Telos,* no. 7 (1971): 128–36.

―――, and Breines, Paul. *The Young Lukács and the Origins of Western Marxism.* New York: Seabury Press, 1979.

Bahr, Ehrhard. *Ernst Bloch.* Berlin: Colloquium Verlag, 1974.

————. *Georg Lukács*. Berlin: Colloquium Verlag, 1970.

Balogh, Eva S. "The Turning of the World: Hungarian Progressive Writers on the War." In *The Habsburg Empire in World War I*, edited by Robert A. Kann et al., pp. 185–201. Boulder: East European Quarterly, 1977.

Barany, George. " 'Magyar Jew or: Jewish Magyar'?" *Canadian-American Slavic Studies* 8, no. 1 (1974): 1–44.

Baumer, Franklin L. "Twentieth-Century Version of the Apocalypse." In *European Intellectual History since Darwin and Marx*, edited by W. Warren Wagar, pp. 110–34. New York: Harper & Row, 1967.

Bellér, Béla. "Tanácsköztársaság és erkölcs" [Soviet republic and morality]. *Világosság* [Clarity] 10, nos. 8–9 (1969): 519–26.

Benseler, Frank, ed. *Festschrift zum achtzigsten Geburtstag von Georg Lukács*. Neuwied: Hermann Luchterhand Verlag, 1965.

Benz, Ernst. *Les sources mystiques de la philosophie romantique allemande*. Paris: Librairie Philosophique J. Vrin, 1968.

Berdyaev, Nicolas. *The Origin of Russian Communism*. Ann Arbor: University of Michigan Press, 1960.

————. *The Russian Idea*. New York: Macmillan Company, 1948.

Bettelheim, Bruno. *The Uses of Enchantment: The Meaning and Importance of Fairy Tales*. New York: Alfred A. Knopf, 1976.

Boella, Laura. *Il giovane Lukács*. Bari: De Donato Editore, 1977.

Bori, Imre. "Lukács György és a magyar irodalom [György Lukács and Hungarian literature]. *Híd* [Bridge] 29, no. 4 (1965): 441–63.

Borkenau, Franz. *World Communism*. Ann Arbor: University of Michigan Press, 1962.

Borsányi, György. "Az emigráció első éve: Fejezetek Kun Béla életéből" [The first year of exile: chapters from the life of Béla Kun]. *Valóság* [Reality] 20, no. 12 (1977): 36–49.

Bosnyák, István. "Lukács György tanácsköztársasági messianizmusa" [György Lukács's messianism during the Soviet republic]. *Valóság* [Reality] 22, no. 8 (1979): 51–55.

Bourdet, Yvon. *Figures de Lukács*. Paris: Éditions Anthropos, 1972.

Breines, Paul. "Marxism, Romanticism, and the Case of Georg Lukács: Notes on Some Recent Sources and Situations." *Studies in Romanticism* 16, no. 4 (1977): 473–89.

————. "Young Lukács, Old Lukács, New Lukács." *Journal of Modern History* 51, no. 3 (1979): 533–46.

Breuer, János. "Babits és Lukács vitájához" [On the Babits-Lukács debate]. *Irodalomtörténet* [Literary history] 8, no. 3 (1976): 745–48.

Campbell, T. M. *Hebbel, Ibsen and the Analytic Exposition*. Heidelberg: Carl Winters Universitätsbuchhandlung, 1922.

Camus, Albert. *The Rebel*. Translated by Anthony Bower. New York: Vintage Books, 1956.

Charzat, Michel. *Georges Sorel et la révolution au XX siècle*. Paris: Librairie Hachette, 1977.

Cohn, Norman. *The Pursuit of the Millennium: Revolutionary Millenarians and Mystical Anarchists of the Middle Ages*. New York: Oxford University Press, 1970.

Congdon, Lee. "Lukács, Camus, and the Russian Terrorists." *Continuity*, no. 1 (1980): 17–36.

————. "The Making of a Hungarian Revolutionary: The Unpublished Diary of Béla Balázs." *Journal of Contemporary History* 8, no. 3 (1973): 57–74.

————. "The Tragic Sense of Life: Lukács's *The Soul and the Forms*." In *Austrian Philosophy*, edited by J. C. Nyíri, pp. 43–74. Munich: Philosophia Verlag, 1981.

———. "The Unexpected Revolutionary: Lukács's Road to Marx." *Survey* 20, nos. 2–3 (91/92) (1974): 176–205.

Copleston, Frederick, S. J. *A History of Philosophy.* Vol. 7, Part 1. Garden City, N. Y.: Image Books, 1965.

Csanak, Dóra F. *Balázs Béla hagyatéka az akadémiai könyvtár kézirattárában (MS 5009–MS 5024* [Béla Balázs's literary remains in the manuscripts archive of the academy library]. Budapest: Bibliotheca Academiae Scientiarum Hungaricae, 1966.

Cushing, G. F. "Problems of Hungarian Literary Criticism." *Slavonic and East European Review* 40, no. 95 (1962): 341–55.

Czigány, L. G. "Hungarianness: The Origin of a Pseudo-Linguistic Concept." *Slavonic and East European Review* 52, no. 128 (1974): 325–36.

"Der Mann mit dem Koffer." *Der Spiegel,* 27 August 1973, pp. 100–1.

Faesi, Robert. *Paul Ernst und die neuklassischen Bestrebungen im Drama.* Leipzig: Xenien-Verlag, 1913.

Fehér, Ferenc. "Am Scheideweg des romantischen Antikapitalismus. Typologie und Beitrag zur deutschen Ideologiegeschichte gelegentlich des Briefwechsels zwischen Paul Ernst und Georg Lukács." In *Die Seele und das Leben: Studien zum frühen Lukács,* edited by Ágnes Heller, pp. 241–327. Frankfurt am Main: Suhrkamp, 1977.

———. "Balázs Béla és Lukács György szövetsége a forradalomig" [The Béla Balázs–György Lukács alliance until the revolution]. *Irodalomtörténet* [Literary history] 1, no. 2 (1969): 317–46; 1, no. 3 (1969): 531–60.

———. "Die Geschichtsphilosophie des Dramas, die Metaphysik der Tragödie und die Utopie des untragischen Dramas. Scheidewege der Dramentheorie des jungen Lukács." In *Die Seele und das Leben: Studien zum frühen Lukács,* edited by Ágnes Heller, pp. 7–53. Frankfurt am Main: Suhrkamp, 1977.

———. "Lucien Goldmann, the 'Mere Recipient' of Georg Lukács." *Philosophy and Social Criticism* 6, no. 1 (1979): 1–24.

———, et al. "Notes on Lukács' Ontology." *Telos,* no. 29 (1976): 160–81.

Fekete, Éva. "Lukács esszékorszaka" [Lukács's essay period]. *Mozgó Világ* [Restless world] 2, no. 6 (1976): 85–95.

———. "Lukács György az első világháború éveiben" [György Lukács during the years of the First World War]. *Valóság* [Reality] 20, no. 2 (1977): 33–44.

Földényi, F. László. *A fiatal Lukács* [The young Lukács]. Budapest: Magvető Kiadó, 1980.

———. "Az egyértelműség igézetében: Az etika és esztétika a fiatal Lukács gondolkodásában" [Under the spell of harmony: ethics and aesthetics in the young Lukács's thinking]. *Világosság* [Clarity] 20, no. 5 (1979): 304–10.

Fuerst, Norbert. *Ideologie und Literatur: Zum Dialog zwischen Paul Ernst und Georg Lukács.* Emsdetten: Verlag Lechte, 1976.

Gluck, Mary. "Politics versus Culture: Radicalism and the Lukács Circle in Turn-of-the-Century Hungary." *East European Quarterly* 14, no. 2 (1980): 129–54.

Goldmann, Lucien. "The Early Writings of Georg Lukács." Translated by Joy N. Humes. *Tri-Quarterly,* no. 9 (1967): 165–81.

———. "Georg Lukács: L'essayiste." In *Recherches dialectiques,* pp. 247–59. Paris: Librairie Gallimard, 1959.

———. *Lukács et Heidegger.* Paris: Éditions Denoël, 1973.

Hanák, Péter. "Kései rehabilitáció" [Belated rehabilitation]. *Világosság* [Clarity] 10, no. 3 (1969): 158–61.

———, ed. *Magyarország története, 1890–1918* [History of Hungary]. 2 vols.

Budapest: Akadémiai Kiadó, 1978.

Hanák Tibor. *A filozófus Lukács* [Lukács the philosopher]. Párizs: Magyar Műhely, 1972.

_____. "Lukács György hite" [György Lukács's faith]. *Új Látóhatár* [New horizon] (1976): 206–20.

_____. *Lukács war anders*. Meisenheim am Glan: Verlag Anton Hain, 1973.

Hegyi, Béla. "A fiatal Lukács György" [The young György Lukács]. *Vigilia* [Vigil] 36, no. 9 (1971): 609–18.

_____. "Lukács György nézetei" [György Lukács's views]. *Vigilia* [Vigil] 35, no. 6 (1970): 401–6.

Heller, Ágnes. "A kötelességen túl: A német klasszika etikájának paradigmatikussága Lukács György életművében" [Beyond duty: the paradigmatic character of classical German ethics in György Lukács's life-work]. *Korunk* [Our age] 33, no. 1 (1974): 31–41.

_____. *Portrévázlatok az etika történetéből* [Portrait sketches from the history of ethics]. Budapest: Gondolat Kiadó, 1976.

_____. " 'Von der Armut am Geiste': A Dialogue by the Young Lukács." *Philosophical Forum* 3, nos. 3–4 (1972): 360–70.

Hermann, István. "A misztikus és a mitikus" [The mystical and the mythical]. *Valóság* [Reality] 24, no. 3 (1981): 20–26.

_____. *Lukács György gondolatvilága* [György Lukács's world of thought]. Budapest: Magvető Kiadó, 1974.

Horowitz, Irving Louis. *Radicalism and the Revolt against Reason.* New York: Humanities Press, 1961.

Horváth, Zoltán. *Magyar századforduló: A második reformnemzedék története, 1896–1914* [Hungarian fin de siècle: history of the second reform generation]. Budapest: Gondolat, 1961.

Johnston, William M. *The Austrian Mind.* Berkeley: University of California Press, 1972.

József, Farkas. *"Rohanunk a forradalomba"* [We are rushing headlong to revolution]. Budapest: Gondolat Kiadó, 1969.

Kadarkay, Arpad. "Georg Lukács's Road to Art & Marx." *Polity* 13, no. 2 (1980): 230–60.

Katona, Ferenc, and Dénes, Tibor. *A Thália története, 1904–1908* [History of Thália]. Budapest: Művelt Nép Könyvkiadó, 1954.

Kaufmann, Walter. "Martin Buber." *Encounter* 52, no. 5 (1979): 31–38.

Kelly, George Armstrong. *Idealism, Politics and History.* Cambridge: Cambridge University Press, 1969.

Kenyeres, Zoltán. "Lukács György és a magyar kultúra" [György Lukács and Hungarian culture]. *Kritika* [Criticism] 8, no. 12 (1970): 1–10; 9, no. 3 (1971): 4–15.

_____. "Lukács György útja a forradalomig" [György Lukács's road to revolution]. *Kritika* [Criticism] 3, no. 10 (1965): 41–46.

Kettler, David. "Culture and Revolution: Lukács in the Hungarian Revolutions of 1918/19." *Telos*, no. 10 (1971): 35–92.

Kiss, Endre. "Néhány motívum a fiatal Lukács Nietzsche-ábrázolásából" [Several motifs in the young Lukács's portrayal of Nietzsche]. *Magyar Filozófiai Szemle* [Hungarian philosophical review] 23, nos. 3–4 (1979): 529–32.

Knight, Amy. "Female Terrorists in the Russian Socialist Revolutionary Party." *Russian Review* 38, no. 2 (1979): 139–59.

Kolakowski, Leszek. *Main Currents of Marxism.* 3 vols. Translated by P. S. Falla. Oxford: Clarendon Press, 1978.

Könczöl, Csaba. "Stílus és korszak—Lukács György: A lélek és a formák" [Style and era—György Lukács: the soul and the forms]. *Valóság* [Reality] 18, no. 3 (1975): 48–57.

Köpeczi, Béla. "Lukács in 1919." *New Hungarian Quarterly* 20, no. 75 (1979): 65–76.

Laqueur, Walter. *Terrorism*. Boston: Little, Brown and Company, 1977.

László, Anna. *Hevesi Sándor*. Budapest: Gondolat, 1973.

Lendvai, L. Ferenc. "A drámakönyv történelemképe és helye a fiatal Lukács munkásságában" [The historical aspect of the drama book and its place in the young Lukács's work]. *Magyar Filozófiai Szemle* [Hungarian philosophical review] 21, no. 1 (1977): 1–27.

———. "A fiatal Lukács történetfilozófiájához: Magyarország és Kelet-Európa" [On the young Lukács's historical philosophy: Hungary and east Europe]. *Világosság* [Clarity] 16, no. 6 (1975): 344–51.

———. "Hatvan év után: Lukács művészetfilozófiai-esztétikai kéziratainak kiadásához" [Sixty years after: on the publication of Lukács's art-philosophical and aesthetic manuscripts]. *Világosság* [Clarity] 17, no. 6 (1976): 376–84.

———. "Lukács György és Seidler Irma" [György Lukács and Irma Seidler]. *Világosság* [Clarity] 16, no. 1 (1975): 34–36.

———. "Weininger és Lukács" [Weininger and Lukács]. *Világosság* [Clarity] 22, no. 1 (1981): 35–37.

Lengyel, András. "A fiatal Révai 'etikus' nézeteiről: Adalék Lukács György és Révai József 1919-es kapcsolatához" [On the young Révai's ethical views: data on the relationship between György Lukács and József Révai in 1919]. *Irodalomtörténet* [Literary history] 5, no. 2 (1973): 281–311.

Lenk, Kurt. "Das tragische Bewusstsein in der deutschen Soziologie." *Kölner Zeitschrift für Soziologie und Sozialpsychologie* 16, no. 2 (1964): 257–87.

Lichtheim, George. *Lukács*. London: Fontana/Collins, 1970.

Litván, György. "Apáink válaszútja: Tallózás a 'Szabadgondolat' 1918–1919-es számaiban" [Our forebears' crossroads: gleanings from the 1918–1919 numbers of Free Thought]. *Új Írás* [New writing] 12, no. 3 (1972): 109–17.

———. "A századelő magyar szellemi életéről" [On Hungarian intellectual life at the beginning of the century]. *Arion*, no. 10 (1977): 15–21.

———. "Egy magyar tudós tragikus pályája a század elején: Somló Bódog, 1873–1920" [The tragic career of a Hungarian scholar at the beginning of the century: Bódog Somló]. *Valóság* [Reality] 16, no. 8 (1973): 32–42.

López Soria, José Ignacio. *De lo tragico a lo utopico: Sobre el primer Lukács*. Caracas: Monte Avila Editores, C.A., 1977.

———. "L'expérience théâtrale de Lukács." *L'homme et la société*, nos. 43–44 (1977): 117–31.

Löwith, Karl. *Meaning in History*. Chicago: University of Chicago Press, 1949.

Löwy, Michael. *Pour une sociologie des intellectuels révolutionnaires: L'évolution politique de Lukács, 1909–1929*. Paris: Presses Universitaires de France, 1976.

"Lukács." *Revue Internationale de Philosophie*, no. 106 (1973).

"Lukács György emlékszám" [György Lukács memorial issue]. *Híd* [Bridge] 36, no. 4 (1972).

Lukács, József. "A vallás és az irracionalizmus problémái Lukács György életművében" [The problems of religion and irrationalism in György Lukács's life-work]. *Valóság* [Reality] 18, no. 8 (1975): 1–9.

McCabe, Bernard. " 'Necessary Murder': Spender and Auden in the 30's." *Commentary*

67 (1979): 51–57.

McCagg, William O., Jr. *Jewish Nobles and Geniuses in Modern Hungary*. Boulder: East European Quarterly, 1972.

———. "Jews in Revolutions: The Hungarian Experience." *Journal of Social History* 6, no. 1 (1972): 78–105.

Maerker, Peter. *Die Ästhetik der Südwestdeutschen Schule*. Bonn: Bouvier Verlag Herbert Grundmann, 1973.

Malter, Rudolf. "Heinrich Rickert und Emil Lask." *Zeitschrift für Philosophische Forschung* 23, no. 1 (1969): 86–97.

Marck, Siegfried. "Neukritizistische und Neuhegelsche Auffassung der marxistischen Dialektik." *Die Gesellschaft* 1, no. 6 (1924): 573–78.

Márkus, György. "Lukács' 'erste' Ästhetik: Zur Entwicklungsgeschichte der Philosophie des jungen Lukács." In *Die Seele und das Leben: Studien zum frühen Lukács*, edited by Ágnes Heller, pp. 192–240. Frankfurt am Main: Suhrkamp, 1977.

———. "The Soul and Life: The Young Lukács and the Problem of Culture." *Telos*, no. 32 (1977): 95–115.

Matzner, Jutta, ed. *Lehrstück Lukács*. Frankfurt am Main: Suhrkamp, 1974.

Mészáros, István. *Lukács' Concept of Dialectic*. London: Merlin Press, 1972.

———, ed. *Aspects of History and Class Consciousness*. London: Routledge & Kegan Paul, 1971.

Mitzman, Arthur. *The Iron Cage: An Historical Interpretation of Max Weber*. New York: Alfred A. Knopf, 1970.

———. *Sociology and Estrangement*. New York: Alfred A. Knopf, 1973.

Molnar, Thomas. *Utopia: The Perennial Heresy*. New York: Sheed and Ward, 1967.

Nagy, Magda K. *Balázs Béla világa* [Béla Balázs's world]. Budapest: Kossuth Könyv-kiadó, 1973.

Nisbet, Robert. *The Quest for Community*. London: Oxford University Press, 1969.

———. *Sociology as an Art Form*. New York: Oxford University Press, 1976.

Novák, Zoltán. *A Vasárnap Társaság* [The Sunday society]. Budapest: Kossuth Könyv-kiadó, 1979.

———. "Lukács György a filmművészet elméleti problémáiról" [György Lukács on the theoretical problems of cinematic art]. *Magyar Filozófiai Szemle* [Hungarian philosophical review] 19, nos. 5–6 (1975): 552–73.

Nyíri, Kristóf. "Ady és Lukács" [Ady and Lukács]. *Világosság* [Clarity] 19, no. 2 (1978): 65–71.

———. "Az orosz irodalom hatása Lukácsra és Wittgensteinra" [The influence of Russian literature on Lukács and Wittgenstein]. *Világosság* [Clarity] 22, no. 1 (1981): 38–40.

———. "Kemény, Eötvös és Madách" [Kemény, Eötvös, and Madách]. *Valóság* [Reality] 21, no. 5 (1978): 20–35.

———. "Lukács 'Die Seele und die Formen' c. esszékötetének fordítástörténetéhez" [On the translation history of Lukács's essay volume, Die Seele und die Formen]. *Magyar Filozófiai Szemle* [Hungarian philosophical review] 18, nos. 2–3 (1974): 401–4.

———, and Kiss, Endre, eds. *A magyar filozófiai gondolkodás a századelőn* [Hungarian philosophic thought at the beginning of the century]. Budapest: Kossuth Könyv-kiadó, 1977.

Pályi, András. "Hevesi Sándor öröksége" [Sándor Hevesi's legacy]. *Vigilia* [Vigil] 35, no. 7 (1970): 452–58.

Parkinson, G. H. R. *Georg Lukács*. London: Routledge & Kegan Paul, 1977.

————, ed. *Georg Lukács: The Man, His Work and His Ideas*. London: Weidenfeld and Nicolson, 1970.

Passuth, Krisztina. *A Nyolcak festészete* [The painting of The Eight]. Budapest: Athenaeum Nyomda, 1967.

Pastor, Peter. *Hungary between Wilson and Lenin: The Hungarian Revolution of 1918– 1919 and the Big Three*. Boulder: East European Quarterly, 1976.

————. "The Vix Mission in Hungary, 1918–1919." *Slavic Review* 29, no. 3 (1970): 481–98.

Percy, Walker. *Lancelot*. New York: Farrar, Straus and Giroux, 1977.

Perneczky, Géza. "Egy magyar művészetfilozófus" [A Hungarian art philosopher]. *Magyar Filozófiai Szemle* [Hungarian philosophical review] 14, nos. 3–4 (1970): 621–55.

Raddatz, Fritz J. *Georg Lukács*. Reinbek bei Hamburg: Rowohlt Taschenbuch Verlag, 1972.

Radnóti, Sándor. "A szenvedő misztikus" [Suffering mystic]. *Vigilia* [Vigil] 40, no. 5 (1975): 317–27; 40, no. 7 (1975): 470–81.

————. "Bloch and Lukács: Two Radical Critics in a 'God-Forsaken World.' " *Telos*, no. 25 (1975): 155–64.

Rochlitz, Rainer. "Lukács et Heidegger." *L'homme et la société*, nos. 43–44 (1977): 87–94.

Rockmore, Tom. "Activity in Fichte and Marx." *Idealistic Studies* 6, no. 2 (1976): 191–214.

————. "Lukács on Classical German Philosophy and Marx." *Idealistic Studies* 10, no. 3 (1980): 209–31.

Rosshoff, Hartmut. *Emil Lask als Lehrer von Georg Lukács*. Bonn: Bouvier Verlag Herbert Grundmann, 1975.

Sándor, Pál. *A magyar filozófia története, 1900–1945* [History of Hungarian philosophy]. 2 vols. Budapest: Magvető Kiadó, 1973.

Scherrer, Jutta. *Die Petersburger Religiös-Philosophischen Vereinigungen*. Berlin: Osteuropa-Institut, 1973.

————. "Pour une théologie de la révolution: Merejkovski et le symbolisme russe." *Archives de Sciences Sociales des Religions* 45, no. 1 (1978): 27–50.

Schlett, István. "Szabó Ervin és az 'etikai idealizmus' vitája 1918-ban" [Ervin Szabó and the ethical idealism debate in 1918]. *Valóság* [Reality] 11, no. 10 (1968): 95–101.

Schmidt, James. "The Concrete Totality and Lukács' Concept of Proletarian *Bildung*." *Telos*, no. 24 (1975): 2–40.

Schmithals, Walter. *The Apocalyptic Movement*. Translated by John E. Steely. Nashville: Abingdon Press, 1975.

Scholem, Gershom G. *Major Trends in Jewish Mysticism*. New York: Schocken Books, 1954.

————. *The Messianic Idea in Judaism*. New York: Schocken Books, 1971.

Schorske, Carl E. "Politics and Patricide in Freud's *Interpretation of Dreams*." *American Historical Review* 78, no. 2 (1973): 328–47.

Siklós, András. "Károlyi Mihály lemondása" [Mihály Károlyi's resignation]. *Élet és Irodalom* [Life and literature] 28 April 1979, p. 2.

Sommerhäuser, Hanspeter. "Emil Lask, 1875–1915." *Zeitschrift für Philosophische Forschung* 21, no. 1 (1967): 136–45.

"Special Lukács Issues." *Telos*, no. 10 (1971); no. 11 (1972).

Stromberg, Roland N. "The Intellectuals and the Coming of War in 1914." *Journal of European Studies* 3, no. 2 (1973): 109–22.

Sükösd, Mihály. "Sinkó Ervin." *Valóság* [Reality] 18, no. 11 (1975): 23–39.

Szabolcsi, Miklós. "Út a magánytól a közösségig: Balázs Béla" [The road from loneliness to community: Béla Balázs]. In *A magyar irodalom története 1919–től napjainkig* [History of Hungarian literature from 1919 to the present], edited by Miklós Szabolcsi, pp. 245–62. Budapest: Akadémiai Kiadó, 1966.

Szekfű, Gyula. *Magyar történet* [Hungarian history] Vol. 5. Budapest: Királyi Magyar Egyetemi Nyomda, 1936.

Szerdahelyi, Edit. "Irodalom és politika 1918–1919-ben" [Literature and politics in 1918–1919]. *Valóság* [Reality] 12, no. 6 (1969): 41–47.

Tar, Judith. "Georg Lukács, Thomas Mann und 'Der Tod in Venedig.'" *Die Weltwoche*, 2 July 1971, p. 31.

———. "Thomas Mann und Georg Lukács." Ph.D. dissertation, University of Kansas, 1976.

Tertulian, N. "Bevezetés Lukács György esztétikájába" [Introduction to György Lukács's aesthetics]. *Magyar Filozófiai Szemle* [Hungarian philosophical review] 17, nos. 1–2 (1973): 141–58; 18, no. 6 (1974): 808–23.

———. "Lukács György szellemi fejlődése" [György Lukács's intellectual evolution]. *Magyar Filozófiai Szemle* [Hungarian philosophical review] 14, nos. 3–4 (1970): 401–26.

Tímár, Árpád. "Hauser Arnold pályakezdése" [Arnold Hauser's early career]. *Ars Hungarica*, no. 1 (1974): 191–204.

Tőkei, Ferenc. "Lukács György, a filozófus" [György Lukács, the philosopher]. *Új Írás* [New writing] 11, no. 8 (1971): 4–5.

Tőkés, Rudolf L. *Béla Kun and the Hungarian Soviet Republic.* New York: Frederick A. Praeger, 1967.

Tömöry, Márta. *Új vizeken járok: A Galilei Kör története* [I move on new waters: history of the Galileo circle]. Budapest: Gondolat, 1960.

Vajda, Mihály. "Law, Ethics and Interest." *Telos*, no. 34 (1977–78): 173–79.

Varga, Csaba. "A jog helye Lukács *Ontológiá*jában" [The place of law in Lukács's *Ontology*]. *Valóság* [Reality] 22, no. 8 (1979): 39–50.

———. "Az ifjú Lukács és a jog" [The young Lukács and law]. *Világosság* [Clarity] 20, no. 11 (1979): 664–71.

Vekerdi, László. "A fiatal Fülep" [The young Fülep]. *Valóság* [Reality] 17, no. 4 (1974): 9–25.

Vezér, Erzsébet. "Hajós Edit halálára" [On the death of Edit Hajós]. *Élet és Irodalom* [Life and literature] 23 August 1975, p. 8.

———. *Lesznai Anna élete* [Life of Anna Lesznai]. Budapest: Kossuth Könyvkiadó, 1979.

Völgyes, Iván, ed. *Hungary in Revolution, 1918–19.* Lincoln: University of Nebraska Press, 1971.

Watnick, Morris. "Georg Lukács: An Intellectual Biography." *Soviet Survey*, January–March 1958, pp. 60–66; April–June 1958, pp. 51–57; July–September 1958, pp. 61–68; January–March 1959, pp. 75–81.

Wessely, Anna. "Antal and Lukács—the Marxist Approach to the History of Art." *New Hungarian Quarterly* 20, no. 73 (1979): 114–25.

———. "A Szellemi Tudományok Szabad Iskolája és a Vasárnapi Kör" [The Free School of the Humanistic Sciences and the Sunday circle]. *Világosság* [Clarity] 16, no. 10 (1975): 613–20.

Zipes, Jack. "Breaking the Magic Spell: Politics and the Fairy Tale." *New German Critique*, no. 6 (1975): 116–35.

————. "The Revolutionary Rise of the Romantic Fairy Tale in Germany." *Studies in Romanticism* 16, no. 4 (1977): 409–50.

Zitta, Victor. *Georg Lukács' Marxism: Alienation, Dialectics, Revolution: A Study in Utopia and Ideology.* The Hague: Martinus Nijhoff, 1964.

I·N·D·E·X

Abraham, 68
Adorno, Theodor W., 23
Adventurers of the Spirit, The (Ritoók), 135, 187
Ady, Endre, 73, 124, 133, 165; and Hungarian intellectual life, 56–57; and mysticism, 75; and World War I, 97, 110; and socialism, 105
Aesthetic Culture, 32, 53–54
"Aesthetics of the 'Romance,' The," 80
Age of absolute sinfulness, 98, 100, 109, 132, 140, 143, 148
Alexander Bernát, 24–25, 35, 58, 61, 82–84, 120–21
Alienation, ix, 20, 22, 24, 29, 43, 48–49, 51, 67, 80, 93–94, 98–100, 108, 114–15, 121, 125–26, 148, 158–59, 179; in Lukács's home, 4; in Hungary, 9; in modern world, 10; and Western culture, 11, 25, 27, 86; Lukács's, 30, 40; of ordinary life, 32; Balázs's, 34; and ethics, 68, Buber's, 76; Lesznai's, 79; of intellectuals, 96; and Sunday Circle, 119; and Free School of the Humanistic Sciences, 123; and the "new culture," 157; resolution of, 183
Anabaptism, 130
Analytic drama, 21
Andrássy, Gyula, 7, 189 (n. 21)
Antal, Frederick, 118, 123, 125–26, 157
Antigone (Sophocles), 26, 31
Anti-Semitism, 8, 76, 84, 200 (n. 63)
Antoine, André, 16, 31
Apocalypse, 69, 103, 109–10, 135, 143
Apponyi, Albert, 7
Arany, János, 53, 193 (n. 41)
Ariadne auf Naxos (Ernst), 81
Aristotle, 74
Ästhetik, 41
Athenaeum, 58, 120–21
Augustine, Saint, 101, 109
Ausgleich, 6–8, 10
Azev, Yevgeny, 102–3, 197 (n. 31)

Baal Shem, Israel, 76, 78, 188
Babits, Mihály, 53–54, 57, 127, 157; and antiwar movement, 133–34
Balázs, Béla (Herbert Bauer), 46, 50, 54, 57–59, 61–62, 78–79, 81, 112–13, 117, 122, 129, 132, 169–70, 201 (n. 80); and Thália Society, 17, 36; sense of alienation, 34; *Dreaming Youth*, 34–35; *Death Aesthetics*, 36, 38; *Dr. Margit Szélpál*, 38–39; *The Wanderer Sings*, 39; affair with Irma Seidler, 66; and fairy tales, 80; and Ljena Grabenko, 89–90; *Soul in War*, 97; and Sunday Circle, 118–19, 121, 175–76; and Free School of the Humanistic Sciences, 120, 123, 125–26; and Dostoevski, 127–28; and antiwar movement, 133–34; joins Hungarian Communist party, 139; during Hungarian Soviet Republic, 157–60

Balzac, Honoré de, 97, 176–77
Bánóczi, József, 16, 84
Bánóczi, László, 16–19, 23, 42, 47, 58
Bartók, Béla, 36, 119, 124, 126, 157, 159
Bauer, Ervin, 34
Bauer, Herbert. *See* Balázs, Béla
Bauer, Hilda, 22, 34, 46, 90
Baumgarten, Franz, 62, 84, 168–69, 194 (n. 84)
Beer-Hofmann, Richard, 48–51, 53, 65, 169
Before Sunrise (Hauptmann), 16
Being and Time (Heidegger), 36
Béla Balázs and His Detractors, 126
Belgrade Convention, 153
Benedek, Marcell, 7, 16–17, 58, 157
Beneš, Eduard, 164
Beöthy, Zsolt, 9, 83–84, 156
Berdyaev, Nicolas, 108
Berinkey, Dénes, 152
Bloch, Ernst, 81–84, 108, 160, 179, 196 (n. 49); meets Lukács, 73–74; atheism of, 75; and Weber Circle, 85; on Lukács and Russia, 92, 136; *Geist der Utopie*, 110–11, 121; and Emma Ritoók, 195 (n. 40), 200 (n. 63)
Böhme, Jakob, 74, 76, 148
Bolshevism, 137–39, 141–43, 152–53
"Bolshevism as a Moral Problem," 138–40
Bolzano Circle, 120, 126
Bordiga, Amadeo, 173
Bortstieber, Gertrúd, ix, 11, 147–48; personality of, 149; marries Lukács, 170, 204 (n. 10)
Brahm, Otto, 16, 31
Brecht, Bertolt, 160
Brilliant, Dora, 201 (n. 79)
Brothers Karamazov, The (Dostoevski), 88, 100, 105–6, 149, 159
Brunhild (Ernst), 33, 63, 81
Buber, Martin, 75–79, 110, 195 (n. 17)
Bubnoff, Nikolai von, 87–88
Bureaucracy, 86, 172–74
Burtsev, Vladimir, 197 (n. 31)

Calvinism, 87–88
Capitalism, 11, 25, 27, 86, 180–81; and Protestant ethic, 87–88, 91; and alienation, 179, 183
Cézanne, Paul, 41–42, 58, 60, 74, 97, 122–24
Characteristics of the Present Age (Fichte), 109, 148
Christianity, 81, 105, 109, 171
Circle of Hungarian Impressionists and Naturalists, 60
City of God (Augustine), 109
Class consciousness, 151, 162, 164, 174, 180–81, 186; as ethics of the proletariat, 182
Clemenceau, Georges, 162–64
Cohn, Norman, 109
Commissariat of Public Education, 156, 158–60

Community, 49, 76, 79, 96–97, 108, 110, 119, 150, 182, 186, 188, 192 (n. 31); quest for, 10, 39, 93; Lukács and, 45–46, 92, 101; and socialism, 105; and Free School of the Humanistic Sciences, 126. See also *Gemeinschaft*
"Conservative and Progressive Idealism" (Fogarasi), 128–29
Counterculture (Hungary), 19, 54, 56–58
Crime and Punishment (Dostoevski), 108, 139
Critique of Judgment (Kant), 114, 199 (n. 87)
Critique of Practical Reason (Kant), 131, 184
Croce, Benedetto, 60

Dante, 26, 31, 43, 63
Deák, Ferenc, 6, 8
Death, 63–64, 110, 120, 191 (n. 65)
Death Aesthetics (Balázs), 36, 38, 120
Death and the Fool (Hofmannsthal), 36
Death of Ivan Ilyich, The (Tolstoi), 36
De Tolnay, Charles, 41, 93, 126, 175, 200 (n. 24)
Dialectics, 11, 142, 148, 151, 160, 179, 184, 186, 204 (n. 37)
Dilthey, Wilhelm, 26, 74–75, 125
Documents of Unity, The, 155
Dohnányi, Ernő, 157, 159, 202 (n. 33)
Doll's House, A (Ibsen), 30
Dostoevski, Fyodor, ix, 10, 68, 104, 111, 119, 124, 135, 159, 201 (n. 71); and Max Weber, 88–89, 196 (n. 70); and Lukács, 92, 98–102, 105, 107, 109–10, 112, 134, 140, 160, 177–78, 198 (n. 54), 199 (n. 85), 203 (n. 53); and Balázs, 127–28
Dreaming Youth (Balázs), 34–35
Dr. Margit Szélpál (Balázs), 38–39

Eckhart, Meister, 59–60, 74–76, 78, 124; and origins of the dialectic, 148
Eigenart des Ästhetischen, Die, 92
Eight, The, 32, 60, 66, 193 (n. 72)
Either/Or (Kierkegaard), 149
Engels, Friedrich, 172–73
Enneads (Plotinus), 59, 61, 86
Entartung (Nordau), 189 (n. 25)
Eötvös, József, 6, 10, 35
Eötvös Collegium, 35
Erlebnis und die Dichtung, Das (Dilthey), 26
Ernst, Paul, 74, 98, 104, 118, 124, 136, 169–70, 197 (n. 89); and neoclassic drama, 33; and Lukács, 62–65, 81; and atheism, 197 (n. 27)
Eschatology, 75, 109
Ethic of responsibility, 88
Ethic of ultimate ends, 88–89
Evangelical Gymnasium, 6, 9
Existentialism, 36, 49, 64
Expressionism, 176–77

Fackel, Die, 41
Fairy tales, 79–81, 87, 158–59
Fáklya (Torch), 156, 158

Father, The (Strindberg), 17
Fear and Trembling (Kierkegaard), 68
Fehér, Ferenc, 100, 191 (n. 77)
Féjerváry, Baron Géza, 7, 189 (n. 21)
Fenyő, Miksa, 54, 57
Ferenc Prenn's Storm-Tossed Life (Lengyel), 163, 187
Fichte, Johann G., 47, 73, 85, 98, 143, 184; and ethical idealism, 74–75, 129; and apocalypse, 109; and Marxists, 148–49
Foch, Marshal Ferdinand, 162
Fogarasi, Béla, 157; and Sunday Circle, 118, 175; and Free School of the Humanistic Sciences, 120, 123, 125–26; lecture on idealism, 128–32; joins Hungarian Communist party, 139
Form, 20, 30, 32, 41–42, 47, 50–52, 57, 60, 63, 67, 77–78, 99, 115; literary, 26–28; and necessity, 33, 49; and tragedy, 38, 68; of society, 92, 128; and art, 122; cultural, 125
Franz Josef, 7
Free School of the Humanistic Sciences, 122–23, 126, 147; organized, 119; first semester, 120; second semester, 125
Free School of the Sociological Society, 56, 119
Freie Bühne, 16–17, 31
Fülep, Lajos, 75, 78, 157; and *A Szellem*, 58–61; and Sunday Circle, 118; and Free School of the Humanistic Sciences, 122–23, 128

Gábor, Andor, 157, 175, 202 (n. 33)
Galileo Circle, 56, 166
Gauguin, Paul, 58, 60
Geist der Utopie (Bloch), 110–11, 121
Gemeinschaft, 77, 99, 102, 139, 175, 186; utopia of, 78; Lukács and Gertrúd, 148; and Communist party, 174. *See also* Community
Gemeinschaft und Gesellschaft (Tönnies), 10
Genoveva (Hebbel), 81
George, Stefan, 44, 48, 50, 53, 65, 85, 95
Gergely, Tibor, 175, 200 (n. 24)
"German Intelligentsia and the War, The," 96
Geschichte des Rabbi Nachman, Die (Buber), 76
Geschlecht und Charakter (Weininger), 54
Ghosts (Ibsen), 15
Giotto, 47, 58
Goethe, Johann Wolfgang von, 17, 29, 159–60, 178
Gogh, Vincent van, 58
Goldmann, Lucien, 64
Göndör, Ferenc, 160
Grabenko, Ljena, ix, 90, 92, 98, 101–2, 104–5, 109, 148, 177, 179; as terrorist, 89; marries Lukács, 91; and Sonia, 108, 198 (n. 54); and Bruno Steinbach, 116–17; joins Hungarian Communist party, 139; end of marriage to Lukács, 147; and Sunday Circle, 175
Grace, 64, 68–69, 81, 104, 107
Groundwork for the Metaphysics of Morals (Kant), 131
Gundolf, Friedrich, 85
Gyulai, Pál, 9

Habsburg monarchy, 136
Habsburgs, 8
Hajós, Edith, 117–19, 132, 175
Hasidism, 76–78. *See also* Mysticism
Hatvany, Lajos, 79
Hauptmann, Gerhart, 9, 16, 19–20, 31, 81, 177
Hauser, Arnold, 61, 92, 157, 175; and Sunday Circle, 118–19; and Free School of the
    Humanistic Sciences, 122–23, 125; on impressionism, 191 (nn. 53, 57)
Hebbel, Friedrich, 9, 18–19, 32, 64; and modern drama, 30; and necessary evil, 140–41,
    201 (n. 76); and atheism, 197 (n. 27)
Hegel, Georg Wilhelm Friedrich, ix, 59, 61, 73–75, 143; Lukács's criticism of, 109,
    115–16; and conservatism, 129; and the dialectic, 142; Lukács's defense of, 148–51,
    181, 184
Heidegger, Martin, 36, 64, 110, 193 (n. 79)
Heidelberg Aesthetics, 93, 112–17, 119, 125, 199 (n. 85)
Heidelberg valise, ix, 93, 100, 117
Heller, Ágnes, 100, 131, 200 (n. 45)
Herder, Johann Gottfried von, 9
Heuss, Theodor, 85
Hevesi, Sándor, 17–19, 58–59, 190 (n. 18)
Hippius, Zinaida, 103
History and Class Consciousness, 179–86
History of the Evolution of the Modern Drama, 21, 24, 27–34, 40, 52, 55, 62–63, 80,
    112, 125, 140, 176
Hofmannsthal, Hugo von, 33, 36
Homer, 100
Honigsheim, Paul, 85, 87–88
Horthy, Miklós, 170–71
Horváth, János, 53
Hungarian Communist party, 90, 139, 141, 149, 166, 174; organization of, 137; merger
    with Social Democratic party, 154–55
Hungarianness, 9
Hungarian Party of Socialist-Communist Workers, 154–55
Hungarian Philosophic Society, 120–21
Hungarian Soviet Republic, 141, 153, 161–64, 167, 171; and Béla Kun, 156; and avant-
    garde, 160; collapse of, 165
Husserl, Edmund, 58, 113, 115, 125, 193 (n. 79)
Huszadik Század (Twentieth Century), 53, 56, 126, 128; and counterculture, 54; and
    positivism, 55, 59, 82

Ibsen, Henrik, 9, 15, 17–19, 31–32, 42, 159; Romanticism of, 20–21, 147; and aliena-
    tion, 22; and modern drama, 30; meets Lukács, 190 (n. 24); and atheism, 197 (n. 27)
Idealism, 81, 85, 119, 128–29; ethical, 74, 130–31; and mysticism, 75; abstract, 99
Ignotus (Hugó Veigelsberg), 54, 97
Illusions of Progress, The (Sorel), 134
Impressionism, 49, 58, 60, 119, 122; Lukács's attack on, 31–33; Viennese, 54; and
    Nyugat, 59; Hauser's attack on, 191 (nn. 53, 57)
Influence on the State of the Ruling Ideas of the Nineteenth Century, The (Eötvös), 10
In the Beginning Was the Garden (Lesznai), 187

"Iron cage" (Max Weber), 11
Istóczy, Győző, 8

Jánossy, Imre, 148
Jaspers, Karl, 85, 116–17
Jászi, Oszkár, 57, 137–38, 151, 167, 170–71; and *Huszadik Század*, 55; and Sociological
    Society, 56; and World War I, 97; and Free School of the Sociological Society, 119; and
    idealism, 128; and antiwar movement, 133–34; emigration of, 157
"Jewish Mysticism," 78
Jews, 35, 78, 97; in pre-World War I Hungary, 7–8; in Hungarian universities, 83–84; and
    capitalism, 88; restrictions lifted on, 189 (n. 12)
Joachim of Floris, 109, 143
Judith (Hebbel), 149, 201 (n. 75)
Juhász-Nagy, Sándor, 154

Káldor, György, 175
Kaliayev, Ivan, 101, 104, 107, 167, 187, 201 (n. 79); atheism of, 102; death of, 103
Kant, Immanuel, 22, 59, 62, 74, 85, 113–15, 123, 125; and ethical idealism, 129;
    Lukács's defense of, 131–32; as bourgeois thinker, 181, 184
Károlyi, Mihály, 136, 150, 162; government of, 137–38, 142, 152–54; resignation of,
    202 (n. 21)
Kassák, Lajos, 139, 157, 159–60, 170–71, 176
Kassner, Rudolf, 43, 48–49, 51, 53, 65
Kéri, Pál, 159–60, 203 (n. 45)
Kerr, Alfred, 15, 169
Kierkegaard, Sören, 20, 48, 52–53, 65, 68–69, 124; and Lukács, 49–50; and faith, 143
Kisfaludy Society, 19, 23, 156
Knights of Europe, The, 133–34, 136
Kodály, Zoltán, 17, 36, 119, 123, 126, 157, 159
Komját, Aladár, 157, 202 (n. 32)
Kommunismus, 172
Korvin, Ottó, 165–67
Kossuth, Ferenc, 7–8, 189 (n. 21)
Kraus, Karl, 41
Kristóffy, József, 189 (n. 21)
Kun, Béla, 138, 142, 149, 154, 166, 171, 174, 201 (n. 85); arrested and beaten, 152–53;
    leader of Soviet Republic, 156, 162, 164–65; extradition demanded, 168; on *Ma*, 203
    (n. 50)
Kunfi, Zsigmond, 152, 156, 170, 202 (n. 27)
Kutasi, Elemér, 53

Landauer, Gustav, 76
Landler, Jenő, 153, 171–72
Láng, Júlia, 118
Lask, Emil, 84, 92, 113–14, 120, 124; and Lukács, 85–86; and World War I, 97–98; on
    Lukács, 112
Lederer, Emil, 84
Lederer, Emmy, 84
Left-Wing Communism—an Infantile Disorder (Lenin), 172–73
Legende des Baalschem, Die (Buber), 76–77

"Legend of King Midas, The," 45–46, 50
Lengyel, József, 149, 163, 170, 187
Lenin, Vladimir I., 117, 136, 138, 143–44, 153, 160, 164; and Sorel, 135; *State and Revolution*, 142; and left-wing communism, 172–73; and avant-garde, 175
"Lenin Boys," 166
Lesznai, Anna (Amália Moskovits), 62, 97, 139, 187, 200 (n. 24); and fairy tales, 79; and Sunday Circle, 118–19, 175
Liberal party, 3, 6–8
Lloyd George, David, 162
Logik der Philosophie und die Kategorienlehre, Die (Lask), 86
Logos, 58–59, 63, 78, 88, 115, 124
Lőwinger, György Bernát. *See* Lukács, György
Lőwinger, József. *See* Lukács, József
Lueger, Karl, 8
Lukács, Anna, 204 (n. 9)
Lukács, György, 3, 6, 19, 31, 33, 43, 46, 55–56, 82–83, 90, 118, 142, 153, 167, 169, 172, 190 (n. 21); dislikes mother, 4; and Hungarian culture, 9; and German culture, 10; quest for community, 11; and Thália, 17–19, 28; "The New Hauptmann," 19–20, 177; "Reflections on Henrik Ibsen," 20–22, 147; *History of the Evolution of the Modern Drama*, 21, 24, 27–34, 40, 52, 55, 62–63, 80, 112, 125, 140, 176; "The Main Directions of Dramaturgy during the Final Quarter of the Last Century," 23–24; "Notes toward the Theory of Literary History," 25–27, 54; *Aesthetic Culture*, 32, 53–54; alliance with Béla Balázs, 34; *The Soul and the Forms*, 36, 40, 43, 48–54, 61–67, 74, 85, 98; *Ästhetik*, 41; "The Legend of King Midas," 45–46, 50; "On Poverty of Spirit," 59, 67–69, 77, 79, 85, 140; "Jewish Mysticism," 78; "The Aesthetics of the 'Romance,'" 80; "The Problem of the Untragic Drama," 80; marries Ljena Grabenko, 91; *Die Eigenart des Ästhetischen*, 92; *The Philosophy of Art*, 92–95, 98, 111, 113–14, 197 (n. 100); *Heidelberg Aesthetics*, 93, 111–17, 119, 125, 199 (n. 85); "The German Intelligentsia and the War," 96; opposes World War I, 97; *The Theory of the Novel*, 98–100, 109, 111, 114, 122, 132, 150; "The Subject-Object-Relation in Aesthetics," 115–16; and Sunday Circle, 118–19; and Free School of the Humanistic Sciences, 119–23, 125–26; *Béla Balázs and His Detractors*, 126–28; on ethical idealism, 130; and antiwar movement, 133–34; "Republican Propaganda," 136–37; "Bolshevism as a Moral Problem," 138–40; joins Hungarian Communist party, 139, 149; "Tactics and Ethics," 140–41, 149, 182; end of marriage to Ljena Grabenko, 147; "The Question of Intellectual Leadership and the 'Intellectual Workers,'" 151; "What Is Orthodox Marxism?," 151–52; "Party and Class," 155–56; as cultural dictator, 156–61; "The Role of Morality in Communist Production," 161; as political commissar, 163–65; marries Gertrúd Bortstieber, 170, 204 (n. 10); "On the Question of Parliamentarianism," 172; "Marxism and Literary History," 177; "On Hauptmann's Evolution," 177; "Stavrogin's Confession," 178; *History and Class Consciousness*, 179–86; and Romanticism, 190 (n. 25); meets Ibsen and Björnson, 190 (n. 24)
Lukács, János, 4, 189 (n. 5)
Lukács, József, 4, 6–7, 66, 83–84, 91–92, 170; ennobled, 3; and Leó Popper, 192 (n. 10)
Lukács, Mária (Mici), 24, 41, 66, 90–91, 147, 189 (n. 5)
Lukács, Pál, 189 (n. 5)
Luxemburg, Rosa, 141, 181

Ma (Today), 159–60, 170–71, 176, 203 (n. 50)
Mácza, János, 159–60

Madách, Imre, 10
Magic Mountain, The (Mann), 188
Magyar Szalon (Hungarian Salon), 16, 19
"Main Directions of Dramaturgy during the Final Quarter of the Last Century, The,"
    23-24
"Man in Inhumanity" (Ady), 110
Mann, Heinrich, 169
Mann, Thomas, 22, 96, 169, 187-88
Mannheim, Karl, 61, 128, 157, 167, 175; and Sunday Circle, 118-21; and Free School of
    the Humanistic Sciences, 122-26
Marie Donadieu (Philippe), 62
Márkus, György, 93, 116
Marx, Karl, ix, 25, 74-75, 110-11, 135, 138, 143, 150, 152, 159, 173, 178-80, 185,
    200 (n. 30); method of, 151; and category of totality, 181
Marxism, 135; Lukács's early view of, 31; Bloch on, 111; Hungarian, 126; Lukács's,
    149, 151-52, 172, 180, 186
"Marxism and Literary History," 177
Mary and Martha (Eckhart), 124
Mary Magdalene (Hebbel), 18
Mary Stuart (Schiller), 29
Masaryk, Thomas G., 98
Máté, Olga (Mrs. Béla Zalai), 166
Materialism, 119, 122, 128, 180
Medveczky, Frigyes, 83-84
Merezhkovski, Dmitri, 103, 197 (n. 20)
Metaphysics of Morals, The (Kant), 131-32
Metempsychosis, 77, 110-11
Michelangelo, 47, 58
Mistbeet plan, 132-33
Misunderstanding (in art), 42, 94
Mortal Youth (Balázs), 128
Moskovits, Amália. *See* Lesznai, Anna
Müntzer, Thomas, 143, 167
Mysticism, 60-61, 87, 89, 96, 121; Jewish, 75-79, 136. *See also* Hasidism

Nachman, Rabbi, 77-78
Narodnaya Volya (The People's Will), 102
National Theater (Hungary), 16-17, 19
Naturalism, 31, 42, 54, 63, 177
Naumann, Friedrich, 85
Nechaev, Sergei, 187
Neoclassicism (drama), 33, 63
Neo-Kantianism, 74, 84
Neoplatonism, 86
Népszava (Voice of the People), 152, 154
Neue Gemeinschaft, 76
"New Hauptmann, The," 19-20, 177
New Verses (Ady), 56-57
Nicholas of Cusa, 76, 148
Nietzsche, Friedrich, 52, 64

Nihilism, 10, 32–33, 102, 104, 108, 110
"Notes toward the Theory of Literary History," 25–27, 54
Nouvelle Revue Française, 124
Novalis, 48–49, 53, 65
Nyugat (West), 48, 53, 79, 97, 126, 128; and counterculture, 54; and Ady, 57; impressionism of, 59, 82

Oblomov (Goncharov), 127
Oedipus Rex (Sophocles), 21, 26, 80
Olsen, Regine, 49–50
"On Hauptmann's Evolution," 177
"On Poverty of Spirit," 59, 67–69, 77, 79, 85, 140
"On the Question of Parliamentarianism," 172
Optimists (Sinkó), 141–43, 187
Osvát, Ernő, 54–55

Pale Horse, The (Savinkov), 103–4, 109
Pannekoek, Anton, 173
Parerga und Paralipomena (Schopenhauer), 64, 194 (n. 95)
"Party and Class," 155–56
Pater, Walter, 44, 52
Pauler, Ákos, 84
Petőfi, Sándor, 171, 204 (n. 13)
Petz, Gedeon, 82–83, 156
Pfeiffer, Franz, 75
Philippe, Charles-Louis, 62–63, 65
Philosophie des Geldes (Simmel), 24–25
Philosophy of Art, The, 92–95, 98, 111, 113–14, 197 (n. 100)
Pikler, Gyula, 55–56
Plato, 52, 99, 116
Plotinus, 59–61, 86, 148
Pogány, József, 153
Polanyi, Karl, 42, 56, 151, 192 (n. 11)
Polanyi, Laura, 42, 192 (n. 11)
Polanyi, Michael, 42, 119, 126, 192 (n. 11)
Pollacsek, Mihály, 43, 192 (n. 12)
Pólya, György, 157, 202 (n. 31)
Popper, Leó, 40, 43, 46–48, 50–52, 56, 58, 64–65, 67, 74, 192 (n. 10); and thought of
    form, 41–42; death of, 66; and *The Philosophy of Art*, 94
Positivism, 10, 55, 59, 74, 119, 122, 128–30
Possessed, The (Dostoevski), ix
"Problem of the Untragic Drama, The," 80
Proletár (Proletarian), 167, 172
Proletariat, 138, 152, 155, 157, 161–63, 175–77, 188; class struggle of, 150; class
    consciousness of, 151, 181, 183; dictatorship of, 154; as universal class, 156; utopian
    mission of, 173; as subject and object of history, 180; standpoint of, 185
Protestant Ethic and the Spirit of Capitalism, The (Weber), 87–88
Pulszky, Ágost, 55–56

"Question of Intellectual Leadership and the 'Intellectual Workers,' The," 151

Radbruch, Gustav, 190 (n. 21)
Radványi, László, 175, 200 (n. 24)
Rationalization, 11, 78, 86–87, 183
Raw Youth, A (Dostoevski), 159
"Reflections on Henrik Ibsen," 20–22, 147
Reinitz, Béla, 157, 202 (n. 33)
"Remembrance of a Summer's Night" (Ady), 110
Renaissance, 57–58, 193 (n. 64)
"Republican Propaganda," 136–37
Réthy, Károly, 44, 47, 66
Révai, József, 157, 160, 175, 203 (n. 48)
Révész, Béla, 157, 202 (n. 32)
Révész, Géza, 119, 199 (n. 3)
Revolutionary Governing Council, 156, 165
Rickert, Heinrich, 58, 84, 112–14, 116, 125
Riegl, Alois, 124
Ritoók, Emma, 53, 61, 135, 187, 195 (n. 43); and Ernst Bloch, 73–74, 81, 83, 195 (n. 40); and Sunday Circle, 118; and Free School of the Humanistic Sciences, 123
Roland-Holst, Henriette, 173
"Role of Morality in Communist Production, The," 161
Romance, 79–81. *See also* Untragic drama
Romanticism, 20–21, 30, 93, 99, 147, 190 (n. 25)
Ropshin. *See* Savinkov, Boris
Rosmersholm (Ibsen), 31
Rote Fahne, Die, 176
Rote Hahn, Der (Hauptmann), 20
Rousseau, Jean Jacques, 186
Russian Revolution, ix, 135–36, 143
Russland und Europa (Masaryk), 98

Sardou, Victorien, 16, 29
Savinkov, Boris (pseud. Ropshin), 102, 109, 140–41, 150, 201 (n. 79); and terrorism, 103–4, 127; death of, 147, 202 (n. 2)
Sazonov, Yegor, 102, 201 (n. 79)
Schelling, Friedrich Wilhelm Joseph von, 73–74, 129
Schiller, Friedrich, 29, 178
Schlamadinger, Anna, 118–20, 132, 175
Scholem, Gershom, 76
Schopenhauer, Arthur, 20, 22, 36, 38, 52, 64, 194 (n. 95)
"Science as a Vocation" (Weber), 86, 92
Seidler, Ernő, 142, 149, 166, 201 (n. 85)
Seidler, Irma, ix, 23, 40, 42, 46–47, 50, 63, 67, 69, 84, 89–90, 142, 148, 194 (n. 99), 200 (n. 51); meets Lukács, 43; marries Károly Réthy, 44; and *The Soul and the Forms*, 48, 62, 64–65, 98; suicide, 66, 73, 143, 187
Sein, 95
Serge, Victor, 167, 171
Sergei, Grand Duke (Russia), 102–3
Shakespeare, William, 21, 42, 59, 80–81, 158–60, 178
Shaw, George Bernard, 18, 33

Simmel, Georg, ix, 11, 23, 28, 32, 41, 58–59, 74, 84–85, 191 (n. 65), 194 (n. 113);
  alienation and tragedy, 24–25, 27, 86, 100; and Béla Balázs, 36; and Ernst Bloch, 73;
  and Karl Mannheim, 121
Sinkó, Ervin, 141–42, 175, 187, 201 (n. 81)
Smuts, General Jan, 162
Social Contract, The (Rousseau), 186
Social Democratic party (Hungary), 18, 105, 152, 154–55, 166
Socialism, 31, 63, 104, 111, 129, 136, 138, 151, 182; metaphysics of, 105; bureaucratic,
  161
Socialist Revolutionary party (Russia), 89, 102
Sociological Society, 56, 120, 128–29
Socrates, 52, 62
Sollen, 95
Somló, Bódog, 19, 56, 190 (n. 21)
Sophocles, 80
Sorel, Georges, 132, 134–36, 143
Soul and Culture (Mannheim), 123–25, 128
Soul and the Forms, The, 36, 40, 43, 48–54, 61–67, 74, 85, 98
Soul in War (Balázs), 97
Spencer, Herbert, 55
Spirit of Russia, The (Masaryk). See Russland und Europa
Spitz, René, 119, 199 (n. 3)
State and Revolution (Lenin), 142
"Stavrogin's Confession," 178
Stein, Ferenc, 203 (n. 72)
Steinbach, Bruno, 116–17, 147, 168
Stepun, Fedor, 88
Sterne, Laurence, 48, 50–51, 53, 65
Storm, Theodor, 48, 51, 53, 65
Strindberg, August, 17, 19, 177
"Subject-Object-Relation in Aesthetics, The," 115–16
Sunday Circle, 125, 128–29, 132, 139, 142, 165; organization of, 118; and problem of
  alienation, 119; in Vienna, 175
Susman, Margarete, 67, 194 (n. 113)
Suso, Heinrich, 60
Symbolism, 31, 33, 54
Syndicalism, 132, 135, 174
Synthetic drama, 21
Szabadgondolat (Free Thought), 137, 139, 151
Szabó, Ervin, 126, 132–34, 200 (n. 51)
Szamuely, Tibor, 153, 202 (n. 16)
Szekfű, Gyula, 157, 202 (n. 30)
Szellem, A (Spirit or Mind), 58–63, 74–75, 78, 82, 122, 124
Szemere, Samu, 84
Szende, Pál, 170–71, 204 (n. 11)
Szilasi, Wilhelm, 61, 193 (n. 79)

"Tactics and Ethics," 140–41, 149, 182
Tempest, The (Shakespeare), 80

Terrorism, 103
Terrorist Brigade (Russia), 102
Thália Society, 17, 28
Thália Theater, 17–19, 57, 124, 158, 190 (n. 18)
Théâtre Libre, 16, 31
Theory of the Drama, The (Balázs), 120
Theory of the Novel, The, 98–100, 109, 111, 114, 122, 132, 150
Tisza, István, 7, 137
Tisza, Kálmán, 6, 8
Tiszaeszlár, 8
Tolnay, Charles de. See De Tolnay, Charles
Tolstoi, Leo, 36, 88, 99, 111, 159–60, 178, 189 (n. 25), 196 (n. 70)
Tönnies, Ferdinand, 10–11, 25
Totalitarianism, 186
Totality, 152, 162, 181–82, 184, 186
Tragedy of Man, The (Madách), 10
Troeltsch, Ernst, 25, 58, 84–85, 112, 169, 194 (n. 84), 197 (n. 20)
"Trumpet of God, The" (Ady), 75

Untragic drama, 79–81. See also Romance
Utopia, 74, 78–79, 95, 111, 115, 127, 132, 149, 173; Lukács's turn to, 67; of untragic
    drama, 81; and Russian Revolution, 136; Lukács's turn from, 148; as reality, 150;
    Dostoevski's, 160, 203 (n. 53); Lukács's opposition to, 172, 177, 179

Varga, Jenő, 120, 153, 161–62
Varjas, Sándor, 126, 156
Vedres, Márk, 167
Világosság (Clarity), 170
Vörös Újság (Red Gazette), 139, 158–60
Vyx, Lieutenant Colonel, 153–54, 162

Waard, Beatrice de, 41, 192 (n. 10)
Wanderer Sings, The (Balázs), 39
Weavers, The (Hauptmann), 16
Weber, Alfred, 84–85, 112, 169
Weber, Marianne, 85, 90, 92, 95–97, 141
Weber, Max, 11, 25, 58, 82, 84–86, 92, 111–13, 143, 169, 173; and mysticism, 87;
    interest in Russia, 88–89, 196 (n. 70)
Weininger, Otto, 52, 54, 66
Werk (work), 22, 25, 40, 43–44, 47–48, 50, 52, 67–68, 115, 124, 148; and alienation,
    51; of goodness, 69
Wertheimer, Adél, 4, 11, 148
"What Is Orthodox Marxism?," 151–52
Wilde, János, 119, 199 (n. 3)
Wilson, Woodrow, 136, 162
Windelband, Wilhelm, 84, 112–13, 125
Wohl, Cecile, 43, 66
Wooden Prince, The (Bartók-Balázs), 159
World as Will and Representation, The (Schopenhauer), 64, 194 (n. 95)
Würdigkeit (dignity), 129, 131

Zalai, Béla, 59, 61, 83–84, 120, 201 (n. 63); Lukács on, 60; death of, 98; and Karl
    Mannheim, 122; and Free School of the Humanistic Sciences, 124–25; and Lukács,
    197 (n. 10)
Zionism, 76

QUE